MONARCHY, REVOLUTION AND REFUGEES

Laos • Thailand • Argentina • Kampuchea

MONARCHY, REVOLUTION AND REFUGEES

Laos • Thailand • Argentina • Kampuchea

Walter Irvine
A personal view

RIVER
BOOKS

To Pietro Andruccioli

First published in Thailand in 2022 by
River Books Co., Ltd
396/1 Maharaj Road,
Phraborommaharajawang,
Bangkok 10200 Thailand
Tel: (66) 2 225-4963, 2 225-0139, 2 622-1900
Fax: (66) 2 225-3861
Email: order@riverbooksbk.com
www.riverbooksbk.com

Production: Narisa Chakrabongse
Editor: Narisa Chakrabongse
Design: Ruetairat Nanta

ISBN 978 616 451 065 4

Front cover: Relaxing after a day's work in the fields, Thailand.

Frontispiece : A procession at Vat Xieng Thong.

Opposite page: Thailand and Indochina, an area of important new beginnings.

Printed and bound in Thailand by Sirivatana Interprint Public Co., Ltd

CONTENTS

INTRODUCTION

I have been fortunate to have lived in many countries, starting in Mexico where I was born, and the UK where I studied. Among the many work-related locations that followed, those I consider in this book, Laos, Thailand, Argentina and Kampuchea, with some references to Vietnam, are all linked to my early beginnings in Southeast Asia, and to the radical political dislocations and refugee movements that took place in Indochina in the 1970s.

Drawing from my diaries and my memory, I give my personal view of the complex changes that each country underwent in that period, placing myself in the account as an observing protagonist. The process of writing has allowed me to relive the extraordinary events I witnessed, but it has also been self-revealing. For putting down on paper my own involvement, has shown the strong impact which the events had on me, exercising a long-lasting influence.

Living in each of those countries has left its mark. But among them, I give pride of place to Laos and to Luang Phrabang, its former royal capital and first among my Southeast Asian destinations. I give an account of the three momentous years I spent there in Part I of this book, but I wish to mention here the causal link which I believe exists between that time, and a chain of subsequent personal choices made between 1972, when I reached Luang Phrabang, and 2008, when I retired from professional life, and beyond.

Laos exposed me to Theravada Buddhism and to its beneficial stabilizing influence, and encouraged a serious interest in its practice, which I have kept to this day. It stimulated a passion for scholarly understanding of different cultures, that of Laos first, followed in Southeast Asia by Thailand, Vietnam and Cambodia. It provided a unique opportunity for political maturation: living in the protective bubble of Luang Phrabang at a time of war, and observing the monarchy moving inexorably towards its final dissolution, was a ground-breaking learning experience. Last but not least, among the various aspects of Laos' legacy, was the sad spectacle it provided, once the communist regime had been established, of a substantive number of its people fleeing the country. The flight of many of my former students with thousands of other Laotians to Thailand's refugee camps, gave me my first personal exposure to forced exile. A movement that included persons I had known in Luang Phrabang strongly impressed me. It created an interest in and concern

Buddha statues in Vat Visun Luang Phrabang 2016.

for refugees which eventually led to a career with the Office of the United Nations High Commissioner for Refugees (UNHCR), and to a life of mobility from one refugee job to another – for twenty-seven years. As a UNHCR official, I served in Southeast Asia (Vietnam, Thailand and Cambodia), Latin America (Argentina, Nicaragua and Costa Rica), the Balkans (Croatia, Bosnia and Herzegovina and Kosovo) and Western Europe (Italy, covering the Vatican, Cyprus, Malta and Portugal).

* * * * * * *

From a personal point of view, the text offers a sample of the nomadic existence I have led during my entire professional life. I like to see my early years in Laos as a time of preparation for my chosen peripatetic lifestyle. Once I joined UNHCR, the wished-for rhythm of constant movement was structured by the Agency's requirement that its professional staff move from one post to another, at intervals of between two to four years. This itinerant existence has suited me down to the ground. There may be deep personal/psychological reasons for this; simply stated, these could hinge on an ever dissatisfied need to escape from a sense of confinement which developed during my early days at home in Mexico, inside a strongly protective and conservative Scottish and Franco-Mexican family.

Whatever that may be, a never diminished urge to move led me towards an outlet, and a kind of resolution, in a life of changed locations and repeated new beginnings. A first move took place when I left Mexico at age 17, travelling to England for a time at boarding school, followed by a three-year stint reading for my first degree at the University of Kent at Canterbury. Movement continued when, having graduated at age 24, I approached the Voluntary Service Overseas at its London Office. This was key, for its offer of a teaching post in Laos, and consequent three years living in Luang Phrabang led me eventually to join the one UN Agency who could provide precisely what I wanted. UNHCR offered adventure in constantly changing environments, away from the stability and confinement of a single place, coupled with the security of a job and a life-long career. Of course, the extraordinary enrichment and sense of freedom that accompanies a nomadic existence comes at a cost. It comes with the repeated severance of all links; links to a location, a culture and a language, to a job and a group of colleagues, to a home and to all manner of personal relationships. And each move demands an extraordinary outlay of energy, combined with the flexibility and openness of mind required to start anew. Like any life option, the nomadic way of life, and the choice to escape from a sense of confinement has its downside.

* * * * * * *

I have noted the key importance I attach to my years in Laos. From the perspective of a place of adventure which offered uncertainty rather than stability, no other country could have provided more. Laos had been seriously affected by the Vietnam War, which raged along its eastern border, and had on occasion spilled over onto its territory in the form of US bombing. Also, it had for years been facing a long-drawn civil war which opposed the country's US-backed Royal Government and the Pathet Lao, an insurgency movement with communist sympathies and strong historical links with North Vietnam. The small kingdom and former French colony was caught in one of the most intractable conflicts of the Cold War. As a result of geography, it stood dangerously between two historical rivals, communist North Vietnam, a client of the Soviet Union, and the Kingdom of Thailand, a close ally of the US.

I learnt these basic facts as I considered the Luang Phrabang-based teaching job which VSO offered. Living in a war zone was the one issue which made me think twice before agreeing to go, but VSO assured me that Luang Phrabang was safe. It was one of five Laotian towns which stood protected by the Royal Lao Government and its army, and although large parts of rural Laos were under Pathet Lao control, the movement had never seriously threatened any of these towns, nor ever sought to enter the royal capital. I would be living there without risk, if I followed security instructions and kept within the town's boundaries.

I did not hesitate for long. To move to a country on the other side of the planet, which was also known as the Kingdom of the Million Elephants and White Parasol, seemed irresistible. Concerning the job itself, teaching English at the Lycée of Luang Phrabang, I had the required skills. I was familiar with the French school system from my own school days at the French Lycée in Mexico City. I had spoken French since childhood and would be able to use it in Laos; the language was still widely used by the bureaucracy as a remnant of the colonial period, and was the medium of instruction at the Lycée. As for English, it had come to me early on at home, where a tri-lingual system operated, French being spoken with my Franco-Mexican mother, English with my Scottish father and Spanish with my brother and three sisters, and all others. I felt well equipped for the job.

On December 1972, therefore, I found myself sitting with four other volunteers on a flight from London to Bangkok, and thence to Vientiane, the administrative capital of Laos. One or two escapades gave us a glimpse of the dusty capital, its run-down colonial architecture, almost empty streets, well-worn cyclos and monasteries. But the first real contact with Laos came a week later, when we newcomers set off to our respective destinations, in my case to Luang Phrabang. My life's adventure had begun.

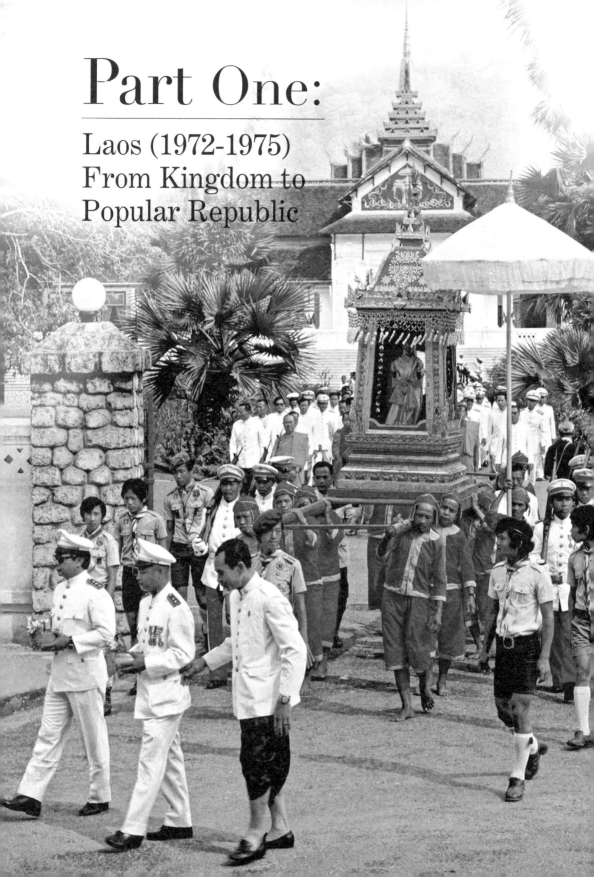

Part One:

Laos (1972-1975)
From Kingdom to
Popular Republic

1

NEITHER WAR NOR PEACE

The Royal Palace built by the French in 1904 for King Sisavangvong.

I reach my destination (1 October 1972)

As the plane approached Luang Phrabang, I got my first glimpse of its spectacular setting, the blue mountains, the lush vegetation, and the confluence of the Mekong and Namkhan rivers, which bounded the town at its eastern end. Just before landing, I caught sight of the palm trees, the temples, the up-turned roofs and, at the town's centre, the famous hill. And as the plane touched down, and approached the air terminal, I smiled at what I had just seen, free from my fears about Laos as a country at war.

Upon arrival, the Lycée provided me with a home, the ground-floor of a two-storey French colonial house. With the help of Richard Cooke, VSO and Luang Phrabang long-timer, I found it at the end of a narrow lane, towering over my neighbour's low-lying houses. Two steps away was vat Sen, my own monastery, where an imposing standing Buddha, ten meters tall, stood alongside the main temple, close to the monk's living quarters.

Walking down my lane and away from the *vat,* at the crossroads with a wider street, a corner shop hinted at the town's diluted French flavour – a bakery which offered sweet cakes and the local version of a baguette which became Laotian when

Opposite page: The Phra'Bang is carried from the Palace to Vat Mai.

The heart of my neighbourhood, Vat Sen.

I settled in the ground floor of the only colonial-style house in my lane.

eaten with pork sausage and fish sauce. Walking beyond, I would soon discover the town's other neigbourhoods. Like mine, they were separate villages, which were built around their own perfect monastery, and conducted separate lives amid a similar mix of houses – modest, low-lying affairs made of pale masonry, or tall, spacious structures built entirely of teak, or solid but slightly decaying French or Chinese villas. The first time I walked to my new lodgings, a group of children surrounded me, peering insistently at my unusual appearance – I was a '*falang dang moo*', a 'long-nosed foreigner'. In time, their parents also took a good look, initially outside the house, and later, as they became more confident, inside. For their initial curiosity eventually led to visits at all times, at the expense of my westerner's obsession with privacy. I started by resisting, locking my front door and keeping my shutters tightly fastened. But I gradually gave in to my neighbours' good humour, and kept my front room permanently unlocked.

Rural inroads in town: vegetable gardens and buffaloes at Vat That Luang.

Both the town's rivers were within easy reach – the abrupt banks of the quick-flowing Namkan river, and the Mekong's lazy embankment. Sitting there in the late afternoon, there was something deeply rural about the fishermen catching their prey.

I soon discovered other countryside inroads close to the centre: gardens showing perfect rows of vegetables near the house clusters; a man walking his buffaloes past the white-washed walls of a royal *vat*. There was no clear-cut break between town and countryside. The only solidly urban area started at the Palace, from where it stretched to the south; to the east, it followed a succession of monasteries and ended up at the confluence. The rest of town moved smoothly away from the centre, past a succession of neighbourhoods which gradually linked up with the ricefields and the villages outside.

My inquisitive neighbours.

The Lycée

I moved about town in a motorized three-wheel taxi until I got hold of a Honda 70, a motorbike small and light enough to maneuver with my polio leg. I needed it to get to my teaching job at the Lycée, on the outskirts of town. Driving along, you could see the school enclosure at the top of the road, the walls and tall trees partly hiding the whitewashed two-story buildings. The privileged site pointed to the Lycée's high standing, but it took a little time before I saw just how much the school was marked by the stamp of the country's colonial past. This was indeed a French Lycée, where mostly French teachers taught the French curriculum in the French language. And though Lao language and culture were not entirely absent, coverage

My students taught me that the best depiction of Lao lore could be found on certain temple doors.

was modest and was carried out by only a sprinkling of Lao teachers. The Laotian Francophile director – the *proviseur* – presided alongside a French *censeur* who clearly enjoyed wielding his authority, and oversaw his French teachers' performance at close quarters. As for the two English teachers – an American Fulbright scholar and myself – we were lucky to be left to our own devices, outside the *censeur's* supervision and under the *proviseur's* vague control.

I asked myself how far teaching English in such a foreign set up, could possibly benefit this very poor country at war. There was one easy answer. Although the Lycée harked back to the country's colonial past and privileged the French language over Lao, it offered good academic standards which many considered the best in town, superior to those offered by other schools: the Roman Catholic 'Daohung' or the proudly Laotian 'FaNgum'. Also, the Lycée's teachers, whether French, British or American were relatively young and mostly progressive, had a taste for controversy, and encouraged the students to be critical. Some French teachers were more explicitly political than others, among them, those who had participated in the 1968 student movement, and were conscientious objectors teaching in Laos instead of military service. In tacit opposition to the local, highly unequal social hierarchy, they sympathized with the Pathet Lao and questioned the social privileges which some of the school's students vaunted. Others, myself included, were less clear about what the Pathet Lao represented, but were equally keen to encourage students to think critically. However, that approach was not always easy to follow.

It went against the Lao tradition of learning by rote, and contradicted the tacit rule that a teacher's knowledge is always valid, and should never be questioned.

Teaching English language and literature was my first job. It was my first attempt to teach, and all in all, I think it went well. With the beginners, I used lively language games, confident that Laos' unconditional respect for teachers would keep my students' enthusiasm within bounds. The games never led to problems of discipline, as would probably have been the case in the West, and I was thrilled to learn that my classes were being described as '*muan*' – a lot of fun – the best Lao compliment one could ever get. I gave my teaching a Lao flavour by fitting in the basic points of a Lao myth or story into language drills and tongue twisters. And to make sure that I learnt Lao, I asked students to translate and record the drills which I later repeated at home as a daily language-learning routine. In this way, the students learnt English in real or imagined Lao contexts, while I learnt Lao and got to know the best examples of Lao lore, including stories of abducted princesses rescued by fearless heroes with the help of wise men living meditative lives in the forest. It helped that some of the characters were depicted on the door carvings or the facades of certain temples. The students directed me to them for visual reinforcement, thus teaching me in passing that the *vat* is a transmitter of myths as well as a bastion of Buddhist practice.

The method of mutual learning between teacher and students was a dynamic system of give and take inside school. This soon developed into real camaraderie outside, with occasional group outings and picnics in areas close to Luang Phrabang which were safe from the war.

A picnic with my students close to Luang Phrabang.

First Contact with the War (15 October 1972)

A French fellow-teacher called Antoine invited me to visit Pak Ou village, some 15 km. out of town. It had been attacked by the Pathet Lao two years before but, Antoine said, a visit there was perfectly safe and did not require official authorization. I had only been in Luang Phrabang for a fortnight, and felt a bit nervous about the plan, surprised that one could just move out of town into areas which were close to the fighting with little official control. Perhaps the laxity in security matters followed from the Royal Lao authorities' cavalier conviction that the Pathet Lao did not pose a threat, and from the assumption by the British Embassy in Vientiane, by my employer (VSO) and by the US Embassy that the Pathet Lao could never win.

Antoine and I left on our motorbikes early, skidding all the way on roads which the monsoon rains had made slippery with thick red mud. There was heavy Royal Army presence on the way, a sign that the Pathet Lao could be close, and as Antoine insisted that moving quickly would make us less of a target, we drove as fast as the mud permitted, just in case. Although my mind was busy with the effort not to skid, I was fully aware of the extraordinary surrounding beauty – the lush vegetation, red roads, luminous skies and the magnificent feathered bamboos.

All of this accompanied us until the road reached the river, and took us to the small village of Pak Suang. Having planned to continue by boat, we left our motorbikes with the boatman's family, boarded the dugout, and slowly moved up-river, against the current, towards our destination, Pak Ou.

The village stood by the confluence of the wide Mekong and the smaller river Ou, close to the westernmost limit of Pathet Lao territory. It was perched high on the embankment, where it looked down on the brown flow of both rivers. Across the Mekong on the opposite bank, a massive cliff fell almost vertically into the water, showing the entry to its caves, famous as a shrine of countless Buddha statues. The boat reached the river bank. We jumped into the mud and followed our boatman up the steep slope towards the village. He carried a rice basket in his left hand, but had lost his right forearm during the war, and so held his stump straight before him to keep his balance. I just managed to keep up with my polio leg, watching my every step to avoid slipping. Just behind me, Antoine hung on to our precious cameras which we were determined to use. As soon as we reached the village, we saw that the number of families far exceeded housing capacity: some of the original houses on stilts, roofed with brand-new corrugated iron, had been rebuilt to a smaller size. But beyond, smaller homes, built close to each other, were inhabited by families who, we learnt, had fled from other villages. Everywhere in Pak Ou, displacement had taken its toll: there was a listless air about the people, some sitting on their small stools by the makeshift homes, the old women chewing betel nut, some of the children sleeping inside. One little girl stared at us, holding a pink-skinned, golden-haired doll. Nearby, the village temple was still standing, but its walls bore the scars of bullets.

In the large clearing overlooking the river, the villagers had been collecting rice rations which Air America had just dropped. Antoine explained what the American airline did. It provided rice supplies for displaced persons who had escaped from Pathet Lao aggression, or had abandoned areas devastated by American bombing. But besides such humanitarian work, for years Air America had provided logistical support to the CIA's covert activities. In this role, the airline delivered military material to the US surrogate army which the CIA had created in the early 1960s, one aspect of US anti-communist efforts in the region. Faced with a US Congress unwilling to approve the grounding of US troops in Laos, the CIA had turned to the Hmong to man a brand-new anti-communist force. The Hmong were the country's largest mountain-dwelling people, otherwise known for the fighting capacity of its men. Standing in Pak Ou, therefore, we were witnessing one of Air America's more open, publicized interventions, which served as a cover for that other activity – to provide support to Hmong forces (see Stuart Fox 1986:30).

As Antoine and I walked on, a villager told us not to take photographs. We gave him our cameras for safe-keeping, and in his rudimentary Lao, Antoine explained who we were. In turn, the man said he had been displaced from his village, could not return to his home and his rice field, and had no land to cultivate in Pak Ou. He only hoped that the village would remain safe, that rice would continue to be provided, that he would one day be able to go back home. Others told similar stories in words and signs simple enough for us to understand. We thanked them, slowly got away and walked down the slope to the boat, carefully carrying our unused cameras, our minds full of the village's sad resignation.

Our boatman took the boat across the Mekong to reach the Pak Ou caves, a site of high religiosity, a point of reference for the whole region. On the bank, we walked in the mud to reach a steep set of steps, and climbed up, holding on to a white-washed balustrade. Once at the

First impact of the Luang Phrabang countryside

Across the Mekong, the Pak Ou caves hide inside the cliff-like mountain.

Pak Ou: view of the Buddha statues from the back of the main cave.

top, and looking inside from the cave's very edge, we could see far into the back. We were overwhelmed by the sight of hundreds of Buddhas facing us from all sides. They rested against each other in tight groups, or stood alone, meditating or staring into space. Some were intact, but many were wasting away, following their own process of disintegration. The place of veneration had been hit by the passage of time – the advanced state of decay of some Buddhas attested to it – but it had not suffered the effects of war.

As we drove back to Luang Phrabang, I kept asking myself the same question. Why had Pak Ou village been devastated, while the caves and Luang Phrabang itself had been left untouched? After all, both locations represented the two main sustaining pillars of the old society, the monarchy and the Buddhist Sangha. Why had the Pathet Lao spared them? The Pak Ou Buddhas had been left at peace, sufficiently so to keep transmitting the sense of quiet serenity which Antoine and I had felt. Why?

A dazzling spectacle in the midst of war (22-23 October 1972)

My students said I could not miss the Festival of the Candlelit Boats – it would show Luang Phrabang at its most magnificent, for this year the spectacle was expected to be more splendid than ever, even as the fighting was getting closer to town.

The festival started at dusk. I stood at the top of Sisavangvong Road long before the crowds gathered, early enough to watch the floats being dragged to their designated place within the upcoming procession. On each of them, a huge bamboo boat carried multi-coloured mythical beings which sat among giant, pale yellow lotus flowers. Once fully lit, the floats were ready to move. The first one carried a peacock with the features of a swan. A loudspeaker, placed under the animal provided the music, which at this early stage was already loud, and encouraged the gathering crowd to clap to the rhythm of the dancing and singing. Shortly after sunset, the impressive succession of moving platforms moved along the lantern-lit road past the palace gardens, advancing towards the town's easternmost end, where Vat Xieng Thong, the most magnificent of the royal temples looked out onto the Mekong. By this time, the town's heartbeat had quickened, as if each house that stood by the road, each golden temple, each tree, each flower, each speck of dust had decided that evening to abandon the austerities of the rains' retreat, and throw themselves into the moving crowd. Under the mellow-mooned sky, lanterns in pairs and threesomes glowed green and yellow and red, against the tiled roofs and solid fronts of the Vietnamese merchants' houses. Strings of multi-coloured bulbs, set up by the monks, pulled entire monasteries into the stream of excitement. Young novices – heads shaven and orange-robed – sat on the white outer wall of that other royal temple, Vat Mai, and watched the floats passing by, as if propelled by the crowd of dancers.

As I approached Vat Xieng Thong, an old lady intensified her pace, clapping rhythmically to the right and left. She beckoned me to follow her into the sanctuary, where each building glowed under the late evening clouds, all of them bluish-white, the colour of lead. The stream of dancers entered the enclosure, as the floats were carried in, one by one. Out of the crowd, a group of girls came towards me, calm and composed, holding small banana-leaf boats, which contained a red flower, a candle and incense sticks. Manivane was among them. She recognized me as her teacher, approached me timidly and asked me to accept her own small boat as a gift. She explained in French: 'The flower and the candle are used to venerate the Buddha, although some may tell you they are offerings for the spirit of the river. When you are ready to place the boat on the water, bow your head, bring your joined hands to your forehead as a sign of respect. Put your anger, your hatred, your defilements on the raft, which you should then place gently on the water. Let go then, let go, let go of your past wrongdoings, let them float away and

Vat Xieng Thong.

disappear into the river. It is the same with the procession's floats; their lights and their beauty are there to venerate the Buddha, and to defer to the river Mekong's powerful *naga* spirits; but they also carry the transgressions of their own neighbourhoods, and take them away, down river, far away'.

Still in the monastery, the procession's barges had been placed next to each other, in a row. Some monks stood squarely in front of them, and pronounced powerful *mantra* to pull the negative karma of their own neighbourhoods onto them. Once loaded with their karmic cargo, they were carried along the temple compound towards the steep set of steps that led them down to the Mekong below. Each one of them, a heavy weight even for several men, swung dangerously as it descended between the white, snake-shaped balustrades and then, once on the bank, advanced over the mud until it reached the dark mass of water below. One by one the barges floated away, gleaming, some the colour of gold, others bright pink. They drifted silently, carrying away the town's wrongdoings. Soon, the Mekong had caught the faint glimmer of the candles, just visible against the broad dark stream, against the outline of the mountains, under a full moon now partly hidden by the strange lead-coloured clouds. The boats gradually disappeared. Some people said humorously that they would not sink into the Mekong nearby, but would instead float all the way to Vientiane, the much derided administrative capital which, they said, could not compete with Luang Phrabang's royal and Buddhist traditions. It would instead serve as a dumping ground where the floats would drop their cargo of Luang Phrabang wrongdoings. One hoped in silence that the collective movement of all of the festival's floats in the country, moving away with their heavy load of national angers and hatreds – their 'bad karma' – would mark the start of a new lunar year of new beginnings without war.

My students had explained that the festival was primarily a Buddhist celebration which marked the end of the rainy season, and the completion of the monks' yearly monsoon retreat – a time of strict confinement in the *vat*, full-time study of the Buddha's teachings, and meditation. But having participated in the procession, and listened to Manivane, I was convinced that the festival was more than a pageant within the Buddhist calendar. It contained a mechanism which was put in motion each year to rid the town of evil influences – an exorcism which served to cleanse the town, and by this token, strengthen it. This was my first contact with the practice. By ritually expelling negative forces, it served to restore the balance and fortitude of a community (a town such as Luang Phrabang or a village, or a house) and recover the health of an individual (a man, a woman or a child). This was an essential concept, which stood at the centre of a person's worldview, both in rural areas and in town, throughout Laos and beyond, including in neighbouring Thailand and in Kampuchea.

* * * * * * *

The celebrations which had so impressed me did not end that evening, nor remained confined to town. They spilled out onto the surrounding villages, including Xieng Ngeun. This was located in the town's surrounding safety belt, well outside the reach of war. On the following day, the closure of the festivities was celebrated there with a boat race. While the procession in Luang Phrabang had combined individual devotion to the Buddha with a communal exorcism of evil, the Xieng Ngeun boat races were mainly an opportunity for fun. I joined a group of my students and spent most of the day there. The races showed the canoes of rival villages competing hard against each other, and their fans cheering loudly from the water's edge. Once done, the boats came close to the bank. The rowers jumped into the shallow water and danced their way towards the muddy riverside, clapping their hands rhythmically to the sound of music which blared forth from the top of the bank's ridge. From there, both fans and spectators invited the rowers to walk up and join them. Having reached the ring of dancers, the rowers each chose one of the village girls who had been sitting on a long bench by the side, waiting. The couples moved within the circle of the *lamvong*, the 'circular dance', feet and hands being drawn by the music's regular beat, the drink and the intense April heat.

It was clear nobody in Xieng Ngeun could be thinking about the war. But that afternoon, once back in Luang Phrabang, I learned that a nine o'clock curfew had been announced, while news circulated that the PL was about to attack.

The war gets closer (23 October 1972)

Early that evening, I went to the Tokyo restaurant, a favourite place, where Lycée teachers met for dinner. The talk turned to Pak Suang, where Antoine and I had left our motorbikes some days before, on the way to Pak Ou. The village had just been evacuated, and a large contingent of Royal Lao Army soldiers was stationed there. The Pathet Lao had taken several neighbouring villages, and were keeping villagers hostage, with the alleged (but improbable) help of North Vietnamese soldiers.

Mauro, an Italian teacher from the Roman Catholic School took the floor. With many years in town behind him, he was a mine of information. He spoke with emphasis and delivered quickly with real authority. Since he could remember, it had been Pathet Lao practice to advance towards Luang Phrabang and then withdraw, momentarily controlling the same areas close to town, but never entering it. The main objective of these movements was solely to provoke the Americans and, if possible, to damage some of their installations and aircraft. Mauro had heard that the US embassy and USAID mission were worried and were preparing to evacuate their volunteers. Speaking as a European, he said such caution was a good example of American over-reaction, and should not concern other nationalities. He insisted: taking military possession of Luang Phrabang was not a Pathet Lao aim. The Popular Lao Army had fixed its military objectives elsewhere, in the Southern province of Champassak, where it actively supported the North Vietnamese along the Ho Chi Minh trail, and in northeastern Laos, where it fought against the Hmong-led, American-backed resistance. In Luang Phrabang, the PL's aim was political: to gain the rural population's support by continual presence in the villages. Concerning the monarchy, the PL did not seek to abolish it. In fact, it had always acted respectfully towards royal property, even outside the town's boundaries. For instance, it had sometimes entered the royal garden at Pak Suang, but when doing so, it had not stolen, but had simply collected eggs and oranges, and left them behind in baskets for the royal table. For the Pathet Lao, Luang Phrabang was a place to be respected, a recognized centre of traditional power and religion which could eventually serve as a rallying point for the new Laos. It was not another town to be conquered militarily.

It was getting late and, as the 9 o'clock curfew approached, we all left. I jumped on my motorbike, expecting to find a mood of alarm. But the only reminder of war I could find was an unusual number of soldiers doing the rounds. Otherwise, everything was calm. More than that, I sensed a lazy, incongruously happy mood, which could, however, be easily explained: this was the one-day holiday which was granted each year to recover from the Boat Festival. There were a few lanterns still hanging from the house fronts along the main street, and the shopkeepers were chatting, enjoying the evening air. The lighthearted atmosphere lingered on. It was proving stronger than the rumours of a Pathet Lao attack.

Pathet Lao Attack (13 November 1972)

The people of Luang Phrabang could shift easily from the reality of peace to that of war, watching the latter as a privileged spectator, from a safe distance. The mood of the town was not that of a town under siege, but that of a strong self-contained royal capital, which the Pathet Lao occasionally frightened, but left untouched.

Having visited the devastated village of Pak Ou, lived through the rumour of a Pathet Lao attack, and followed the Boat Festival, I too, was developing the ability to move from peace to war, though any signal of combat still caused a nervous reaction. As was the case on 13 November 1972, when belying everything Mauro said about Luang Phrabang's immunity, the Pathet Lao attacked.

At 4 o'clock in the morning, a loud, metallic crash woke me. 'It's my upstairs neighbour', I thought. I heard the hum of a plane, and another crash. Forgetting that the Pathet Lao had no planes, I asked myself 'Is this the Pathet Lao attacking? A hum and a crash, a hum and a crash, again and again, at regular intervals. My heart beat fast and loud as I lay motionless in bed, waiting. I got up and groped for the light, but there was no electricity. I could see nothing in my pitch-black room. I found the doorway, groped my way through the corridor and into the bathroom. I went up the two steps to the toilet to look out of the window behind. Another hum and crash, and a flash of light, just enough to get a glimpse of my neighbour's house. I stood there listening to every sound, watching the sky, feeling my feet getting cold on the bare tile floor, mentally separating the hums from the crashes: 'The hums are an airplane, maybe an American T-28, flying out to get at the Pathet Lao, but the crash? '. I went back to bed, until only the planes could be heard.

In the morning I was ready by seven to go to the Lycée, feeling safe and sound in the ground floor flat of this my solid colonial-style house, but anxious to share the night's events and find out what had happened. I was convinced that everyone would be suitably alarmed, my neighbours to start with. But no sound came from the flat above. I could only hear a wireless blaring outside, and my Lao neighbours' children playing – all sounds of normality. I took my motorbike out of the back of the house and drove straight to school, looking forward to a good talk. But all I found was the guard standing by the gate. Looking surprised, he asked why I had come. 'Nobody will be here today, we're celebrating the king's birthday. Maybe you'd like to join the celebrations at Vat Xieng Thong?' I had forgotten the holiday. But rather than dwelling on that, I asked him about the attack. He had nothing to say but 'bo pen nyang' – 'it was nothing, never mind'.

I could not leave it at that, and so decided to call on Jacques and Luce Ripoche, both Lycée teachers. I was glad to find them, relieved to be able to talk. They had been shocked themselves, but they had been in Luang Phrabang long enough to take such events in their stride. The occasional sound of gunfire was part of the local normality. 'You will get used to it' Luce said, 'as you probably have accepted the occasional earthquake in Mexico…' Over coffee, they told me what they knew: the area near the airport had been hit by several Pathet Lao rockets. An American T-28 and some houses had been hit. We drove to the spot near the airport where the rockets had landed. In one field, two Americans were digging out an iron tube of roughly 10 cm diametre, a Soviet-made rocket; they said eight people had ended up in hospital, but would be fine. We drove on further, towards the airport. Off the main road, two houses had suffered: one, a small home, stood abandoned. Next to the other – which looked like an office – a green safe had survived. We speculated that the Pathet Lao had probably missed their targets, the airstrip perhaps, or the barracks that stood opposite the bombed office, or the 'secret' American military base beyond the airport. The Pathet Lao's respect for Luang Phrabang and the monarchy was not as absolute as Mauro had claimed, and it was surely not by chance that the attack had taken place on the day the king was celebrating his sixty-fifth birthday.

Jacques, Luce and I did not quite know what to do next. We did not want to dwell on the rocket attack, so rather than going home, we followed the Lycée guard's advice and went to Vat Xieng Thong.

Vat Xieng Thong, access from the west.

The king's birthday (13 November 1972)

We approached the monastery with some hesitation, but there was no one checking the entry, and we walked straight in, and headed for the main temple. The monks were chanting, and we supposed that the king and his party were inside. Outside, long, straw mats had been placed for the guests. Every so often, a royal guard walked past, casually and barefoot. Here and there, children played freely, while another group of guards, in their French-style red berets, squatted in the shade of a large bougainvillea. We sat by the temple's large drum, close to the king's musicians who sat cross-legged on their mats, two of them ready to hit the xylophone keys. They played whenever the monks' chanting stopped. We were fascinated by what we could see, but as the main event was taking place inside the *vihaan* we started to wonder how long it would last. For a very long time! Only some two hours and a half later did the king's guests finally come out of the temple. The men, in formal white jackets and loose silk trousers, puffed at their pipes or cigars, waddling down the steps. The women, in their heavy silk skirts followed, their hair tied in typical Luang Phrabang fashion into an identical knot, above the right ear. The king, in yellow trousers and white shoes came last, with the queen at his side, small and quiet, her grey hair streaked white. They moved casually towards the monastery's main gate, where the royal car – a white Edsel – waited. A guard in his dark red beret opened the car door, and they were off. The sovereign's simple manner fitted the casual and relaxed mood of the occasion. On that day he acted as if Luang Phrabang were a large village under his benevolent protection, its people a part of his extended family.

I expected the celebration of the king's birthday to last only that morning. But I learned at the *vat* that the monks' prayers for the king would continue for another three days, the celebrations ending with a small procession of the royal elephants on the third. That, I thought, I could not miss. The news put the PL's attack further into the back of my mind, and though the spectacle would be taking place on a school day, I started making plans to attend.

Two days later, therefore, I rushed into town after teaching, in time to catch up with the expected grand procession of mahout-ridden elephants. I found instead the more modest spectacle of only two elephants ambling down the main street. Still, I was totally taken by the spectacle. The mahouts came straight out of pre-modern times, dressed as the guards of a great king of the past. In their red, loose-fitting outfits, their caps tightly fastened over their heads and ears, they sat on the elephants' backs, making them move by pressing a short dagger against the small of their necks, pushing their bare calves and feet against their sides. The small procession was led by a frail, elderly man in a mauve *sampot*, white stockings, a walking stick and an incongruous pair of white tennis shoes. He was the *panya sang,* the elephant ritual specialist, and head of the mahouts. Four men followed, dressed in black, a red cloth tied round their heads into a knot at the back. There was a moment of real solemnity when the elephants stopped by a red wooden structure, in front of Vat Mai.

Like other such structures facing other important *vat,* this *lak koi* had been a mounting-rail for the

King Sisavang Vathana.

A royal elephant enjoys tasty delicacies (left) which are placed by a monk on the *lak koi*, an H-shaped support, formerly used by the sovereign as a mounting stand. (Above) Vat Mai.

sovereign. Shaped like an H, the *lak koi*'s transversal bar was now used as a shelf on which the monks placed small balls of sticky-rice, and banana-leaf cornucopia, each filled with candles and flowers and incense. Before being offered these delicacies, the elephants were approached by the *panya sang* who spoke into their ears in a solemn tone to remind them of their duties: to stand firm, protect the king, ensure his longevity and save the town from the scourge of evil influences. The same entreaty had been delivered into the elephants' ears earlier, in front of Vat Xieng Thong.

The spectacle was at its end when the elephants were led back to the Royal Palace. But they did not miss the chance for yet another munch, and stopped on the way by the silver shops, where the merchants fed them with bananas and sugar cane. Walking behind, the three musicians continued to play. The sound of their drums and brass plates lingered behind the small procession, the two beasts a pale reflection of the royal elephants of the mythical past, when the kingdom at its most powerful had been defended by legions of fierce elephant-riding warriors. There was a magic about this Luang Phrabang of ritual, stronger in even its more modest expression than the impact of rockets, and T28s, and flattened buildings, and fear.

New Pathet Lao Attack (17 December, 1972)

There had been a lull in the fighting, and news that the Royal Army had managed to push back the Pathet Lao further away from town allowed for a momentary breathing space. Antoine and I decided to revisit Pak Suang, the village we had gone to shortly after my arrival, and whose attack and evacuation had been discussed at the Tokyo. When we got there, it was deserted. Next to the temple compound, we met a group of government soldiers. They were friendly, but with our limited Lao and their own reluctance to speak, we could only determine that the area was not yet safe for the villagers to return. They would have to stay away for at least another week. We felt like cutting the visit short, but the soldiers retained us for a smoke. The ice had been broken, and as we were leaving, they pointed to some caves on the elevated part of the river bank – the spot from where they had launched their attack, pushed the PL away and recovered full control. Turning towards the Mekong, I noticed some boys swimming. They were not older than thirteen or fourteen, but they were soldiers.

Antoine and I drove back, certain that the Pathet Lao had been successfully pushed back, at least for a time. We were wrong. The next day, they struck again. The sound of gunfire woke me in the early hours. This time the rockets had fallen on Ban Hat Hien, a village behind the airport. Later in the morning, according to what was now a macabre routine, I called on Jacques and Luce and drove with them towards the airport. We spotted a small group of Royal Lao Army soldiers. They were standing beside the house where the rocket had hit. One of them wore dark glasses, and a heavy pilot jacket with 'Vietnam' written on the back. He had enough English to explain: 'One rocket landed in the middle of the road, the other hit the house and killed three children and their mother. She and two children were caught running to the shelter behind the house, but the other child didn't even have time to get out of the house: there's blood inside, next to the bed where she died.' We felt sick to the stomach, and looked at each other without saying a word. We went into the house. On the floor, next to the pool of blood, was a small hole where the rocket had hit. The hole wasn't big (a rocket hits the ground and explodes horizontally, sweeping everything on its way, sideways). Above the bed, a poster showed the caption 'virtuous soldier' in English, under the image of a US soldier. Outside the house: pieces of furniture, a suitcase, a pot, some photographs. A small building attached to the house next door had also been blown up. We walked to our motorbikes, past the soldiers, in silence, and drove away. We avoided two rocket holes, one in the middle of the road where there were no houses, the second at a cross roads, where a small café and two houses had been slightly damaged.

The terrible episode forced me to reflect on what I had been living through. Only two months had passed since my arrival, but I had been moving without pause from a Pathet Lao attack, to the king's birthday's, from teaching English to following an elephant's procession, from driving close to the front line to witnessing another attack, from living a teacher's routine to having a distant feel of the fighting. I had a strong sense of the people's gentleness, which I could not reconcile with their taking part in a violent war. I needed to collect my thoughts and put the pieces of the Laotian puzzle into some kind of order. Fortunately, the December break was only a few days away. I had one week at my disposal and decided to travel out of Luang Phrabang.

2
I WIDEN MY HORIZON (1972-1973)

The war in southern Laos – in and around Pakse
(December 1972-January 1973)

While no instructions defined where I could safely go near Luang Phrabang, no set of clear rules existed regarding travel to other parts of Laos. These, I was surprised to learn, could be visited at will. I took note, and with the December holiday before me, and wishing to break away from my Luang Phrabang confinement, I made myself ready to travel to Pakse, the capital of the southern province of Champassak.

There was no way of travelling there directly – I had to pass through Vientiane. Commercial flights were functioning, but I wondered whether they were safe. A plane flying back to Vientiane from the South had crashed in early 1972, killing all passengers. However, as Royal Air Lao had been operating smoothly since the accident, I went ahead and booked. I flew to Vientiane on 27 December, but once there, rather than risking another Air Lao flight to the south, I chose to travel by road. But the road network inside Laos was by all accounts rudimentary, and so I was advised to cross over into Thailand, travel south on that side and cross back into Laos when I reached the border crossing point closest to Pakse.

I reached Thailand by crossing the Mekong from Vientiane. This turned out to be easier than the political differences between Laos and anti-communist Thailand had led me to expect. All the same, the contrast could not have been sharper between the two countries' checkpoints: relaxed on the Lao side, punctiliously bureaucratic in Thailand. My passport was stamped as a matter of course in Thadeua, the Lao river port. Not so, on the Thai side, in Nong Khai. Once there, I climbed up the bank and reached the immigration office where the officials took forever to examine my passport. They were self important in their well-pressed uniforms, the bars on their shirt pockets reminding me of their rank. This was a world where bureaucratic smugness coexisted with the cult of the uniform, excessive rigor and strict anti-communist vigilance. That could only be expected, for I was travelling at the height of the Vietnam war, when Thailand hosted US air bases on its territory, and provided mercenaries to fight alongside US forces in Vietnam.

The contrast with Laos continued when I crossed Nong Khai town on my way to the bus station. I sat at the back of my *samlor,* a three-wheel rickshaw. The town was clean, with a feeling of hygiene which permeated the neat asphalt of the roads, and the modern government buildings – everything was well pressed and starched, like the immigration officials' uniforms. I was far from the dilapidated colonial charm of dusty Vientiane, and the aging *stupas* and burnished gold leaf temples of Luang Phrabang. Here the monastic compounds and the temples inside them seemed brand new, shining brightly when the sun hit their glossy fronts. This was the culture of newness and modernity which had not reached Laos.

I continued my journey and passed through Udon town, where Thailand's commitment to anti-communism and the US was immediately apparent. The restaurants showed large 'Harry's Bar' or 'Joe's Bar' signs, reminding clients of the large American military base which stood outside town. This was a far cry from Laos, where Americans were careful to camouflage their military activities, while advertising their development and humanitarian aid programmes. There was no civil war here, no Laotian sharp conflict between the government and the Pathet Lao, and although the Thai Communist Party did show itself sporadically in some areas of Thailand (the North East particularly), the country was dominated by a strong authoritarian government who imposed its will by means of highly effective military and police forces.

The people I met in Thailand had little information about Laos. Their minds were full of stereotypes of 'dangerous' communists, and so could not believe I was living there. When I reached Ubon, another major town further south, the abbot of the monastery where I spent the night wanted to know everything about Laos, and called in other monks to listen. But that wasn't the end of that. Having satisfied their curiosity, the abbot focused on my being a teacher and asked me to give the group a quick English lesson, there and then. I felt at home! Often, when entering a *vat* in Laos, I had been welcomed with a similar mixture of curiosity and language-centred self-interest. I finished my tale about living in a communist-ridden conflict zone, gave my lesson and was finally allowed to collapse under a mosquito net.

I was up early. The monks had gone out for their daily round of alms, I washed up, ate the dried meat and sticky rice they had left for me, and left. Travelling long hours by bus, I finally reached the Thai immigration office on the Thai-Lao border further south, at Chong Mek. At this particular spot, the international border is not the river Mekong, it is a land boundary – the river flows some fifty km. to the east inside Laos, with both its banks standing firmly inside Lao territory. To get to Pakse, I still had to travel east for an hour or so, on a bumpy road, reach the Mekong and find a boat to finally cross over into town. It had been a long journey, but I felt free, free to go wherever I pleased, without worrying about whether to drive along this road or that, about security or the Pathet Lao or the Royal Lao Army. I loved Luang Phrabang, but it was great to be away.

From the boat, the Mekong seemed huge, four times as wide as it is in Luang Phrabang. But it moved more lazily than it did in the North, and seemed to barely advance between its low river banks, and long-drawn bends. I got off the boat, walked up another steep bank to the edge of town, and stopped to look back at the river and beyond, to the wide plain and the mountains on the western bank. As the sunlight hit the water, the view was magnificent. But the town itself was the opposite of that, being squat and run down. I walked down the main street, along the river. On one side, some dilapidated houses on stilts pointed the way to the market pavilion; on the other, I saw a row of dusty cafés, shops and restaurants, remarkable for the number of black-trousered Vietnamese women who served lemonades, or coffee and cake among swarms of flies. Further down, I reached an untidy public garden, where items of artillery were displayed. The faded lettering on a sign said that the Royal Lao Army had seized them from the North Vietnamese. This makeshift military exhibition, the town's large military headquarters on the east bank, the Supreme Command Building on the right bank, and the sound of T-28s taking off at regular intervals, all led to the same conclusion, unlike Luang Phrabang, the war had penetrated Pakse to its very centre.

I asked myself the question: did the war explain Paksé's run-down condition? Was this the temporary result of the war? Or was it the permanent expression of chronic social inequality and widespread corruption, which was known to be rampant? The massive but still unfinished cement palace being built for the local prince, Bounoum na Champassak, was more than perplexing in its ugliness, and in the unnecessary extravagance it represented at a time of war. The visible carcass of the huge unfinished palace was pregnant with meaning about the kinds of abuses which the war permitted; in this respect, the rumour in Luang Phrabang was that US Development Funds had been appropriated for its construction. It was also said that the people of Paksé publicly deferred to the prince's authority (as the son of Prince Nhouy, non-royal but supreme over-lord of the area under the French) but privately did not spare him for this and other alleged malpractices – his connection with the opium trade, his involvement with a number of casinos, and his having placed, on the Bangkok antique market, large numbers of Buddha statues and ancient inscriptions vandalized from the ancient Khmer ruins of Vat Phou. I took the accusations with a grain of salt, since they came from those among my Luang Phrabang friends who favoured the Pathet Lao, and strongly resented the obstructionist political Right which Prince Boun Oum represented. But the rumours reinforced my perception of Pakse as a town where war and generalised profiteering fed into each other. To complete the picture, the claim was made that the Prince profited directly from the secret sale of rice to the Pathet Lao, or turned a blind eye to the practice among wealthy Chinese merchants[1]. In either case, the covert sale of rice meant that the PL obtained the rice they needed, and in exchange spared Pakse from a major attack.

But there were other likely reasons why the town's integrity had been spared.

---

1   For the close relationship between the Na Champassak family and the Chinese business community see Evans 2009: 251.

The area to the east of Pakse in the direction of Vietnam comprised the strategic Bolovens Plateau where the Laotian conflict was entangled with the Vietnam War. Indeed, the plateau was flanked to the east by a section of the Ho Chi Minh trail, the North Vietnamese logistical corridor which had been targeted by American bombers from the air, and by American-paid mercenaries from the ground, most of whom were Thai. Pakse was an important military base; and though American air sorties did not necessarily originate there (they came from Thailand or further afield), it was a major Royal Lao Army Centre of Operations from where the Pathet Lao was targeted on two counts – as Lao enemies and as sustainers of the North Vietnamese. That being the case, why had Pakse not faced a major Pathet Lao offensive? Although the Vietnamese were operating on Lao territory along the Ho Chi Minh trail 'secretly' (as 'secretly' as the Americans were bombing them) they could have backed the Pathet Lao against Pakse. Why had this not happened? Was it fear of retaliation from Thailand? Since Pakse was located close to the land border with Thailand, it was likely that Thailand's well-known military capability had a strong dissuasive effect on the PL/Vietnamese's possibly belligerent intentions. Also, at a time when efforts towards a political settlement were progressing, a consensus may have developed that while fighting could not cease, a major military conflagration involving Thailand and North Vietnam had to be avoided at all costs.

* * * * * * * *

I wanted to visit the Khmer ruins of Vat Phou. The closeness of war in Pakse compared to Luang Phrabang made me hesitate, but the pull of the famous archaeological site was strong, and on second thoughts, remembering a tourist guide's note that a southbound road had linked it to the mythical Angkor Wat, I decided to go. The journey started early the following morning in a low-roofed boat which forced all passengers to crouch down, creating a feeling of intimacy. But neither this, nor the presence of two elderly men and several young women, travelling with small infants or very young children, managed to dispel my nagging concern about security. The feeling persisted after we set off, and as the put-put of the boat showed we were moving too slowly, I knew that we could never get away if ever we were targeted from the river bank. For more than an hour we carried on at the same pace, until the boatman brought us close to the bank where the water was shallow. Then the engine's groan turned to a splutter and we came to a stop. I felt trapped. But the others didn't – they were all smiles, and when the boatman said 'it'll take time before we can start again', they exclaimed '*Bo pen nyang*! – 'nevermind'. Soon the women (except those who were breast-feeding) got into the water, away from the midday heat, which the low roof of the motionless boat was

The god Indra riding
Airavata (Lintel Detail)
Vat Phou, Dec 1972.

quickly transforming into an oven. They called me to join them. Still upset, I chose
not to move, but their contagious good humour got the best of my bad mood, and
when they decided to get back on, I gave them a hand. When the boat moved again,
I sat right at the front. Two small boys stood beside me, giggling and braving the
wind which pushed the heat hard into their eyes …. until they accepted defeat and
sat low, huddling together against the wall of the boat. The war was out of my mind.

It was a five-hour journey down the Mekong to the small town of Champassak.
I was the only one to get off the boat, and soon found a local bus for the short ride
to the ruins. We drove past another of Prince Bounoum's houses, which overlooked
a large pond, and stopped near the foot of Phou Kao (the Ancient Mountain) on
which the religious site had been built. Shortly after, the rattle of a machine gun
broke the silence. The sound seemed to come from the other side of the mountain.
I walked up regardless, beginning the stiff climb uphill, along a path of steep
steps that ascended between two impressive structures (perhaps praying halls for
pilgrims) and led past a succession of terraces to the main shrine at the top.

I approached a red stone building which stood one fifth of the way up. On
either side of a doorway, multiple-headed water snakes – the *naga* – carved in
stone, threatened the intruder with fierce open jaws. Walking on, I stopped to look
at the crisp carvings on the frame of another doorway. At the centre of the lintel,
a man sat cross-legged directly above me, wearing a necklace and a loin cloth. Had
I known anything about the Khmer who built the site, and the Hindu identity of
the gods they depicted in stone, I would have identified the god Indra riding the
three-headed Airavata in the figure above me. In my ignorance, all I saw was that
the figure was fierce, as fierce as the menacing *naga*.

What I later learned about the Khmer's tumultuous history would tempt me to
say that their architectural complexes, built to impress and to attest to the might
of the polity and its sovereigns (but mellowed plastically by religious sentiment

and masterful decoration) captured the essentially war-like nature of the Khmer people. The politico-religious sites were the work of a military people accustomed to assert their authority over their own territories, over those of their vassals and other subjected peoples. At the time of my visit, however, I was entirely focused on understanding Laos, and wrote in my diary that the carvings expressed the latent aggressiveness not of the Khmer, but of the Lao people, that aspect of their character which was displayed daily in the war, but contrasted sharply with the gentleness which I had learned to appreciate. When I eventually restored to Vat Phou its Khmer identity, I retained the site's capacity to express bare political power in the softening idiom of religious conviction, in a way that had fitted the paradox of Laos as it appeared to me in 1972 – its people had seemed kindly and compassionate in all ways, but had been fully engaged in a conflict in which the enemy was never spared.

Two monks joined me as I reached the top, and pointed to the shrine. I took my time taking photos, and slowly went back down with them as they showed me some features I had missed. Having reached the road, we walked to where a local bus was expected, and as we lazily stood waiting, and watched two soldiers who drove past on their motorcycles, the sharp sound of a machine-gun made us start. There was a moment of nervousness, but my companions just laughed it away with a cheerful 'bo pen nyang'. We continued to wait, but the bus never turned up, and so we waved for a ride on a small roofless truck, and got on. Off we went, holding on tight, as millions of mosquitoes blinded us, got into my hair and skidded off the monks' shaved heads. I had got used to the occasional rattling of the machine-guns.

I stayed the night at a monastery in Champassak, and caught the first morning boat back to Paksé. Before going to Vat Phou, I had been struck by the presence of the Vietnamese and Chinese, but while the Vietnamese in the market and coffee shops were modest in their dress and manner, the Chinese, as I now confirmed, had looked prosperous. They were part of a community that counted – their strong commercial and cultural presence, their elaborate temples and the white mass of the Chinese Cultural Centre showed it.[2] Compared to Luang Phrabang, Pakse had struck me with a strong Sino-Vietnamese feeling, an impression that tallies with the fact that the town's population at that time (some 70,000) was equally divided among the lowland Lao, the Vietnamese and the Chinese. In Luang Phrabang, both communities were prosperous and readily identified, by the Chinese-owned

---

2   Urban Laos comprised a dominant class of politicians and civil servants of low-land Lao ethnic origin (extended in Luang Phrabang by the court) and a commercial class of Vietnamese and Chinese merchants and petty traders (extended by a small Indian group). The relative weight and visibility of each group could vary, influencing a town's general atmosphere in fundamental ways.

silver shops on Sisavangvong Avenue, and the magnificent Vietnamese monastery, Chua Phat Thich, which offered spectacular views over the Mekong at sunset. But the communities' imprint did not alter the town's essentially Lao character as unlike had seemed to occur in Pakse.

Another point of comparison: northern and southern Laos differed in terms of their ethnic minorities. In Luang Phrabang, I had noted their occasional presence, and though security conditions had prevented me from visiting their villages, I knew they were culturally and linguistically diverse, and a major factor in the dynamics of war. The absence of the hill tribes in Pakse caught my attention. I had read that some of the area's ethnic minorities lived on the Boloven Plateau. Did they not wear distinctive clothing? Did they choose to remain in their villages? Or had I had simply missed them? In any case, I wondered whether they were playing a role in the war, as did the Hmong in north and north-eastern Laos. It turned out that the Laven, the Suay, the Alak and other minorities of the Plateau lived close to the worst-hit areas, where American B-52 carpet-bombed Vietnamese forces along the Ho Chi Minh trail, or where the Royal Lao Army confronted the Pathet Lao. But the communities' imprint did not alter the town's essentially Lao character, as had occurred in Pakse.

* * * * * * *

I had little time to get back, and decided to fly – this time braving three Air Lao flights, one to Savannakhet, the next to Vientiane and the last to Luang Phrabang. I had managed a good break and had learned a great deal.

I now knew that the country's leadership at its highest levels was in the hands of the old feudal class, regardless of political orientation. The South operated under the non-royal but politically and economically dominant Na Champassak family. Prince Bounoum had played and continued to play a central role in national politics as a member of the intransigent Right, rivalling with the neutralists and obstructing as much as possible any kind of understanding with the Pathet Lao. His position was considerably strengthened by Champassak's historically rooted tradition of autonomy combined with solid links with anti-communist Thailand. Prince Bounoum's dominance among the rightists was paralleled at the political Centre and on the Left by two other princely leaders whose origin was in the North but whose relevance, like Prince Boun Oum's, was national. They were both from Luang Phrabang, were members of the vice-royal branch of the royal family and were half-brothers. One was the committed neutralist Prince Souvannaphoumma, Prime Minister in my time. The other was Prince Souphanouvong, the most internationally visible member of the Pathet Lao leadership. I did not know yet that the brothers would be key to the political evolution of the conflict, against the perennially obstructionist presence of the Right.

Pakse's Sino-Vietnamese flavor and the presence of its own ethnic groups had sharpened my awareness of the country's ethnic make-up, and of the complex social dynamics behind the war. This was not a unified royalist side fighting a nationalist liberation movement with communist sympathies. The Lao people were not only sharply divided politically among Rightists, Neutralists and the Pathet Lao, they were also composed of numerous ethnic groups who were linked in a maze of inter-ethnic rivalries and alliances which varied among the regions and related differently to the conflict. I had some idea of how this complex set of relationships operated in the South. I needed to find out how they functioned in the North.

Back in the North (January 1973)

The security situation had seriously deteriorated during my absence: on January 3, 1973, an Italian priest who worked closely with the Roman Catholic Bishop of Luang Phrabang, Alessandro Staccioli, had been shot dead on the Vientiane-Luang Phrabang road. On the same day, another calamity struck when the Pathet Lao took the Hmong village of Ciugna. Faced with these facts, my plan to visit the hill peoples had to be postponed.

The priest's death was a major personal loss for the bishop, and for the priest's students at the Catholic School. As for the fall of Ciugna, it was a disaster. The village functioned as a buffer, and without it, the town became vulnerable to a Pathet Lao attack. The PL's move had caused a terrible panic in the village, making most women and children, and some men flee into town. Once there, they described how families had run away frantically, trying to escape from PL gun fire. Five children had been killed. It was not clear how many men had been hit, or had remained in the village or had fled.

Luang Phrabang responded by providing food and shelter. Astonishingly, however, the opinion started being voiced by the town's authorities that help should be given out in small doses – too generous a response, they said, could induce the displaced Hmong to stay on in town, and encourage the men who remained in the village to join them. If that happened, Ciugna would no longer serve as a buffer, and Luang Phrabang would be made permanently vulnerable to direct attack. Ciugna could not be dispensed with. This meant that the displaced group, including the women and the children would be encouraged to go back as soon as the Royal Lao Army drove the PL away.

The Vientiane Agreement (21 February 1973)[3]

From the time I set foot in Laos, the war had been an unmovable background to everything I did. Its impact had varied in intensity, but in the absence of information about what was being negotiated behind the scenes, I regarded it as a permanent fact of life. However, intense peace discussions had in fact been progressing, and following difficult negotiations, the warring parties had finally agreed on a number of points. The resulting historic document showed the way towards a gradual resolution of the conflict, in a process which was the hope of those who welcomed or at least accepted the Pathet Lao, but a reason for resistance among members of the political Right. For apart from providing a road map of constructive action, the Vientiane Agreement could be seen as the culmination of a long-drawn out process, extending over decades, in which the Pathet Lao had gained international legitimacy. The fact was celebrated by the movement's sympathizers, but bitterly lamented by its detractors.

Significantly, the signature of the Agreement in February 1973 followed the Paris Agreements on Vietnam. These had ended the Vietnam War on January 27 and provided the Pathet Lao with a precedent on which to claim international recognition, based on its considerable military capability (increased from 24,000 in 1962 to some 48,000 men in 1973) and on the political control it now exercised over four fifths of the country's territory, and over two fifths of its population. For the Pathet Lao, the Agreement was a major breakthrough, which was celebrated accordingly among its ranks.

As with the 1954 and 1962 Geneva Agreements before it, the 1973 Vientiane Agreement incorporated a key component: the eventual creation of a Coalition

Pathet Lao leaders Phoummi Vongvichit, Souphanouvong and Politburo members celebrate the February 1973 Agreement. (photo of Photo in the Houaphan Province Memorial Sites Committee museum)

Government. The Agreement otherwise required the strict application of the 1962 Geneva Agreements which forbade all military activity by foreign powers, specifically the United States and the Democratic Republic of Vietnam. This was key, since it addressed the factors which had made Laos into a pawn in the Cold War.

While the PL had good reasons to rejoice, responses on the Royal Government side were nuanced and differed by location. In Luang Phrabang, they were surprisingly subdued, compared to the strongly voiced opposition reported from Vientiane. Among Luang Phrabang's highest authorities, a carefully phrased optimism hid a wide range of opinions, from reluctant acceptance to downright hostility. A similar ambiguity existed at the Lycée. The students were on the whole reluctant to say what they thought. Some of those who spoke seemed out of touch with the Agreement's significance, one student even deploring that the end of the war would take Laos out of the international scene, and make it sink into insignificance… But even among those who were in favour, initial enthusiasm soon grew thin and was gradually replaced by cautious skepticism, based on the suspicion that neither side would respect the terms of the Agreement, and that the Right would boycott it, as had occurred previously, after the 1954 and 1962 Geneva conferences.

In fact, news reached Luang Phrabang shortly after the Agreement's signature that right-wing groups had demonstrated violently against the terms of the document in Vientiane. It was also said that the PL had broken the ceasefire in some twenty locations. Under such circumstances, it was feared that the Agreement would be a dead letter. As it turned out, it took fourteen months of difficult negotiations and continued fighting, before a Coalition Government was finally established, in April 1974.

The Lycée in a changing political context (9 March 1973)

In the polarized environment which the Agreement exacerbated, my Lycee students and colleagues began to speak more willingly about politics. By comparison, the school administration's attitude vis-à-vis the Pathet Laos' political advances was noncommittal, while it fully supported the *status quo*. This was shown at the school's annual Teachers' Day, a formal affair which was attended by well-known public figures and upholders of the current system: the City Mayor, several Luang Phrabang National Assembly representatives, and the Supreme Patriarch, pillar of the Buddhist hierarchy of monks, the Sangha. The room where the main event took place had been prepared with extreme care. It was dominated by the image of the Buddha. On either side, the teachers were invited to sit on chairs which had been set up in a circle.

---

3   For the full contents of the Agreement, see Stuart Fox 1986: 31.

All male and female students sat on the floor in two separate groups, the boys in their usual school uniform, the girls wearing their best silk *psins,*the traditional embroidered Lao skirt. The girls had also adopted the traditional dress code of religious deference by placing a narrow silk scarf over one shoulder, tying it under the other arm, at the waist. After a long wait, the Patriarch entered, accompanied by three monks. He greeted us all, gave some words of advice to the students, and provided us teachers with a booklet of Buddhist maxims, and a photograph of himself. To pay homage to teachers collectively, the girls approached in pairs, carrying offering bowls which contained flowers, candles and incense sticks. We were then invited to move outside to receive a further blessing. The Patriarch and a monk approached us as we sat in rows, waiting. Holding a silver bowl filled with water, the Patriarch started to sprinkle us lightly. But the water droplets kept falling, longer than expected; on our heads and shoulders, again and again, while the students giggled and kept shifting on their chairs, and the Patriarch kept sprinkling. He was enjoying himself, and so were we …

The gesture was a fine conclusion to a day of mixed fun and formality. Having taken leave from the religious and lay authorities, we thanked the students for their hospitality, the care with which they had decorated the school, the flower arrangements and elaborate offerings.

* * * * * * * * *

Lycée students on Teachers' day.

The Supreme Patriarch sprinkles teachers and students with blessed water.

Back at home, I paused to reflect on the day's events. Ever since my arrival, I had been surprised by the students' deference. The gestures of respect had been pleasing to watch, but from my foreigner's perspective, had sometimes seemed excessive. I understood that teachers were regarded as holders of knowledge and moral authority, and had to be treated accordingly. But the day's ceremony had pushed that attitude to a kind of cult. As with other traditional ceremonies, the school ritual seemed yet another carefully orchestrated rehearsal for a hierarchical society. And in the context of the Vientiane Agreement and increasing Pathet Lao power, it had political significance. The enhancement of deference as a value, placed the school at the centre of the old social order, where deference was a central axiom, with the full authority of the monks and the town's highest authorities. To that extent, the Lycée functioned as a counter to the Pathet Lao's more egalitarian model.

The day's events, and my role as a Lycée teacher were a subject of further reflection some days later, when I talked to one of my middle-level students. Thongsouk was a lowland Lao. But he was an outsider in Luang Phrabang, a country boy who had come from the village of Pak Ou, memorable for my first ever trip out of town. Thongsouk was more communicative than most, and spontaneously disclosed his anger about the war. In Pak Ou his family had owned a large teak house, which the Pathet Lao had burned down. In the family's efforts to save the building, his mother's brother had been killed. The survivors were devastated, and he had been deeply affected, becoming temperamental and irascible. Sometimes, when feelings of anger came to the surface, he found he could not keep his cool. Apart from the family tragedy, he was worried about the future – the Lycée was a dead end for people like himself who lacked important family connections. His only chance was to follow the one model of success to which he had access, to become a T28 pilot. He said this just after the display of privilege which I had seen on Teachers' Day.

In my first months of teaching, I had found value in providing the élite of a poor, small, land-locked country with a foreign language, and encouraging its members to think independently. But to help educate the future élite of a highly structured, unequal society when the foundations of that society were about to collapse, that was another matter. Was the job a waste of my time? Was it a waste of my students' time? As for students from simpler backgrounds and no connections, like Thongsouk, was the job a hoax? Was it a misleading performance that made them believe that studying English, and French and all other subjects of the French curriculum had a future to offer?

The sharply hierarchical nature of the society was one of the issues which the Pathet Lao wanted to address. Their objective of a less unequal, more just environment, was directly relevant to students with a specific grievance such as Thongsouk. And as awareness of PL objectives grew, and knowledge of corruption among politicians and the commercial class increased, the PL gained in student support, even among the more privileged. In time students as a group would become one of the movement's key sustainers, not only in Luang Phrabang but in Laos as a whole.

Beyond the lowland Lao: my first visit to a Hmong village
(15 March, 1973)

The Vientiane Agreement was signed on 21 February. The ceasefire it proclaimed gradually improved security conditions around town, thus allowing me to drive farther than had been possible before. The areas I could reach included Ciugna, the village which the PL had taken on the third of January. Two months had elapsed since then, and just under a month after the Vientiane Agreement was signed; it was high time I moved out of lowland Lao territory, and got to know more about other ethnic realities.

As I knew no Hmong and my Lao language was still rudimentary, I asked a Hmong student called Moua to be my interpreter. We set off soon after Teachers' Day driving straight there until we reached a bend outside Ciugna, where the road ran horizontally past the village's long line of houses. We looked for evidence of the attack, but there was nothing to show for it – it had all happened more than two months before. On either side of the road, the Hmong homesteads stood directly on the ground, unlike Lao houses which are built on stilts. The rough wooden planks of the walls, and the straw roofs looked stark and sad against the mist, blending well with the villagers' weather-beaten faces and faded clothes. They also fitted in with the yellow-brown dampness of the fields behind the houses – a steppe-like landscape, where the horses stood their ground against the wind that pushed the pale-green grass blades to the side. The village was isolated and peaceful, surrounded by fields and towering mountains, a suitable setting, I thought, for the villagers' austere lives and hard work. The place had recovered from the Pathet Lao's attack, but the difficult conditions of its people compared badly with lowland Laos; they seemed worse than those of run-down Pak Ou, the village I had visited upon my arrival in Laos. In retrospect, and though it is hazardous to compare levels of poverty, life seemed to have been less difficult there, despite the concentration of displaced people. War was not after all the great equalizer – the Hmong of Ciugna seemed to have a much rawer deal.

Back in Luang Phrabang the contrast between the town's succession of brilliant ceremonies and the austerity I had just witnessed, gave me a measure of the gap separating the country's ethnic groups. I had seen a Hmong village at close quarters, but that was only one ethnic reality within a total of 68 groups, none of whom accounted for more than 50% of the total, including the dominant low-land Lao (47-48%). The opportunities for social differentiation and exclusion among the groups seemed endless, in a process that systematically made subordinates of the hill-dwelling peoples, placing them beneath the lowland Lao, and under other urban dwellers – Vietnamese, Chinese and Indian merchants.

I had witnessed the mechanism operating occasionally at the Lycée, where I had seen Khmu' students targeted. Their people lived in the mid-level altitudes

Hmong women at the market in Ciugna 1973.

of mountainous areas, and were referred to as 'Kha', which means slave. The term had stuck, partly because the king's barefooted guards, who were recruited from that group, were the archetype of unconditional subservience and a required feature in all public ceremonies centred on the king. Hmong students could also be discriminated against, a fact that no longer surprised me, given the ambiguous manner in which the Hmong from Ciugna had been treated when they had run for safety into town.

For the Pathet Lao, the extraordinary variety and hierarchical differentiation and mutual discrimination among the ethnic groups was a key political issue that required reform. A strong egalitarian conviction lay behind this. But there was another reason: the Pathet Lao were heavily indebted to the mountain peoples who had provided them with indispensable safe havens during the movement's initial stages. As their military and political position prospered, the PL sought to cancel the discriminatory aspects of inter-ethnic relations in the areas under their control, defending the principle that all peoples in Laos should contribute equally to the construction of a new, ethnically unified Laos. After the PL's victory in 1975, the equalizing trend continued, when a policy of integration was applied countrywide to replace the former system of separate autonomies. Accordingly, all 68 nationalities in the country were invited to participate in the creation of a multicultural Lao State, and a new Lao national identity.

The PL's equalizing policy would eventually achieve some results after 1975, when they managed to correct some aspects of the rigid pre-revolutionary ethnic order. But in March 1973, when I visited Ciugna, that utopia had not been attempted, let alone realized. The Vientiane Agreement was in place to promote the cessation of hostilities, but was not expected to modify the social order. Seen from Luang Phrabang, a chasm continued to separate the town from the countryside, and among rural villages, in the mountainous areas particularly, each ethnic group continued to stand its ground in opposition to all others.

3

NEW YEAR RITUALS AT A TIME OF WAR

Pi Mai (new year) celebrations (April 1973)

The war had not prevented Luang Phrabang from celebrating any of its renowned ceremonies. But as Pi Mai approached, the persistence of the conflict despite the Vientiane Agreement was creating tension and this, I felt, was encouraging the authorities to exert more zeal than ever in preparing for the New Year. Perhaps especially brilliant festivities could help counter what was regarded as the Pathet Lao's growing influence, and strengthen the essential components of an unmovable Lao identity. Officials who were for or against the Agreement both indicated by their efforts that the traditional order had to be maintained more firmly than ever. As for ordinary people, war seemed to have intensified their belief in the efficacy of the upcoming rituals. It was said that the ceremonies had remained unchanged from time immemorial, and provided similar benefits year after year, but in the presence of war, they were expected to help heal the deep national divisions which were tearing the country apart. In my case, however, the relevance of the celebrations to current affairs was not my primary concern. I expected that the ceremonies would reveal a great deal about the Lao worldview, and so I focused on their hidden meanings and extraordinary aesthetic appeal.

As I would soon discover, the celebrations accommodated two contradictory

My houseguests and I get prepared for the water throwing.

aspects, the sacred and the profane. The sacred dimension appeared in formal rituals which purified the town, confirmed the sanctity of its institutions and strengthened the moral value of the social order. The playful, profane dimension showed itself at all other times through song, dance and play, encouraged by the season's intense heat and, among the men, by liberal amounts of drink. But the latter aspects never reached a state of orgiastic abandonment. They were kept in check by the domesticating influence of Buddhist devotion, by the intimidating presence of the town's religious and civil authorities and, at the festivities' highest moments, by the over-arching authority of the King.

* * * * * * * *

New Year in Luang Phrabang was famous countrywide, and although political and military conditions made access difficult, visitors from outside town, including expatriates and diplomats, managed to participate. I had my own share of guests, a group of VSOs from Vientiane, Savannakhet and Pakse, who braved the obstacles, some of them even travelling 210 miles on the Vientiane/Luang Phrabang road by motorbike. Among them my friend Raymond Hall, a fellow volunteer who was teaching in Pakse, arrived with a badly injured leg – determined to make it, he had covered the full distance on his own, had lost his balance, and fallen off his motorbike when the New Year merrymakers of a village had hurled buckets of water on him. When Ray finally arrived, other colleagues such as Mike, posted in Savannakhet, and Margaret and Olwyn and Joanna, who worked in Vientiane, had already transformed my house into a chaotic inn. Once settled, we threw ourselves into the festivities. My students warned us that there would be much rowdy water-throwing and we should have our water-filled buckets at the ready to retaliate whenever we were targeted. It was not long before we joined in.

Temporary *that* were built with sand to honour the Buddha.

Freeing birds and fish, and building *that* for the Buddha (13 April 1973)

We started on the last day of the dying year, joining the entire town as it focused on the morning markets. We went to the one at the top of Sisavangvong Road, close to the Palace. Everything worth buying was for sale, handicrafts of all descriptions, all manner of sweet and savoury foods and everything needed for Buddhist worship including scented frangipani flowers, candles and incense sticks. But the most sought-after items, were small live birds in bamboo cages, and fish in small plastic bags, each waiting to be sold and then promptly freed by their momentary owners as a form of merit-making – a poetic expression of the Buddhist virtue of detachment.

On the afternoon of that day, I left my guests to their own devices and joined my students. We boarded a canoe and crossed over to Xieng Men, on the right bank of the Mekong, where sandbanks appear every year in mid-river, when the intense heat of the dry season brings the water down to its lowest level. The purpose of the expedition was both religious and profane: to show devotion to the Buddha by building a *that* with sand, and enjoy some horseplay on the side. Compared to the permanent *that* which are found in monastery courtyards, these smaller ones were temporary, though that did not diminish the merit of making them. I joined my companions as they gathered sand, carried it to a carefully chosen spot, built a mound, made it into a pointed pyramid and smoothed its surface. The finishing touch was to plant elongated flyers on the sides, each of them marked by the signs of the zodiac.

In the overwhelming heat, each group set off to build the tallest, most beautiful structure. The challenging task was met lightheartedly, as a piece of fun, but once the *that* was completed, a more thoughtful mood set in. Squatting, the builders raised their joined hands to their foreheads for a moment's silence, looking the very picture of Buddhist devotion, although just behind, facing the river, other groups carried on with the jostling and water-splashing. But the pause did not last long. The *that* builders soon changed gear again, ran to the river, pushed each other into the water, the young women pulling at the young men's shirts, the men enjoying the women's attention.

On one side of the narrow stretch of sand, the king's youngest son, Sauriyavong Savang (thus spelt to distinguish him from his nephew Suriyavong Savang), known

A refreshing pause in the Mekong after building *stupa* in the heat.

to all for his large size and loud laughter, was busy enjoying himself with his Lao and foreign guests. Standing in full view of all, he and his friends also built a *that,* and once it was finished, threw themselves freely into their own fun, without inhibitions. By acting as a good Buddhist also capable of having a good time, the prince showed his closeness to the people, and strengthened the town's already strong attachment to the royal family. In the present political context, I reflected that the multiple bonds which linked Luang Phrabang to the monarchy were a formidable force whose resilience the Pathet Lao had evaluated correctly. It was not by chance that they had left the royal capital largely untouched; they had only hit the airport with just enough muscle to provide a convincing reminder of their presence.

Inside the procession, each village was led by the abbot of its monastery.

The procession of the palanquins
(14 April)

The day following the stupa building, my guests and I went mid-way up Avenue Sisavangvong, and waited there for a procession which was to move across town, starting at Vat That Noi, and ending at the famous monastic compound, Vat Xieng Thong. The long advancing column included all of the town's neighbourhoods. These were veritable self-contained villages which vied against each other for the supremacy of their monasteries, the scholarship or

I recognised my students among the young women. Protected by their parasols, they carried offerings in a sign of devotion.

magical expertise of their abbots, the beauty of their young women and the antics of their young men. I watched each village showing its riches within the procession. First, came the abbot of the first village, already soaked in his sedan chair, followed by his monks and novices.

Then, the young women and girls appeared, in their silks and brocades, walking under parasols, and carrying elaborate conical flower arrangements in their silver bowls.

Their careful movements and grace contrasted sharply with the group behind them; wild-looking men with faces and bodies smeared with coal or soot. Encouraged by a dose of alcohol, they sang, danced and clapped to the sound of drums, cymbals and the traditional Lao mouth organ, the *khene*. The men were given some license to be wild and rowdy, in this procession and for other carnival-like moments, but not in the evenings, when they could be asked by their families to go to the *vat*, nor during the more solemn rituals.

Men's license to act freely never implied permission for licentiousness. Men were only allowed to swagger and boast in front of young women, or compete noisily against each other, or throw water, but nothing else. As for the women, they could be paragons of correctness, as in the Procession of the Palanquins, although they were permitted to drop their modest attitudes at certain well-defined moments, but always within limits defined by common rules of decency. In short, the New Year allowed for some flexibility in the definition of gender, and in the relation between the sexes, but always within the rules of correctness which the ceremonial renewal of the Kingdom required.

* * * * * * * * *

My friends and I watched the procession from the side of the road, inside the crowd of onlookers. Many were holding buckets of water, ready to hurl over

The young men showed the wilder aspects of the festivities.

The Pou Nyeu Nya Nyeu perform for the passing crowd.

the passing column. As their targets approached, they threw the water, drenching the men with full force, but sprinkling the young women gently. Among the onlookers, the older women approached the monks with restraint – one way of making merit – but the children did not discriminate. They hurled water on the monks and even the abbots, soaking them to the bone. And then I caught sight of two extraordinary beings walking in the middle of the crowd. Close in appearance to gigantic puppets, their huge red heads towered over their long rattan skirts which they dragged forward at every step, as if sweeping the ground.

They were lighthearted and playful, and added a touch of fun, a sight which both children and adults enjoyed. I decided to follow them. They advanced slowly, and then they stopped. Suddenly they had become actors, surrounded by a small circle of spectators. Their improvised dance was followed attentively, with a certain deferential fondness. I wondered why. A spectator told me: 'They are the Pou Nyeu Nya Nyeu' (Grandfather and Grandmother Nyeu). 'They are the ancestors of the Lao people'. I continued to watch the performance even more attentively, promising myself to find out more.

My friends and I were gradually pulled in by the crowd, ending up drenched under the ferocious sun. We kept bumping into my students who did not hesitate to pour more water on us, our soaked clothes clinging to our bodies. We finally reached Vat Xieng Thong. The orderly succession of neighbourhoods dissolved there: the monks moved to one side, and the women sought refuge by one of the monastery's temples. The stage was set for the men to take over noisily as a

The procession dissolved at Vat Xieng Thong: the women stood aside (above) as the men took centre stage (below).

chaotic crowd. They occupied the free space separating the various temples, some doing the sword dance, others pushing and shoving, clapping and singing, while my friends and I joined in as a single body, doing the same.

Outside Vat Xieng Thong, the crowd seemed even freer. As we walked home, my friends and I faced brigades of children or young men in the midst of battle, using water as a lethal weapon which was sometimes mixed with noodles, paper and glue.

Brigades of young boys threatened their victims with a lethal mix of water, rice, paint and glue.

A glimpse of the monarchy and the traditional order
(15 April 1973)

The programme specified that the king would continue at the centre of the most important rituals of purification and renewal. For the time being, however, I was about to see him in a more mundane role, playing host at the Royal Palace where he welcomed the diplomatic corps and the Lao elite every year. Like other foreigners who worked in officially recognised institutions, I was invited. The evening started on the southernmost side of the palace grounds, where I sat next to the other guests. The chairs faced the main façed, and I was close enough to see the kingdom's three-headed elephant clearly outlined in gold on the pediment. Directly behind me, the Phou Si hill's dark presence seemed to be ensuring our protection. On my left, a spacious ceremonial hall and its adjoining elevated terrace dominated the stage where the Royal Ballet would perform. The king's seat was placed at the centre of the terrace, flanked on either side by rows of chairs for the court. More rows of chairs surrounded the stage. All trees and shrubs were floodlit.

As I looked around at my fellow spectators, I saw some of my Lycée colleagues lost in a sea of unknown western faces, probably diplomats who were in town for the occasion, away from their embassies in Vientiane. We sat until the message moved from mouth to mouth that the performance would begin at the top of the Phou Si, behind us. We turned our heads in unison towards it. Although buried in darkness, the bright moonlight showed us the hill's outline. Slowly, we focused on the hill top, where we saw several lights shining dimly through the thick frangipani foliage. As more and brighter lights appeared, we recognized the mythical water-serpent, the *naga*. Everyone in Luang Phrabang knew that the beast had been guarding a treasure for uncounted eons under the hill, until he was tamed by a magically potent monk, on the initiative of a benevolent king. Since then, and until that evening, the *naga* was known to be the fully domesticated protector of the religion and the monarchy close to the palace, traditionally the centre of the kingdom's stability.[4] The lights behind the foliage began to move. Nailed to our seats and mesmerized by the apparition, our eyes followed the large dragon-like serpent meandering its way along the downward path of steps, its long body made up of lotus-shaped, light orange lanterns which were raised and lowered by children to the sound of bells, and the thud of drums. It reached the foot of the hill, crossed the palace gates and entered the grounds, advancing at its own slow pace. Reaching the palace pond, it settled by the water, and placed the lanterns of its body neatly on the ground. As the lantern-carrying children hid behind the shrubs, out of sight, only the _naga_ remained – the revered mythical beast who had been cruel but was now the kingdom's gentle, permanent protector. I reflected that the

The Vat Mai high reliefs: a timeless representation of the palace, traditionally the centre of the Kingdom's stability.

4   There are a number of versions of the myth, some of which include a wealth of detail.
    See Stuart-Fox and Somsanouk Mixay 2010: 34-36.

Hanuman, the monkey commander, and two monkey soldiers in a 2016 performance of the *Ramayana*, Palace Museum Theatre Luang Phrabang.

tale was relevant to the real threats that were destabilizing the kingdom. We needed the undomesticated warring sides to be transformed, like the *naga,* into a factor of peace. Could the king orchestrate that change?

After a long wait, a large group of white-coated dignitaries walked out of the palace, towards the side of the stage. A group of women of the court followed, dressed almost identically in the traditional silk skirt, the *psin*, their hair swept sideways into the same tight chignon, to one side of the head. The ambassadors came later. Again, there was a longish pause, until the king and the royal family finally appeared. Everyone rose; the king sat, everyone followed and the performance could now begin.

Various scenes of the Lao version of the *Ramayana*, the famous Indian epic, were acted out in ballet form, showing Phra Lam, the exiled royal prince setting off with his younger brother to rescue his wife Nang Sida, the unwilling victim of the King of Demons who had ravished her. All Laotians knew the key episodes, and at each performance waited impatiently for Hanuman to appear – the monkey king and commander of the monkey soldiers who, by tricks or by skill, managed to defeat the demons and rescue the princess. The moralizing tale extols the virtues of the ideal husband, brother, wife and king, and celebrates the army, among the kingdom's other defenders. The narrative sets good against evil – dark characters whose only purpose is to bring calamity and chaos. Turning to reality, I wondered about the audience's politics and who among the spectators, Lao or foreign, would identify the saviour monkeys with the Royal Army, or would place them in the ranks of the Pathet Lao. The skill of the dancers, the magnificent costumes, and the beauty of the masks strengthened the monkeys' vigour and fighting skills and perhaps led the spectator to confirm for himself on what side of the conflict he stood. However, the animal elasticity and fanciful gestures of the monkey army brought in a welcome touch of comedy which pulled one back into fantasy.

The concluding moments of the performance were marked by the appearance of a truly fantastic float. On it, the god Indra, holding a lyre, sat on the back of a magnificent buffalo, with six beautiful girls standing on either side. An escort of sword dancers preceded the moving platform, while a second group of men followed, advancing in a loose, dancing walk, throwing their arms forward with upturned fingers. They did this with an air of informality which prevailed on and off stage – Indra's attendants giggled on the buffalo, while the royal children, whom I saw sitting by the king's feet, kept fretting to get more attention from the adults.

The performance came to a close with a women's ballet. This did not represent a well-known myth. It was simply a dance offering to honour the king. Thirty girls, covered in silk and gold advanced towards him, retreated slightly, paused, advanced again, throwing their arms forward at each step, opening their hands to represent blossoming flowers. Having reached the edge of the stage, the young women bent their knees in unison, looked down in deference and saluted the king with joined hands.

The performances were followed by a buffet with Lao and western dishes, served on a wide terrace. Music from the reception hall inside invited the guests to walk in. Wide green sofas had been placed against the walls of the hall, surrounding the large dance floor. At one end, an orchestra played Lao music, encouraging the couples to join the 'circle dance' – the *lamvong*. The white-jacketed men advanced in the inside of the circle, slowly opening and closing their hands; the women on the outside did the same, but more gently, one of them moving her hands and bending her knees imperceptibly under a perfect head kept erect by the tight upward sweep of her hair. The traditional music lasted for as long as the king was present, but once he left, there was western music, and the self-consciousness with which groups excluded each other began to relax. Crown Prince Vongsavang stayed until the end, saying farewell to the departing guests. Among them I could see the ladies of the court approach the prince, only too glad to be deferential for one moment and raise their joined hands.

A scene from a 2016 performance recalls the representation of the *Ramayana* at the Palace in 1973.

* * * * * * * * *

The evening had a strong aesthetic appeal and offered several genuinely magical moments. It had also been politically revealing. It showed that the essentially hierarchical and unequal monarchical system, which I had just seen at its apex, could not easily be reconciled with the Pathet Lao's egalitarian Laos. Beyond that obvious conclusion, the evening and the rest of Pi Mai were an occasion to reflect on King Sisavang Vathana's role in the country's unresolved conflict. Could he play the part of national unifier, could he be the arbiter of a compromise that could lead to peace? At the time, I had too few elements to judge. All I had seen was the king's closeness to the people in town and the unquestioned reverence with which he was regarded. The following stages of the Pi Mai celebrations not only confirmed that, they also showed him as the supreme unifier of cosmological forces at the beginning of the annual cycle. But was this understood beyond Luang Phrabang and the North? And beyond his ritual importance, were the king's authority and his position at the highest point of the social order recognized throughout the country? What I had seen in the South, and what I knew about Prince Bounoum's authority made me doubt it. And I was not sure about the peoples' depth of feeling for the king in Vientiane. All I could say was what the negotiations showed: the Pathet Lao was acting as if the monarchy was a force to be reckoned with everywhere in Laos, and not only in Luang Phrabang.

In 1973, my questions remained unanswered. But there was one certainty; for the duration of Pi Mai, the king would play his expected ceremonial role undisturbed, renewing the solidity of the institutional order, and strengthening the pillars of the old society, the monarchy and the Buddhist Sangha. He would be presiding over a number of solemn rituals, starting with the celebration of the most revered Buddha in Laos – the Phra'Bang.

The King lustrates the Phra'Bang (16 April)

The famous Buddha statue was kept inside the palace for most of the year. But at Pi Mai, it was carried out in great solemnity to Vat Mai, the royal monastery which stands on one side of the palace grounds. Early in the morning, the mayor and other dignitaries walked to the *vat*, where they met the Supreme Patriarch and the town's leading abbots. The group then walked to the palace where they approached the king and invited him to lead the town's collective devotions to the Phra'Bang later that morning at Vat Mai.

While the king and his retinue prepared for the event, the Buddha image, placed in an elaborately carved, golden palanquin, was carried out of the palace by two rows of royal guards. There were signs of hierarchy everywhere. The guards were dressed in red, wore tight caps and were barefoot, to indicate their low status and membership of the demeaned Kha ethnic group. A long line of officials and members of the court followed, all formally dressed, many carrying offerings in silver bowls, having joined the procession according to strict rules of precedence. At Vat Mai, the Buddha image was placed by the main temple, under a protective dark-red dais. Everything was ready for the lustration ritual, the pouring of blessed water over the sacred Phra'Bang.

The Phra'Bang awaits the people's devotions at Vat Mai.

The water bathed the image via two elevated gilded conduits, one of which reached the Phra'Bang from the front, the other from the back. The conduits, carved into the shape of water serpents – the *naga*– received the water at the tail-end, and channeled it towards the beast's mouth or neck, from where it dripped into a narrower funnel, and down on the Buddha below.

I joined a small group of people who had gathered inside the *vat* compound. Most of us were standing, while those closest to the Buddha sat on mats. People waited with quiet impatience, eager to set eyes on the most sacred of all Buddhas, show their full devotion, and become strengthened and renewed for another year by its benevolent influence. As I stood waiting with a small group of bystanders by the compound entrance, not quite knowing what would happen next, the Pou Nyeu Nya Nyeu appeared. We made space for them, and after a moment's respite, they started to dance slowly and clumsily, as I had seen them doing before, on Sisavangvong Road. I was now told their full story and discovered the extent of their importance: they had rescued the Lao people from total extinction by cutting down a gigantic tree whose excessively abundant foliage had blocked out the sun, condemning mankind to freeze, and its crops to wither.[5] The collapsing tree had crushed the old couple to death, but their spirits had remained in Luang Phrabang as the town's protectors, bearing the title of 'Thevada Luang', 'Highest Protective Divinities of the Place'. In that role, they became the object of a cult in which they were presented with offerings through a spirit medium at Pi Mai each year.

5   For a full account of the foundation myth, translated from the Lan Xang Annals, see Finot, in France Asie XII: 1047-1049

Sing Keo Sing Kham performing for an attentive crowd.

Grandmother Nyeu pours scented water into the *naga*-shaped conduit to lustrate the Phra'Bang.

With all this in mind, I stood waiting outside Vat Mai, wondering why the Pou Nyeu Nya Nyeu had appeared at this particular spot, at this particular time, when the king was about to arrive. I later found out that they were there to ensure that all evil influences were kept away from the Sacred Phra'Bang's bathing ritual – a natural activity for the town's principal protectors to perform. In this crucial task, they were accompanied by a small, golden-headed cub lion with a prominent nose and crimson mouth. This was Sing Keo Sing Kham, the couple's small Himalayan lion son, who also danced in its own personal way, snapping rythmically at every step.

All three characters, as the town's protective spirits, participated as an integral part of the morning's proceedings, ensuring that the site remained inviolate and worthy of the solemn ritual which was about to take place.

* * * * * * * * * *

The royal procession was not expected immediately. So, I abandoned the Pou Nyeu Nya Nyeu and walked back to the palace front and waited by the gate. It was some time before I caught sight of the king and the royal family, the royal children and other princes, walking in a truly impressive succession of parasols and silk.

I followed from the sidewalk. Once they reached Vat Mai, the king and queen briefly entered the *vat*'s main temple, came back out into the courtyard and slowly approached the Phra' Bang. They reached the tail end of one of the *naga*-shaped conduits by means of a small ladder, and poured the scented water, King Sisavang Vathana first, and then, Queen Khamphoui. Having done this, they went back into the temple for further devotions. Unexpectedly, the Pou Nyeu Nya Nyeu then came on stage. Having stopped dancing, and left the small lion cub behind, they walked slowly towards the red dais, ascended the set of steps and poured their own

The king and the court walk from the palace to Vat Mai.

offering of scented water into the *naga* conduit. As they did this, they were no longer the half-sacred, half-profane entertainers I had seen mingling freely with the crowd. They were fully the mythical elders of the Lao people, submitting in that role to the over-arching authority of the holy Buddha, within a hierarchical order in which they held rank at the highest level, second only to the king and queen.

The day's ritual came to a close when the king and his party returned to the palace, leaving the Phra'Bang to the people. For an entire day, they queued up to make their yearly devotions, making merit by pouring their share of blessed water. I later learned that this act was also the medium through which the givers of the water received the positive energy contained in the Buddha image – as the water poured over the

Having been the object of the town's devotions, the Phra' Bang was carried back to the Palace.

image, so did the positive energy in the image travel towards the givers, moving in a direction contrary to the water's flow. Merit could also be acquired by bathing other statues of the Buddha, using the water which had touched the Phra'Bang. Indeed, the water was considered to be so holy that. the devout collected it in silver ewers, using it to bathe their own Buddha images at home. But nothing could be better than performing the ritual on the Phra'Bang. The opportunity to do so was unique and short-lived, for the very next morning, a select group of monks placed the sacred image in its golden palanquin for the return journey to the palace, a fit location for the Palladium of the Kingdom for another year.

The people lustrate the king at Vat Sanghalok

The king continued to play his part at the most significant moments. After Vat Mai, he visited Vat Visun, famous for its monumental *that* and its collection of decaying Buddhas, finally reaching the simple surroundings of the more rural Vat Sanghalok. A new ceremony of ritual bathing was about to take place. But this time, rather than the Phra'Bang, it was the king himself who was the object of veneration. This raised the sovereign to the highest religious status, placing him ritually at almost the same level as the sacred Buddha image itself.

The royal party, headed by the king, the crown prince, Prince Khammao and other members of the court walked under white parasols up the dusty slope to the monastery. The bare-foot guards flanked them, but did so in an informal way that suited the relaxed quality of this rural *vat*, in all ways simpler than those in town. The lustration took place by the *vat*'s outside wall, close to one of the main gates, in a small cubicle to which an elevated water conduit had been attached at the back. In keeping with the surroundings, the red wooden conduit had been carved roughly into the shape of a primitive *naga*, a pale reminder of the golden magnificence of the water serpents of Vat Mai.

Under the white parasol, the king walked barefoot towards the cubicle, flanked by his guards. He entered, the door was shut, and he was out of sight, his parasol bearer standing at the ready. At the back of the cubicle, the townsfolk had gathered, waiting by the *naga*-shaped conduit. They climbed a small ladder to reach it, and poured the water which flowed slowly in the direction of the king's small enclosure, eventually falling on the royal person inside. This was done with the same reverence which had been shown to the Phra'Bang itself, emphasizing the king's sacred quality. The ceremony reminded me of an earlier ritual bathing, which had been organized a fortnight before at Vat Mai for the Supreme Patriarch. There was thus a triad of supremely revered points of focus for the people's devotion: the Buddha, the Head of the Sangha and the King.

The king followed by the crown prince (right) and Prince Khammao (behind, centre) arrive at Vat Sanghalok.

In this more rural setting, the king and his party appeared less formal than elsewhere. Though the assembled townsfolk squatted and saluted respectfully as he drew near, no barrier, no royal guards stood in the way. It was a paradox that the

The King is escorted to his closed cubicle for the bathing ritual.

The devotees pour scented water into the *naga*-shaped conduit. The water falls on the king inside the cubicle.

king was most approachable when being venerated as the Phra'Bang had been some days before. By participating in the ritual, ordinary people confirmed his authority as the supreme mediator between them and the forces of good, the sustaining strength behind the social order which many believed was being threatened by the political and military progress of the Pathet Lao.

* * * * * * * * * * *

I had been totally mesmerized by the festivities, the crowd's lighthearted enjoyment, and the collective determination to carry out the yearly succession of elaborate rituals scrupulously, according to custom. It was clear that the ceremonies had achieved their goals. The king's bathing of the Phra'Bang had renewed the kingdom's devotion to the Buddha; the people's bathing of the king had confirmed his secular and other-worldly authority; in turn the building of *that* and the widespread lustration of Buddha images in the *vats* and at home had strengthened the peoples' continued allegiance to Buddhism. Also, the Pou Nyeu Nya Nyeu had linked the present to the mythical past. By including them, the celebrations had brought together three mutually reinforcing sources of renewal and strength, the Buddha, the monarch, and at a lower ritual level, the highest protective spirits of the animistic pantheon. Many devotees probably hoped that the combined effect of such forces would help recover the kingdom's lost stability. But it was now up to politics to show how exactly such desired stability could be defined, agreed and established.

4

DEEPER INTO LAO REALITY
(MAY-NOVEMBER 1973)

An accident and new beginnings

Once the euphoria of Pi Mai had subsided, I resumed my teaching routine, concentrating on my students and the school until an unexpected development forced me to stop. One morning, driving my motorbike to the Lycee, I absent-mindedly moved onto the wrong side of the road, and collided head-on with Somchanh, one of my students from the fifth grade. Having crashed, it was not long before he was back on his feet, but I was not so lucky. The front of his motorbike went straight into my right polio leg, sending me flying into the air and down onto the pavement, a few metres away, unconscious. The leg brace did not stop the femur from being fractured, in fact it gave in, and once the bone had been broken maintained the leg in a twisted position.

I regained consciousness lying on a stretcher, on the floor of Luang Phrbang's main hospital, surrounded by the Swiss medical team. Fearing complications, the doctor decided to leave the leg brace on, and as the case required better facilities than those of the local hospital, advised that I be flown out of Luang Phrabang. I was transferred to Vientiane on the British Embassy plane – the 'beaver' – and put on the first flight to Bangkok. By that time VSO had made arrangements to keep me at the Bangkok Nursing Home, all expenses covered. I was lucky: the brace was removed, the femur was put right, and my leg was soon on the way to recovery inside a full-length plaster cast. There was a hitch, though. I needed to stay in hospital longer than expected, and was requested to come back regularly for periodical check-ups, until the plaster was removed. I reassured my parents via long-distance calls to Mexico and proceeded to accept this unwanted extended holiday.

Conditions at the Nursing Home were first-rate, there was unlimited time to read, and I had many visitors from the British Embassy and the British Council. From the Council, one official and his Japanese-Brazilian wife became good friends, and insisted that I spend my convalescence in their high-rise Bangkok flat. This was a far cry from my simple surroundings and austere living in Laos, and despite the warm hospitality, Bangkok felt like a place of exile. In addition, the constant flow of letters from teachers and students only increased my wish to go back. Two months after the accident, I returned, reaching Luang Phrabang just as the school was breaking up for the long yearly holiday. It was too late to teach, and once

I had attended to some outstanding administrative work, I was free, with several months of leisure before me. I began by moving house, leaving behind what I had come to consider my excessively western-style house at Vat Sen. One of the French teachers who had left Laos for good, Jean Claude de Forceville, had made available a Lao-style house. I rushed to take it over.

Located half way up the Phou Si, its upper floor of polished teak wood offered a view to the roofs of Vat Mai – centre of the New Year celebrations – and beyond, to the farther bank of the Mekong, and Xieng Men. As I was still convalescing, visitors poured in – friends, students, and next-door neighbours. The move to this wonderful Lao-style house opened a new chapter in my Luang Phrabang life. It was so close to Vat Mai, to the magnificent Buddha, the gold-covered bass-reliefs of the *vihaan*, and the extraordinary doors, I felt I had moved deep into the town's very heart.

House-warming party at my new house on the slopes of the Phou Si.

To settle in a new house did not mean severing all links with Vat Sen. I was used to my lane and the monks and the neighbours, and I naturally kept in touch with them, always glad to accept their invitations. I particularly enjoyed a spirit medium possession session. I did not know then that spirit mediums would become a central aspect of my post-graduate studies, but at this first encounter with them, they left me spellbound and aroused a level of curiosity which has never flagged.

Aspects of Vat Mai.

Beyond Buddhism: spirits and spirit mediums (June 1973)

The spirit medium session took place in a simple house on stilts, within walking distance from Vat Sen. I settled on the spacious verandah which occupied most of the upper floor. After a while, a jeep pulled up, and a youngish woman stepped out. This was Khamtun, the spirit medium. She came up to the verandah, followed by a large matron who just managed to drag herself up the stairs, pulling three large plastic bags all the way to the back room. The bags were

Food and drink and the mesmerizing sounds of the *so-i* and *so-u* players got us all to join in.

The spirit medium Khamptun inhales the essential qualities of a rice cake and by this method transmits them to the spirit who has just possessed her.

packed with blouses, scarves and *psin* which Khamtun would be wearing as she became possessed in succession by various spirits. Some of the clothes were truly luxurious; they included several silk *psin,* some of which were embroidered in gold. The woman next to me said that the Queen Mother had lent them for the day, as it to say that everyone in town, high and low, participated.

I had been asked to come at about ten, but we only got started after midday. I made myself busy while I waited, writing notes and taking photos. But as always happened when I was the only *falang* among the guests, I was given special treatment. Khamtun spotted me as soon as she arrived, and got one of the women to give me some sticky rice in a basket, and a bowl of noodles with bamboo shoots. With that, several rounds of pungent *lao lao,* and the music that soon began, I was ready to join in.

The session started close to where I sat, inside a small room at the back of the verandah. Khamtun chose a pink *psin* and turquoise blouse to be possessed by one of the town's main protective spirits, Princess Man. Khamtun appeared on the verandah, and sitting on a square cushion, her legs folded beneath her, she faced a group of four or five ageing women who repeated incantations in monotonous tones to invite the spirit. It took some time before Khamtun started to sway from one folded leg to the other, bent forward, almost touched the ground with her forehead, and continued to sway until settled: we them knew that Princess Man had entered her. The attending women who sat neatly on the floor, with their legs to one side, raised their joined hands towards Khamtun, in a sign of deference. But Khamtun moved violently again, in a new side-movement which this time made her turn and lie flat on her stomach. Again, she recovered, and reaching for her cushion, sat cross-legged once more, indicating that the Princess had finally fully possessed her. Khamtun kept changing her facial expression – one moment she looked calm and relaxed, the next she tightened her lips and tensed her jaw, relaxed again and then pushed betel-nut into her mouth with unexpected energy, and chewed it, with rapid, jerky movements.

By now, some twenty women and four or five men, had filled the verandah. Three women approached Khamtun, lowered their heads and placed their offerings of fruit, candles and large 2,000 kip notes neatly on a tray. Choosing carefully, Khamtun took a small rice cake and placed it in front of her closed eyes. She sniffed the food on behalf of the spirit, absorbing in its goodness.

The crowd was growing by the minute – the majority of elderly women and beside them, some middle-aged men who were there as spectators. Alongside humorous comments and side chatter, there was spontaneous singing and dancing, and some individual performances. One skeletal elderly woman made a few steps, and a thin old man moved his hands with feminine grace, a flower wreath covering his head like a crown. Khamtun faced these side performances calmly, with a patronizing air. She was the centre of attention, while all the others, whether possessed or not, were her subordinates.

Khamtun got up, took a few steps, looking at the participants as if to inspect them, then sat back down on her cushion. The long-awaited consultation session then began: Khamtun listened to question after question concerning health, love, prosperity, political fortune, or personal revenge.

Khamptun's possessing spirits are consulted in succession.

The longish session came to an end when Khamtun, at this point looking tired, went into a sideways contortion which put her flat on her stomach again. Once recovered, she got up and went into the back room. That was it for the first spirit. A further four followed: Khamtun appeared again, dressed in a different combination of clothes, sat on her cushion, gave new signs of possession, responded to further consultations and re-entered the back room. Her exhaustion became more visible with each possession. When the last spirit left her, she looked so helpless, lying motionless on the floor, that the women who sat closest, held her and lifted her head gently until she recovered.

The uninterrupted succession of contrasting scenes had been intensified by the piercing, whistle-like ululations of the women. One of them led and the others answered her call. At one point, the collective cries reached a paroxysm of excitement when the leader, very elderly and blind, produced sounds so loud as to cover the entire chorus. It was astonishing that a sightless old woman, her head shaved, her body doubled up at the waist, could dominate the group with such energy. I was amazed. Far from the gentleness, serenity, composure and infinite calm that Buddhism promoted, I was witnessing an earthy, immediate, primary, visceral form of worship. By means of alcohol, collective invocations, and the drawn-out whistling sounds, a hypnotic atmosphere had been created. The high-pitched noises, eerie and mysterious, came straight from another world. The spirits were miles away from the gentle world of Buddhist contemplation.

The session left me with many unanswered questions, and this led me to consult a senior monk in my neigbourhood monastery. Sathu Boun was a recognized scholar and meditation master. On the subject of spirits, he said they could not be trusted; there were countless numbers of them, and some were evil and dangerous, and should be avoided. He urged me to focus on the Buddha's teachings instead,

 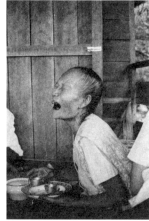

Song, incantations and alcohol generated a hypnotic atmosphere.

to find out about meditation, and learn to practice. But my focus was on how ordinary people related to the world of spirits, what they thought about them, what they expected of them. I needed to delve further into the people's beliefs, rather than step back. I told Sathu Boun that finding out more about the spirits would not prevent me from following his advice.

The standard Lao view was that the world was peopled by an infinite variety of invisible beings who existed at all corners of visible reality, craving attention. They were known as '*phii*' (pronounced pii with an aspirated h after the p). As Sathu Boun had said, some *phii* were unreliable and even malevolent, could be dangerous and impossible to control. The physical appearance of the worst among them was well known, the name of a given *phii* being associated with a specific compilation of images of horror; for instance, a floating head with bulging, phosphorescent eyes dragging its uncovered innards in the dead of night. One of the most feared was the spirit of a person who had died a violent death and harboured an insatiable need for revenge. These horrific beings, however, were fortunately a small minority. Most spirits were seen as calculating profiteers with commercial mentalities to whom a human being could offer a donation, a gift, or an offering in exchange for protection.

Among the almost infinite variety of spirits, there was a moral hierarchy in which the transactional, self-interested *phii* constituted only the middle level. Above them, were the *thevada*, a kind of angel – pure disinterested beings who exerted their benevolent influence from a state of beatitude, and who never entered any kind of transaction with human beings. Below them, but still higher than the mass of *phii,* were spirits who communicated through a medium. They were special because of their desire to help human beings in the role of healer, counselor, folk psychologist or diviner, but they shared a *phii*'s expectation to receive offerings for their intervention. Most of these materialistic but benevolent beings could be contacted through their mediums at any time during the year.

Within this group, a minority had a wider scope in that their benevolent interventions focused on a group of persons, such as the inhabitants of a town or a town's neighbourhood. These spirits acted as protectors of entire collectivities, and in that role sometimes became the object of a cult, which took place at a fixed time of the year, and could attract large numbers of adepts. Such spirits were not referred to as *phii.* Their names were provided by a legend or a myth that elaborated on the origins of a particular location, and on the protective spirit's identity and specific role. This was precisely the case of the Pou Nyeu Nya Nyeu, the elderly couple who had puzzled me during Pi Mai. I finally was able to understand the pair's special position among Luang Phrabang spirits. Their cult was carried out by a group of devotees who communicated with them through a medium each year. Just before the Lao New Year, the devotees presented various delicacies to them through their medium – sweetmeats or fruit or any kind of food that the spirits might relish. In exchange, the spirits promised to protect Luang Phrabang for the coming year.

So outlandish had the Pou Nyeu Nya Nyeu and their cult appeared to me, that I wondered how they related to Buddhism. The answer was simple; they were extraneous to it. For instance, their shrine, a modest structure on stilts, stood in the grounds of a monastery (the well-known Vat Aham), but it had been built at a distance from the *vat*'s main temple, the *vihaan*, and its Buddha image. Also, the shrine's upkeep was entrusted to a lay ritual specialist (not a monk) whose family had held the role for generations. The cult, therefore, was kept firmly outside the religion, although the spirits themselves fell under the Buddha's protection.

The Pou Nyeu Nya Nyeu and their Lion cub were only three of the innumerable protective beings whose spirits were associated with the topography of Luang Phrabang. In fact, the town was thick with them. For instance, in the category of the *naga* (initially rebellious but eventually domesticated and protective water serpents), fifteen were associated with specific rocks lying at the Nam Khan river's confluence with the Mekong. They were believed to temporarily abandon their habitat at certain times of the year to ride all the rivers and tributaries in the area, and ensure that their waters continued to flow. There was also the town's single most important *naga*, who lived under Phou Si, the hill opposite the Royal Palace. Such imaginary protective beings were approached at the sites where their respective legends placed them. They operated alongside real beings of flesh and blood such as the royal elephants who, acting also in exchange for carefully selected delicacies, were entrusted with expelling or at least neutralizing the threats to the town's integrity represented by the marauding evil *phii*.

Purists such as Sathu Boun could choose to focus on the Buddha's teachings and advise that one should ignore the spirits. But he never denied their existence, he just mistrusted them. It would have to wait for the Pathet Lao's political takeover in 1975 to see a policy which denied their existence and aimed at eliminating all practices associated with them. The communist authorities declared that devotion to the *phii* was a backward superstition, was politically undesirable and had to be suppressed. But the policy encountered such resistance, that it had to be reversed, and the beliefs and associated cults reinstated. A similar process of interdiction and subsequent partial restoration occurred in relation to the culture's monarchic and Buddhist aspects, including those expressed during Pi Mai. In both cases, the pervasive presence of pre-revolutionary practices and beliefs were unmovable axioms of the popular culture and were there to stay.

The Luang Phrabang-Vientiane road (November 1973)

Each time I had flown to Luang Phrabang, I had caught glimpses of the magnificent mountains and lush vegetation that surrounded the Vientiane road. I had promised my self that I would drive it one day, but it had long been insecure and strictly out of bounds, and no one could forget the priest who had been shot there, nor the many incidents which had made it a place of danger. When I heard that the road had been cleared for security and was open, I made preparations to drive down. One difficulty, however, was no longer the presence of the Pathet Lao, but my means of transport. I would be driving on my small Honda 70 on a difficult road: some 210 miles of loose earth, gravel and stones, mostly without asphalt. This was bound to be hard on the bike, particularly the tires. Nevertheless trusted it to meet the challenge, as it had been put into good working order after the accident.

On 8 November 1973, therefore, three students, two teachers and I headed south on our motorbikes towards Vientiane. During our stops, we chatted to village café tenders and room-leasers. After the isolation which the war had imposed, they welcomed the arrival of visitors. To them, the end of the fighting meant leaving behind fear, and those terrifying nights when they had carried their small children on their backs to the safety of caves halfway up the mountain. Now they could sleep at home, undisturbed. The warmth with which people welcomed us combined beautifuly with the views I had so wanted to see – the mountains, the luscious valleys and the crystal-clear streams. Vangvieng, a village of rare beauty, has

Spectacularly beautiful Vang Vieng.

remained in my mind as the culmination of the trip, with its impeccable wooden houses that stood by the river, and blended with the uninterrupted mass of palm trees, rich vegetation and giant bamboos.

It was difficult to leave such perfection behind, but we tore ourselves away and faced the last leg of our journey – a final difficult climb before descending towards the Vientiane Plain. This we were relieved to reach, as the soft afternoon light hit the hats of the peasants who were taking in the grain. We were exhausted but exhilarated by our achievement – to have moved freely through previously forbidden territory.

The journey had changed my perception of Laos. Prolonged physical contact with the road that linked Luang Phrabang to Vientiane had reduced the mutual aloofness and irreconcilable differences with which I had regarded them mentally. Driving in very difficult conditions had made me focus on the physical reality of the road, had kept me nailed to it, had made me attentive to the contact between the Honda tires and the unseen surface, had made me painfully aware of the risk of skidding on the loose dirt and gravel. This uninterrupted attention made the road into the single most important connecting link between the two towns, a string, sometimes tense, sometimes loose, which was firmly tied to Luang Phrabang at one end, and to Vientiane at the other. I had always thought of these towns as isolated entities, separated by their fundamental differences – Royal Capital of Tradition versus Administrative Capital and Seat of Government. The succession of obstacles I had encountered, and my final thrilling arrival in Vientiane, had given me a physical sense of their interconnections, and beyond that, of the unity of Laos.

My conclusions were strengthened by the unexpected presence of King Sisavang Vathana in Vientiane, where he was presiding over the yearly festival of That Luang, an imposing gold-leafed *that* and national symbol of Buddhist Laos. The ceremony was attended by a crowd who had gathered along the walls that surround the monument, and make it into a religious fortress. I focused on the king, on how he was approached and on how he behaved. In contrast with the informal gathering I had seen in Luang Phrabang, especially at the more rural Vat Sanghalok, here the police kept the public in check. The king entered the monument's enclosure with his suite, well protected by the police, in addition to his Luang Phrabang guards, with their emerald green or deep-red outfits and tight caps. I waited outside until he and his party finally appeared, but rather than walking slowly and greeting the people, the king moved quickly under a white parasol, flanked on both sides by the royal guards and the police, as if in need of protection. This was so different to his calm, paternal closeness to the people up North.

The king was the same person I had seen many times before, but in Vientiane he seemed more distant, more solemn in his demeanor. People approached him in a more formal way, as perhaps befitted his role as the nation's sovereign, but certainly less warmly than I had observed in familial Luang Phrabang. But regardless of the quality of the link, what mattered politically to many was that no challenge to the king's authority had ever been voiced by the Pathet Lao. There was as yet no indication that they would eventually establish an orthodox communist system to his exclusion. Luang Phrabang's influential Political Consultative Council, led by Prince Souphanouvong, the Pathet Lao leader, continued to confirm that Pathet Lao goals were compatible with the maintenance of the old social order and the monarchy.

That Luang, the symbol of the Nation.

5

POLITICAL AWAKENINGS (1973-1974)

Student activism and Luang Phrabang's political arousal

(February 1974)

As negotiations moved towards the creation of a Coalition Government, and the Pathet Lao gained political ground, student activism grew in most parts of the country. Protest and unrest had been in the air for some time, but the students' first real attempt to voice it coincided with the first anniversary of the Vientiane Agreement on 21 February 1974. Student strikes broke out in the South, showing particular virulence in Paksé town where the students' odium focused on Chinese merchants who were accused of war profiteering – hoarding rice and selling it at exorbitant prices. In order to appease the strikers, the Paksé authorities forbade meetings of more than three Chinese persons, and outlawed the use of any language other than Lao. This sounded an alarm bell among the Luang Phrabang authorities. Led by the mayor, they were determined to quell any sign of criticism. Unlike the South, however, corruption rather than war profiteering was the bone of contention. Accusations were rife against the civil service, targeting specific members of the administration, among them, the mayor. When the municipality raised the price of cinema tickets supposedly to help cover the cost of a new fire engine, and the vehicle could not be seen, he was accused of pocketing the money. And although a brand-new fire engine was eventually seen driving in town, and the authorities tried to improve their public image, accusations of corruption continued. The mayor even started using a bicycle when petrol was rationed, but his reputation did not recover.

As February 21 approached, Lycée students planned to hold a large student rally to denounce corrupt practices, with the participation of two other schools, Fangum and the Ecole Normale. To preempt the damage, the mayor forbade the rally and encouraged each establishment to organize smaller, separate events. He also asked his main advisor to visit the schools, call an assembly of students, and strongly caution against disruptive action. While two directors agreed to the precautionary measure, the Director of the Lycée opposed it. But the mayor stood his ground, and went to the Lycée himself. Resorting to moral-political blackmail, he denounced the planned demonstration as a threat to the Vientiane Agreement and the wished-for Coalition Government. He called in the President of the Students Federation, and acting through him, prevailed upon the students to cancel the rally in the name of political responsibility. He later authorized a smaller gathering and, during a school assembly, he congratulated the school for complying, implicitly shaming the student activists. On that day, separate enclosures were set up in front of the school's main building, one for the teachers and another for the authorities – the mayor, two National Assembly representatives, and some Pathet Lao cadres. A third enclosure accommodated the monks who initially participated as spectators, but later took centre stage when they blessed the guests and the students, thus clinching the authorities' desired consensus with holy water. For the time being, the students' activism had been placed under control.

Most of the teachers, myself included, had a hard time digesting the authorities' manipulative use of the Vientiane Agreement. But their success was short lived, for the mayor's authoritarian prohibition of the schools' rally encouraged rather than dampened the students' activism, and as accusations of corruption continued, the more motivated students reaffirmed their conviction that the only hope for improvement was assertive collective action. In time, the Pathet Lao became a pole of attraction for these activists, in Luang Phrabang and elsewhere, thus providing the movement with an increasingly solid political base.

* * * * * * *

Beyond vocal student circles, and a small group of critically minded fellow-teachers, I noticed a general increased readiness to discuss the terms and implications of the Vientiane Agreement. Also, public opinion was becoming sharply polarized. I saw this in the household of my nextdoor neighbours. There was no conflict between the parents: the father followed a dispassionate form of politics, and a relaxed, wait-and-see attitude to current political uncertainties. The mother expressed no opinion. The differences were between two of the sons, Nooi, who followed the spirit of the Agreement and favoured peaceful coexistence with the Pathet Lao, and his elder brother Nyai whose pro-western orientation, good knowledge of English, and well-paid job inside a foreign-subsidized development program pulled him in the opposite direction. Nooi spoke hopefully of the PL, believed in Prince Souphanouvong's conciliatory words and was glad that Luang Phrabang was getting used to the PL's presence. Nyai bitterly disagreed, and considered current developments a disaster. For Nooi, Vientiane was hostage to an intransigent political Right and could not be trusted. Nyai mistrusted the PL, and as sympathy for them grew in town, he turned increasingly against them.

The PL's increased presence in town was manifested in the camps they had established there. Events held in them, such as the occasional film show, permitted contact with the town's folk and created a certain familiarity, especially with the young and with students. One of the camps stood a short distance from my house,

The Joint Police showed that both sides could work together: a PL soldier (right foreground) and an RLG soldier (with a machine-gun, centre) provide security for the King's Bathing Ritual (in the cubicle, centre). The royal guards, squatting barefoot and dressed in red and green (left foreground) wait for the king. The crown prince stands on the left at the back.

on one side of Phou Si, a strategically placed vantage point which otherwise, some ironic commentators claimed, benefitted the PL with the power of the hill's *naga* and the religious aura of its famous *that*. Apart from being favoured by the camps, the PL's visibility was strengthened by the creation of the so-called Joint Military and Police Force. Comprising Royal Government and Pathet Lao elements, the force had been created to 'neutralize Vientiane and Luang Phrabang' – to transform them into places of political cooperation rather than confrontation. There were many instances when the Joint Force had operated smoothly in Luang Phrabang, not least during the Pi Mai celebrations, when Royal and PL police forces had worked together to ensure the peace. Such instances of cooperation augured well for a possible future of harmonious coexistence between the two sides, despite the prevailing political polarization, including within families. This was still a time of hope.

The new Coalition Government and the Luang Phrabang summary (April 1974)

The intense negotiations that followed the Vientiane Agreement had aimed at a prompt political compromise as their main objective, but it took nearly fourteen months before the difficult discussions led to fruition. Two historic events were the prize: on 3 April 1974, the belated establishment of a Coalition Government; and, on 5 April, the meeting in Luang Phrabang between Prime Minister Prince Souvannaphoumma representing the government, and his half-brother, the PL leader, Prince Souphanouvong. The events intensified the town's politicization, but decreased its polarization. The PL's opponents hardened their position, but the promise that hostilities would cease and that peace would be restored, created a sense of optimism which made many skeptics into new supporters of the politics of compromise. The meeting between the two brothers gave Luang Phrabang a much-needed sense of hope.

Prince Souvannaphoumma believed that the country's independence, and perhaps even its survival, required a coming-together of all political forces. In 1974, in the role of Prime Minister, he continued to stand his neutralist ground, a testimony to his tenacity and life-long efforts to bring the PL into the political fold, despite the uncompromising opposition of the Laotian Right. For the Right, to incorporate the Pathet Lao into the government was an intolerable concession to international communism, a move which would inevitably lead to the country's engulfment by the communist camp. Souvannaphoumma, ever since the 1960s, had been at the centre of the country's internal conflict. He was now ready to fight again.

Within the Pathet Lao, it was not clear who was part of the leadership and how it operated. The identity of its members remained something of a mystery, a nebulous fact hidden in the stronghold of Viengsay, in the distant north east. But everyone knew that Prince Souphanouvong was the PL's most visible representative, the movement's public relations voice and highly visible participant in political discussions with the government. His position had always been on the Left. He had actively opposed the French Colonial Regime in the 1940s and in the 1960s had placed himself in the pro Soviet/North Vietnamese camp, taking a strong stand against the United States' ever-growing presence in the region. In 1974, Souphanouvong's role was that of a conciliator. Thanks to a unique combination of high social status and unswerving political commitment, he could be a useful intermediary, a man who could be trusted by the PL, and enjoy some credibility with the government. The dialogue that developed between the two half-brothers created the hope on both sides that a constructive dialogue for reconciliation could move forward despite the continued intransigence of the political Right and the influence of the more radical members of the Pathet Lao.

Prime Minister Prince Souvannaphoumma and his party being welcomed at the airport.

Prince Souphanouvong arrives at Luang Phrabang airport.

The excitement started at the airport with the arrival of the prime minister. Prince Souvannaphoumma was the epitome of the elderly statesman, a cigar-smoking international figure known to the world's foremost leaders as the champion of the neutralist position. Once on the tarmac, he walked his elderly man's walk towards the Supreme Patriarch, taking time to greet him, and then past a long line of notables, who bowed or squatted before him and presented him with flower offerings. As he walked in his formal way, followed by his wife and some ministers, I saw deep respect among those who were there to welcome him, respect for both the prince and the prime minister.

The arrival later that morning of the Pathet Lao leader, Prince Souphanouvong's was electric. He stepped out of the plane, and immediately greeted all present before even setting foot on the tarmac. I was immediately captivated by his direct approach. He had an instinctive ability to come close to the people, and did not hesitate to almost squat to be level with a group of children. I could see nothing of the arrogance

Prince Souphanouvong engages with a group of children as soon as he sets foot on the tarmac.

for which he was often faulted. Far from appearing superior, he invited proximity and direct contact.

The contrast between the two half-brothers was palpable when they walked together in town, surrounded by the crowd's respectful enthusiasm – the distant, slow-moving elderly statesman, and the vibrant, charismatic innovator. I noticed a group of my students squatting and waving small Lao flags by the side of their path.

The half-brothers are welcomed by an enthusiastic crowd.

A glimpse of the past: Souphanouvong (2nd from the right) and the PL leadership in the heat of the fight: (from left to right) Noukak Phoumsavane (Economics and Finance Minister) Khamtay Siphandone (Supreme Army Commander) and the Secretary General of the Lao People's Party Kaysone Phomvihane / Pathet Lao Fighters. (Photos Houaphan Province Memorial Sites Committee)

An attentive crowd listens to Souphanouvong.

Prince Souphanouvong was permeated by the romantic aura of his adventurous past, and the scarcity value of his rare appearances in towns under Royal Government control. He had the appeal of the aristocrat who had chosen revolution, including the subterranean existence he had shared with the Pathet Lao High Command, avoiding relentless US bombing in the limestone caves of Viengsay.

On the morning of 5 April 1974, the Red Prince's expansive, self-assured manner, his natural charisma, and the words of reconciliation and peace he pronounced in front of the Provincial Office, captivated his audience. Speaking with the authority of the National Political Consultative Council over which he presided, his words fitted the expectations of the crowd, and convincingly transmitted the message that peace could be achieved.

That evening, a carefully prepared programme offered a menu of folk entertainment, revolutionary songs and dance. The public performance was a fitting conclusion to the morning's speech. We saw a succession of scenes which glorified the themes of freedom, independence and national pride, in settings which combined a strongly rural flavor with the inclusion of the ethnic minorities. The performance was well received, and concluded with a good round of applause. I was not sure, however, that the audience who attended that evening from the government side (high-ranking members of the bureaucracy and the army) had identified with the values that had been acted out, including the positive valuation of the hill peoples. For the spectators who were part of the local elite, the dance and the music had probably jarred with their preferred kind of performance, whose highest expression was maintained by the palace and the court. Perhaps some in the audience had not been entirely at ease to see the well-known dance routines of age-old tradition replaced on stage by the energetic regimentation of political art. The public comments that followed were positive, but the opinions voiced privately by some were that national reconciliation among the Lao was one thing, but being subjected to foreign cultural influences was another.

It was not clear whether the evening's performance followed models that came from China or Vietnam, but for those who saw the Pathet Lao as willing instruments of communist domination from the outside, it did not matter which. On the other hand, people who backed the PL emphasized the freshness of the performance. But despite different opinions on the show, the day's events gave rise to a general sense of optimism.

An evening of non-Lao revolutionary culture.

Some political progress in Vientiane; Pathet Lao consolidation in Luang Phrabang

Once the princes had left town, the euphoria gave way to the all-too-familiar reality of political procrastination. Not everything was moving smoothly: towards the end of May 1974, I learned that the peace process had been seriously threatened. The British Ambassador, Alan Davidson who was always attentive to the needs of VSO volunteers, and never failed to check on our well-being, invited me for lunch. He and two Home Office civil servants on official business from London were up in Luang Phrabang for the closing session of the Political Council. They were full of inside news: Phoumi Vongvichit, a key figure within the Pathet Lao leadership, had recently requested the International Commission to put an end to an alleged imminent Rightist coup. He claimed that tanks were ready to enter Vientiane and. specified the names of the principal organizers, including a well-known colonel. The Commission responded immediately, and by 3 am, a Commission Indian general forced his way into the camp where the coup was allegedly brewing. But the accused colonel was found to be fast asleep, and by 4 am the accusation was dismissed as baseless. The conclusion was that the PL had fabricated the story to activate the International Commission as a warning to the Right that a takeover would not be tolerated. The Pathet Lao's rumour-mongering was a dangerous game. The ambassador feared that it could undermine negotiations by creating suspicion, and could provoke the Political Right to stage a real coup. It had to be said, however, that the accusation, though false, made sense when set against the PL's well-based fears of political derailing by the Right, something the country had witnessed more than once. Sounding an alarm could not be taken lightly when coming from a man of Phoumi's caliber and credentials – a man of international political prominence, prolonged revolutionary activism, and active engagement in the defence of Lao culture and language[6]. Such a man was well placed to assess what could be expected from the Right.

* * * * * * *

6   Phoumi Vongvichit was a key negotiator following the Vientiane Agreement; had been Head of the Lao Delegation to the 1962 Geneva Conference, and Minister of Information in the Second Coalition Government. One of a small number of members of the traditional Lao elite with a history of prolonged revolutionary militancy, Phoumi Vongvichit had been been active within the Lao Issara Movement against French colonialism until its dissolution in 1949 when he followed Souphanouvong to North Vietnam. In addition, Phoumi enjoyed the prestige of a man of letters as historian, poet and strong defender of the Lao language and culture. For details of Phoumi Vongvichit's role see Stuart Fox: 1986.

The cremation attested to the Pathet Laos' enduring tolerance of royalist culture at the time. Only in 1975 would that culture be rejected and the monarchy abolished.

Shortly after the ambassador's visit, several urgent personal issues required my presence outside Laos. I was away for most of the summer, staying first with my family in Mexico, and then travelling to the US. With my VSO contract close to expiring, I had decided to change agency. I visited Washington D.C. to join the International Voluntary Service (IVS), once more as a Luang Phrabang-based volunteer teacher, but this time at the IVS-supported Fangum Secondary School rather than at the Lycée. I was back in Luang Phrabang on October 2, 1974.

In my absence, negotiations in Vientiane had continued to move forward, albeit with hitches and momentary impasses. In Luang Phrabang, the PL had consolidated its presence even more. By all accounts, it was fitting in well, and seemed to be accepting the town's traditions. For instance, the Luang Phrabang football pitch, which stretched below one of the larger royal monasteries, Vat That Luang, had been used in the past to carry out royal cremations. It served that purpose once again on 15 October for the cremation of one of the deceased consorts of late King Sisavang Vong, King Sisavang Vatthana's father. The ceremony was conducted with undiminished royal splendour, and was guarded by the Joint Government/Pathet Lao Military Police. The cohabitation of the monarchy and the communist Pathet Lao seemed to be working well.

Nevertheless, the Pathet Lao's cultural influence was growing. The screening of films in their camps had now developed into open air entertainments, including on one afternoon at the same football pitch where the cremation had been organized. This was the third time the show had taken place, and almost all seats were taken. The performers were mainly hill peoples – Lao Theung and pro-Pathet Lao Hmong – whose dancing and singing illustrated the revolutionary virtues with emphatic enthusiasm. I was reminded of the evening that followed Prince Souphanouvong's speech, but there was a difference. The audience consisted of ordinary people – I could see no high-level bureaucrats or politicians – and there was plenty of enthusiastic applause. The PL's innovations in public entertainment had clearly made their mark. They were demonstrating a skill for promoting themselves and their own values, while being conciliatory towards the old society. It was not clear how long the resulting harmony would last.

6

I VISIT THE HMONG'S MILITARY BASTION
(21-22 DECEMBER 1974)

Preparing for Long Cheng

As the Pathet Lao became increasingly visible in Luang Phrabang, I wanted to know how the PL's political progress was affecting the hill-dwelling ethnic groups, the Hmong in particular, who were at the forefront of the government's anti-PL military efforts. With improving security conditions, one could now go to Hmong villages well beyond Luang Phrabang's immediate vicinity, and that included an area I had always wanted to visit: the heartland of Hmong military power in the towering mountains of northeast Laos. Having made up my mind, I convinced two fellow-teachers and good friends, Guy and Brigitte, to join me. Once again, I asked Moua to be our interpreter and guide. He felt it wiser for security reasons to travel in a larger group, and in the end, four teachers, Moua, three other students and I – nine persons in all - left Luang Phrabang on 21 December for a two-day journey.

We met before setting off to agree on priorities. One goal was to better understand how Hmong village life had been affected by the war, but our main objective was to reach Long Cheng, Hmong General Vang Pao's stronghold and CIA Centre of Operations in northeastern Laos. We pooled all available information about the general, a man who had been for years a national figure of some prominence. (Principal source Mc Coy 1972: *The Politics of Heroin in South East Asia*). Vang Pao's fame as a military leader could be traced back to the 1954 battle of Dien Bien Phu, which had ended the French presence in Indochina. At the time, he had led 850 hill tribe guerrilla fighters to relieve the doomed French garrison, and although he failed, his attempt earned him a reputation for courage and anti-communist commitment. A further stage in his career was his enrolment in the Laotian army, in which he prospered, reaching the highest levels. As the US became involved in Indochina, Vang Pao's military career prospered further under the auspices of the CIA.

The Agency had arrived in Laos in the early 1960s with the objective of advancing its anti-communist agenda militarily. But being seriously understaffed, and faced with a US Congress that was unwilling to approve US troops on the ground in Laos, it had turned to the Hmong to set up a surrogate anti-communist fighting force. The CIA co-opted those Hmong clans who inhabited strategically key areas, offering their leaders generous benefits – hard cash and a free hand in the opium trade, a source of wealth which, since the French colonial period, had been central to the political ascendancy of Hmong strongmen. Among them, Vang Pao became a CIA favourite. With his military experience, leadership qualities and close association with the Lao anti communist Right, he became the undisputed leader of the Hmong US surrogate forces, and occupied one of the most critical leadership positions in the Royal Lao Army as Commander of Military Region II. The area had decisive strategic importance, close as it was to the Pathet Lao's High Command in the limestone caves of Houa Phan Province, where the PL political and military leadership had established itself, safely barricaded from US bombing for years. Also, Region II was adjacent to the Lao-Vietnamese border, where the strategic Plain of Jars offered Vietnamese forces a potential point of entry into an area which the Pathet Lao controlled. Given the frequency of military confrontations between the Royal Government's forces and the Pathet Lao in and around the Plain of Jars, Vang Pao established his military base (and the CIA's Centre of Operations) in the very high mountains that overlooked it, in a location which offered strategic advantage over Pathet Lao-controlled valleys and settlements. After 1962, he established his permanent centre of operations in that area at Long Cheng.

* * * * * * *

Our nine-person group was ready to leave before sunrise. When we boarded our small bus, it was already half full. Moua and I sat at the front, next to the driver.

Phou Khoune stands 1393 metres tall.

The others settled in the open part at the back with three other passengers, facing each other on the hard wooden seats that ran parallel to the road, on both sides of the vehicle. We all huddled together to keep warm in the morning chill, as the bus climbed up the steep mountainsides, towards the magnificent Phou Khoune, the tallest mountain in Laos.

Shivering against each other, we moved sideways as a single body at each bend, while the few of us who were not sick, looked in amazement at the magnificent scenery. After Phou Khoune, and a long drive over high mountains and a valley, the road took us to a second valley where we reached the perfection of Vang Vieng, known to me when driving to Vientiane the year before. Moua took the lead and managed to find sleeping arrangements for all nine of us, in three separate houses, one of which had a small noodle shop attached. We were talking noisily there over dinner, when a Lao woman who was sitting alone at her table approached us and started to chat. She had overheard that we were Lycée teachers on our way to Long Cheng, and said she would be travelling there on the same early bus the next day. She was from Luang Phrabang where she worked at the Ministry of War Victims, and was also active in trade, which took her regularly to Long Cheng and its surrounding villages, almost once a month, providing the Hmong with goods which were not available in the mountains. Fat and complacent, she was unnervingly self-assured. 'I never lack clients; everyone in the area knows me, including the General. If you like I can show you how to get to his house once we're in Long Cheng, and introduce you to him'.

The consequences of slash-and-burn cultivation.

Hmong young women display their finery at New Year.

We were up early and ready to head for Long Cheng. The road led us half the way up to an area made momentarily desolate by burnt vegetation, the result of the Hmong's preferred slash-and-burn style of cultivation. Bare, burnt tree trunks projected their sinister shapes onto the inundated land.

Further on, the scenery was spectacular. The neat, well-traced road wound up increasingly steep mountains, taking us to the highest altitudes where the Hmong prefer to settle. There the air was fresh and invigorating, and the houses, the music, the language and the customs were all uniquely Hmong. Occasionally, as if to rest, the road ran horizontally for a longish stretch, although it still progressed dangerously close to the edge which looked down several hundred feet on a valley below. Higher up, we turned a corner and were confronted, unexpectedly, with a group of young women standing close by in a field. Under their bright pink or green parasols, in their turbans, black trousers and silver necklaces, they reminded us that this was the Hmong New Year, and we were in their territory.

During Hmong New Year, we meet General Vang Pao

We drove along a narrow gorge, which led us straight into Long Cheng. The wide valley was almost completely surrounded by mountains. To one side, five or six T-28 aircraft, and a small Royal Air Lao DC3, were parked at one end of a long airstrip. At the centre of the valley, a machine-gun had been placed on the top of a massive rock. As we entered Long Cheng itself, our tradeswoman friend pointed to a very large building – General Vang Pao's house. Further along, beyond a group of small wooden houses, we saw the USAID compound which was probably also the CIA's Operations Centre. More than a village, Long Cheng was a stark military barracks, built for the single purpose of waging war under Vang Pao's uncontested leadership.

We got off the bus, and taking up the tradeswoman's offer to guide us, we followed her to Vang Pao's house. A relaxed group of soldiers greeted her as we entered the receiving hall. In time, a Hmong colonel came to tell us that the general would be glad to see us later in the afternoon. In the meantime, he asked us to leave our backpacks in the hall. We would find them later in our rooms, where we would of course be staying, courtesy of the general. I imagined that being foreign teachers attached to a well-known school in the royal capital had given us special standing. However, it turned out that the general welcomed all foreigners who made it to Long Cheng, and even in his absence, the doors to the hall of his house, large as a warehouse, were always wide open. We were not that special after all…

The colonel apologized for the general's delay, and invited us to wait outside and, if we so wished, to take a walk downhill to the area where the New Year celebrations were taking place – they had been going on for ten full days, since December 12. That *was* a surprise. We knew this was the festive season, but never imagined such prolonged celebrations would be taking place in one of the country's most militarily active areas. We were only too glad to join in and, heading for a level field downhill, we followed three Hmong girls. Under their bright pink and yellow parasols, I could just see the back of their embroidered sashes, standing out against their wide black trousers. They went slowly past the market, down a narrow lane and finally reached the field. Standing behind them, all nine of us found ourselves at the centre of the festivities, but soon dispersed into smaller groups to be less intrusive.

I caught sight of a row of boys and one of girls, facing each other in parallel lines. The boys each wore a black cap or a brown felt hat, while the girls had a black turban – brightened by pompons at the back – which was wound tightly round their foreheads. The youngsters were playing the annual courtship game. Boys and girls, standing in front of each other as a pair, showed their mutual interest by throwing a black cloth ball back and forth. I listened to the regular muffled smack of the ball being caught by the girl's

Hmong woman at New Year 1974.

hand and then the boy's, while the hypnotic, strangely intimate movement went on without stop. They played their part by singing their feelings, often humourously, in a lilting monotonous song. The girls had made the balls by hand, and had kept them until the New Year for their chosen young man.

Approaching the girls' row from the back with my camera, I focused on the boys' earnest faces and then, coming closer, I clicked to capture the small squares of perfect embroidery on the girls' blouses. I tore myself away, slowly moved out of the level field, and headed for a slope where other groups were standing. In one, there was no ball catching, just girls singing and boys listening. In another, the game was being played silently, without songs. From above, a few metres uphill, a group of older men watched, smoked a long water-pipe, or soothed a half-naked child who cried under a black umbrella. Moua and I approached the group of singing girls, and stopped to listen more closely. He smiled, walked towards one of the girls, then said something to another. After a while, I saw the second one looking at me, singing another monotonous lilting song. When she finished everyone was looking at me. Moua later translated the words:

'You are a prosperous merchant who has just come, and
you will soon go back to your own land. When you come
back here again, it will be too late, I will be married'
'What has your mother done, that your face is like
flowers, but I'm sad because the flowers are not for me'.
'I'm sad because you and I can never get married. I cannot
follow you, although I want to, I cannot because of my
father and mother and brothers and sisters. But if one day
you return to come and visit my husband and me,
you will be very welcome and we shall have opium together'.

* * * * * * * * * *

Back in Vang Pao's house, our group stood waiting for the general. He finally appeared, walking down from the first floor, dressed in dark grey. The colonel introduced the group. Vang Pao shook hands with all of us, greeting us in French, and being especially attentive to Brigitte and Monique. His wife followed close behind him, wearing a bright turquoise pullover, gold necklace and careful chignon – the uniform, I thought, of a 'big man's wife' (in lowland Lao style, rather than Hmong). Vang Pao smiled warmly, while she merely smiled, standing one step behind. He had only a short time to be with us, but he invited us into a small room, and offered the available seats to the teachers in the group, leaving the students standing.

Playing catch – a form of courtship.

He answered all our questions willingly, emphasizing the strength of the Pathet Lao. He explained that in 1973, their attacks in areas close to Long Cheng had forced him to move the Hmong New Year celebrations from December to January. When asked how his Hmong villages had fed their families despite the fighting, he said that growing vegetables and maize and raising poultry and pigs had continued to be possible. There was also a question about poppy cultivation. 'As my own family knows from experience', he said, 'it is very hard work for the Hmong who grow it, and it is a gift to the Chinese who buy it cheap, and sell it for a fat profit. Little by little, most people are giving it up. In Long Cheng it hasn't been present since 1960'. Not surprisingly, the General left it at that. I was well aware that poppy growing was hard work – I had seen the poppy latex being collected more than once – but I knew there was much more to the issue than Vang Pao's words conceded. Our meeting with general Vang Pao was coming to an end, and we asked him to tell us about unexploded mines. 'A US team is demining', he said, 'but the problem is huge, even inside Long Cheng. In recent months, as many as ten people have unfortunately been killed, and many others have been maimed. The fighting generally has taken place in the surrounding mountains, but as I said before about 1973, the Pathet Lao sometimes have come close to Long Cheng, even firing against this very house'.

We went out again for a short walk before dinner. The general greeted us briefly when we were back in the house, but excused himself and went upstairs. We were taken into a large room with a long refectory-style table. It was the eating facility for the general's subordinates, the Hmong equivalent of the servants' quarters in a large country house. Our group sat at one end of the table, which was covered with a plastic tablecloth with flower designs, and ate our dinner of sticky rice, pork and boiled cabbage. The tradeswoman was also there, chatting with some of the general's staff. We were all of us benefitting from Vang Pao's condescending hospitality, which later in the evening extended to the sleeping arrangements – rudimentary but comfortable enough, with adequate bathing facilities attached.

The following morning, we had breakfast in the same refectory, and collected our luggage from the entrance hall. The colonel had told us that the general was too busy to see us off. As we walked towards the main door, however, the tradeswoman appeared again, and called out loudly for us to stop "How can you leave without thanking the general?" We left her question unanswered and walked away, leaving her behind with her self-importance, her claim to high status and her tiny audience – a group of soldiers who stood warming themselves by the fire.

Some conclusions

All nine of us boarded the bus, and as we drove away, I thought about Vang Pao's words. They had been short and incomplete, and in some ways misleading. He had talked about the end of opium cultivation, but the practice was still ongoing. He had talked about the backbreaking work, but had not said the women did all the work, prepared the fields, pierced the capsules and collected the produce. He had suggested that people were giving up opium, when I knew from my visits that its use was a regular part of a Hmong's way of life.

General Vang Pao had spoken of opium cultivation with an air of detachment, as if it were dying out and only concerned his people, as if it had nothing do with him. But the facts indicated that he was closely involved. For years, US planes and helicopters had transported the opium out of Hmong villages of the north east to locations where it was sold and distributed[7]. Getting the opium to the market beyond the fighting areas was one of the benefits which the Americans had accorded the Hmong in exchange for fighting, and it was widely known that the general was well aware of the process, having allegedly benefitted greatly from it. But that was something he would never have discussed.

On the bus, we could see the road descending from the highest altitudes, into a scenery of soft rolling hills. We knew we were on our way home. I thought about pampered Luang Phrabang, and the austere world of Hmong women and men we were leaving behind. The New Year festivities I had just seen were full

---

7   See Wekkin in Stuart Fox 1982for an extensive analysis of the issue.

Familiar sights in a Hmong village: weighing opium (left) and opium smoking (right)
(Photo by M. Muecke)

of colour, but otherwise, in Long Cheng and in the Hmong villages I knew, the brown homesteads, the inclement weather, the backbreaking work, the isolation, could be forbidding to the outsider, with perhaps only one compensation – the unrivalled sense of freedom which the highest mountains can offer. And then, there was the war: I had just seen the anti-communist Hmongs' military heartland and could confirm the extent of their involvement and the price they were paying for it – the men's injuries or loss of life and the families' displacement, a cost perhaps equal to that paid by the other Hmong, who had rallied with the Pathet Lao. These sacrifices, the lowland Lao seemed on the whole not to know, or chose to ignore. With two exceptions: the highest military or political circles who could not but value their key military role; and the profiteers, such as the tradeswoman, who cultivated an ongoing relationship with them, whenever economic advantage dictated. Otherwise, the average Lao person was oblivious of the facts, and continued to place all Hmong and their culture, at the bottom of the ethnic hierarchy, as a single, politically and militarily undifferentiated category, failing to distinguish among the Hmong who were non-belligerant, those who followed the PL and the anti-communists who were aligned with the Royal Lao Government.

7

GETTING CLOSE TO
THE PATHET LAO TAKEOVER

The Pathet Lao gains political ground (April-May 1975)

At the end of 1974, political and military conditions seemed stable. Only very few ceasefire violations had been reported, and although some inevitable disagreements over policy had occurred within the Coalition, the Vientiane government was holding. Also, the Joint Military Police was on the whole working smoothly, its Pathet Lao members having become a familiar sight in town – they were taken for granted. People were taking ongoing changes in their stride, although I did detect a certain nervousness among students from political or Chinese or Vietnamese merchant families, who were uncertain about their future and started to talk in private about leaving the country. But beyond such specific worries, public life in town remained unaffected, while the uninterrupted progress of the annual calendar of public festivities had the normalizing effect I had seen before. My own teaching routine continued, and brought me effortlessly to the month of April.

April 1975 was a momentous time for Indochina. This was the month when communist forces entered Phnom Penh and Ho Chi Minh City, the month when the Lao Popular Liberation Army (LPLA) was preparing for decisive militarily offensives which would take place in May. However, in Luang Phrabang, as in most urban, government-controlled areas, it was business as usual. With no alarming, up-to-date news concerning military or political matters, the New Year festivities were prepared with the usual wholehearted participation, absorbing everyone's attention, drawing it away from politics. As for myself, I was so relaxed, so unaware of ongoing events, that I nonchalantly chose to miss the Pi Mai celebrations and enter a monastery for a two-week retreat. I remember sitting in my wooden cubicle, keeping to my meditation practice despite the deafening noise of the cicadas in the late afternoon, and the sound of clapping and singing from passing pick-ups carrying groups of rowdy Pi Mai-celebrating youths. No thoughts of politics entered my mind, and today, it seems uncanny that my retreat ended peacefully on 18 April, one day after the Khmer Rouge took Phnom Penh, and only some days before LPLA military action was stepped up.

By the first week of May, news reached Luang Phrabang that the LPLA had been making progress. It had seriously challenged Royal Army troops in Savannakhet, Central Laos; the Hmong stronghold at Long Cheng, still vivid in my memory, was expected to fall; my one-time host General Vang Pao was no longer Commander of Military Region II. Also, beautiful Vang Vieng had been taken, and the strategic meeting point of routes 7 and 13 had been wrested from government forces. As things stood, the rumour circulated that the capital might fall, until we heard that the LPLA had stopped some 130 km north of Vientiane, and left it untouched. But the expectation of a major military breakthrough returned when we learned of two historic victories: the Khmer Rouge's entry into Phnom Penh on 17 April, and the Vietnamese communists' entry into Ho Chi Minh city on the 30th. In the opinion of many, it was only a matter of time before the communist takeover in the two Indochinese capitals was replicated at home. The work of specialists later confirmed that the unexpectedly rapid victories by the North and South Vietnamese communists and the Khmer Rouge had in fact altered the balance of political power in Laos, polarized opinions regarding change, and favoured the real holders of power within the Pathet Lao – a radical political faction which represented the movement's real voice and decided to seize power militarily. For the time being, and before final victory, however, the Lao revolution progressed according to its own pace and methods, focusing on political conquest, and backing this with a careful dose of military success. Following that line, the PL capitalized on the increasing number of public demonstrations in its favour, many of which were organized by students. Increasing numbers among them were warming to the movement, which they saw as the only force capable of countering corruption, war-profiteering and the unlimited ambitions of strongmen.

On 10 May, news reached Luang Phrabang that students were demonstrating in Vientiane in support of a National Political Consultative Council document. Just issued under the signature of its chairman, Pathet Lao leader Prince Souphanouvong,

An initially peaceful concentration of demonstrating students in front of the Governor's office, Luang Phrabang.

the 'Eighteen Point Programme for the Current Construction of the Fatherland' had two main objectives: to develop a Comprehensive Plan of Economic Development, and to adopt a foreign policy of strict neutrality. Significantly, and to the relief of many, the document confirmed that the monarchy would be maintained. The programme was generally well received, and even acclaimed. Predictably, however, the political Right opposed it, and in response, Pathet Lao supporters took to the streets. Demonstrations mushroomed in several towns. Starting in Vientiane, they attracted unprecedented numbers of sympathisers (one source mentioned 30,000 students[8]) and took a violent turn. One targeted the massive US Development Aid Mission (USAID), and ended with angry demonstrators damaging shop fronts on Samsenthai Avenue, and setting the US flag on fire. Another focused on Chinese and Vietnamese merchants who were accused of rice hoarding; their shops ended up with broken windows and some looting. Another rally was aimed at rightist military officers and high-level government officials.

On 15 May, Vientiane's demonstrations were followed by protests in Luang Phrabang. Students spoke out against high prices and corruption, and seized large quantities of milk and sugar from the storerooms of the wealthier Chinese and Vietnamese merchants. The produce was placed for safekeeping at the Provincial Office, to be sold later at lower prices. Demonstrators stood in front of the building and called for the resignation of various public servants, including the governor.

In the morning, the atmosphere remained calm and relaxed – slogans were sung and demonstrators danced and clapped, in what seemed a political version of Pi Mai. But in the afternoon, the mood changed. Demonstrators entered the USAID compound, destroyed valuable equipment, appropriated the rest, and took money allegedly mounting to over one million kip. That evening, we heard repeated exhortations on the radio that USAID should leave, and that all American activities should be placed under government control.

By 16 May, conditions had settled, and most students and all of us teachers were back at school. Though the surrounding chaos did not encourage work, I managed to make students focus on English conversation and on a written test for most of the morning. But in the afternoon, once I reached home and a USAID messenger delivered an urgent message from my current employer's office in Vientiane (IVS), I stopped pretending that things were normal. The message instructed me to join a small group of USAID staff who would be flown to Vientiane from the nearby town of Xiengeun in the afternoon. I rushed to catch the flight, but despite all efforts, missed it. I was not sorry, though. I knew that anti-American feeling was

---

8   Luang Phrabang USAID official Robello.

on the increase, and that non-essential USAID staff was being evacuated. But the measure seemed premature, certainly for me, a British/Mexican citizen. I was convinced that my British nationality, and the respect I enjoyed as a long-time teacher in town, would protect me.

All the same, I let the IVS office in Vientiane know that I would be flying down to sort things out on the first regular Royal Air Lao flight available. I was determined to convince the IVS director to let me stay on. Once in Vientiane an unexpected piece of news helped: the French and Japanese embassies had agreed that there was no need to evacuate their personnel, including their volunteers. Armed with that argument, and despite IVS' well-meaning American caution, I got what I wanted – I was free to take the first flight back. However, a flight was not immediately available and I was stuck in Vientiane for a few days. As I waited, conditions there got worse, and by 21 May they had seriously deteriorated, for the Americans particularly: the USAID compound was occupied by a joint contingent of students and workers.

Fearing a reversal of IVS' decision, I rushed to the Royal Air Lao office, only to discover that my ticket could not be issued. A new rule had been established that any air travel required a laissez passer, and this needed to be approved by the Joint Police. The Joint Police office was not far, but it took a long time to have the laissez passer issued, to return to the airline office and get an airline ticket for the next day. As I waited at the Royal Air Lao office, I bumped into a VSO volunteer, Mike, stationed in Savannakhet. He described the Pathet Lao's spectacular entry there, complete with flowers, enthusiastic welcoming cheers, and a long line of tanks rolling in. This, Mike said, was the Pathet Lao's response to rumours of an imminent Thai-supported coup. I could not wait to be back in the north to witness my own Pathet Lao entry.

When I arrived back to Luang Phrabang on May 22, everything was in a turmoil. Strike followed strike – at Nam Papa Lao (the Water Company), at the National Bank, at the Office of Agriculture, at the Office of Public Works, at the Royal Air Lao office – alongside protests by mid- and low-level civil servants, and walk-outs from government departments. I learned that the PL was by then fully in control of the rice trade. As the Pathet Lao had gained ground, several Royal Army units had joined them, echoing reports that Royal Lao Army troops garrisoned in northwest and central Laos had mutinied and also joined. Strikers demanded that USAID personnel pack and leave within three days, a deadline which was increased to thirty days after negotiations. USAID buildings were scheduled to come under government control. The *Sat Lao* newspaper staff were told to leave town within the same period as USAID, and ordered to hand over facilities to the government.

Talking to the Hmong on either side of the political divide
(July 1975)

Gradually, the turmoil I faced in May subsided, and as stricter controls were imposed in town, a semblance of normality was restored. Movements out of town were under greater scrutiny than before, but not those of foreigners, and in the absence of obstacles, I took the first opportunity to travel. I chose this time to go down river to Sayaboury Province where my students advised me to visit the Hmong villages of Nala and Namphoui. I asked Moua to come along. As we and other passengers waited for our boat to leave early one morning, the police inspected everyone's identity cards. I knew this newly-introduced measure was resented, but there was no complaint and everyone in the boat complied – Moua and I, one junior Lycée student and his elderly relative, and three Hmong men. The last passenger to get on was a Pathet Lao soldier, also a Hmong. I smiled to Moua. The soldier's double identity, Hmong and Pathet Lao, seemed a contradiction in terms... Although I had always known that some Hmong clans had sided with the Pathet Lao, the strong Hmong/anti-communist association in my mind made a Pathet Lao Hmong seem an anomaly. This made it doubly interesting to get to know our travel companion. He smiled as he boarded and was friendly from the start, even lending me his bowl when the young Lycée student who sat on the side offered to share some noodle soup. Once we got to talk, he could not resist borrowing my sunglasses. He was always relaxed, even when the passengers' chit chat implied criticism of the PL. He listened quietly, and said firmly that the disorganization and corruption which was rife in Vientiane didn't occur on his side. And he left it at that. There was a conciliatory self-assurance about him which inspired respect.

The soldier held a position of responsibility. His duty on the boat was to check the rice being loaded at each stop of the journey, and to record its weight. He was also a member of a *kong pathuang* (strike organization) and, in the role of strong Pathet Lao supporter, travelled widely. As we moved on, he loosened up, and told us about himself. On this trip, he was combining work with a visit to his village. Five years had passed since he had been there. He had left when the PL encouraged him to strengthen his political commitment by studying in Samneua – the Pathet Lao stronghold in the northeast. It took him three months to get there, but it had been worth it, a stepping-stone for greater things. Having done well at the Samneua school, he had been sent to Vietnam for further study. In Hanoi, there had been no problem with the language, since the course (also focused on politics) was taught in Lao by a Lao teacher. He had learnt some market Vietnamese, just enough to get by.

By the time we got off the boat at Nala, we were on excellent terms. We entered the village together, the soldier looking truly thrilled to be back.

He insisted that Moua and I join him at his uncle's house. The family did not know he was coming, and took some time to digest that it was really him. They asked us to sit down, offered a glass of hot tea and got the soldier to tell all about the years of absence. When conversation turned to politics, there was a slight change in the soldier's tone, as had happened in the boat: it became more official as he spoke with his self-possessed voice of authority. He said important changes would take place when the PL really took over, the PL would get rid of the 'ugly' wooden houses and replace them with solid cement structures, build new roads, and organize the village into labour groups of men and women. Group leaders would make sure the sexes worked efficiently and keep relationships proper, with no lingering later in the evenings... I could see he had learnt his Hanoi lesson well: 'progress', 'efficiency', 'hard work' and puritanical morals. I could not entirely identify with his enthusiasm, but kept my peace, while noticing how proud he was to show he was somebody, a full member of the new order. It was not clear what his relatives really thought, they just listened.

As we ate our food, and all felt free to be frank, the uncle, the aunt, their two sons and the soldier were soon talking about their own versions of the Pathet Lao's entry into Nala five years before. Some people had been killed, but they disagreed about numbers. When the discussion turned to details, I wondered how this would end – Moua and I looked down at our food, in silence, and I thought about the PL's

entry at Ciugna, of its families fleeing to Luang Phrabang in a panic. But the conversation continued, as certain details were carefully avoided. After all, the soldier had returned to see them after years of absence. And he was educated, counted for something in the movement, and knew what he was doing. The talk turned to lighter matters, local gossip about old friends, while the mother offered more food. With a PL soldier in the family, it was better to keep things smooth.

Hmong: water-pipe smoking.

At multi-ethnic Namphoui, we were welcomed by Ya Lii and his wives.

Moua and I were glad to accept the family's hospitality for the night. We were up early in the morning, and headed for Namphoui. Moua and I stood at the back of a packed taxi for the entire journey, climbing to a much greater altitude, until we reached the village, famous for being a melting-pot for many groups: lowland Lao, mid-altitude Black Tai and Lao Theung, and top-altitude Hmong. We got off the bus and looked straightaway for Ya Lii, who knew Moua from Luang Phrabang. We approached his house and saw two elder wives sitting in the porch on one side of the door, while the younger woman, strikingly beautiful, sat on the other.

The women made room for us, and we sat with Ya Lii outside, drinking a glass of hot tea. He was sad that most of the Hmong families had left the village. Living in a Thai camp was a good option for many, and he had been thinking about it himself. But his second wife was ill, and could not travel on account of her legs, which were so swollen that she could barely walk. Clearly at a loss about the future, he was not sure whether to stay or pack his things and leave. That afternoon, Moua and I had similar conversations with others who agreed that these were difficult times. Like Ya Lii, they were uncertain about the future and felt increasingly vulnerable after they heard that the Hmong groups with close links with the US had been flown out of Laos. Also, the Americans had recently airlifted General Vang Pao from his base at Long Cheng to their base in Udon, Thailand. They did not need to be Vang Pao followers to feel unprotected by his departure; after all, the PL often associated the Hmong with Vang Pao's strong anti-communists, and could treat them as such regardless of their politics. Moua and I talked to many people, but no one seemed to know how to come to terms with the new Pathet Lao order. Talking in Namphoui was unlike chatting with the soldier's conciliatory family at Nala. Before leaving, I walked down to the river. A Hmong matron sang a sad song while her daughter, a mere child, was busy bathing. A young boy smiled his wide smile and ran into the water. By the water's edge, a fully dressed young woman with rolled-up trousers washed some clothes, while a little girl looked at me out of a strangely aged face from the river bank.

By the river at Namphoui.

More PL presence in town, opposition grows
(mid-July 1975)

On 18 July, the Pathet Lao took over control of Luang Phrabang in a quiet, unobtrusive way, acting as they had as part of the Joint Police, with a soft approach of gradual political persuasion. In time, however, they started introducing rules which seemed invasive and created resentment. Police control over movements out of town was increased, and a system of close surveillance was set up in each neigbourhood by politically co-opted local leaders and their informers.

Arrests on the grounds of supposed counter-revolutionary activities became the order of the day, as were accusations of alleged association with 'American reactionaries'. The supposed culprits were sent to political reeducation camps (euphemistically dubbed 'seminars', pronounced '*samana*') where they followed intensive courses in 'political recycling', or were forced to confess their purported political errors. The length of stay was never specified at entry, and varied from person to person, according to the imputed faults. Living arrangements could be draconian. Initially, the more trusting members of the Royal Lao government and the army, who were especially targeted, went to the camps of their own accord, but as the period of confinement kept being extended, and rumours circulated about the hardship involved, many potential '*samana*' inmates, fearing the worse, crossed over to Thailand, adding to the mounting number of refugees.

One incident that involved one of my students, pointed to the toughening trend. Somphone ran into difficulties by refusing to cut his hair, and by wearing wide, 'elephant-foot' trousers. One morning, the police stopped him at the market and forced him to cut his trouser bottoms with a pair of scissors, on the spot. He was accused of being a negative influence on the revolution, a reactionary, like his father. Within a few days, he was sent away to be reeducated. Before that happened, Somphone's father, a Luang Phrabang member of the National Assembly, had been arrested on the grounds of corruption, and of being a CIA agent. He also was sent to a 'seminar'. Soon after, two of Somphone's sisters, and his younger brother fled to Thailand, ending up in a refugee camp where they were eventually approved for resettlement in Australia. Only Somphone's mother remained in Luang Phrabang.

I knew Somphone and his family well. They had lived close to my first house at Vat Sen, and had become good friends, inviting me to all their family celebrations. They were well-off by local standards, were close to the palace and benefited from the advantages attached to the father's political role. I was shocked. Although I could not judge the merits of the Pathet Lao's case against the father, the accusation of CIA membership which was being made against so many members of the former elite, did not seem credible. As for the accusation of corruption, it had been used for months as an all-purpose term of opprobrium. In any case, I could vouch for Somphone, who unlike many of his classmates, was non-political, though he tended to be saucy. The incident with Somphone was but one example of the new Pathet Lao tendency to focus on petty issues and use them to penalize students, the very group who had been an important source of political support at a key moment in their rise to power. Not surprisingly, many students and previous Pathet Lao supporters were upset and began to be fearful about the direction of change.

I myself was disappointed. Somphone's family was only one of the many who were being broken up by the revolution. As the Pathet Lao's rule hardened, and their presence was resented, an increasing number of families from all ethnic groups faced the dilemma so clearly expressed in Namphoui – to leave or to stay. This was taking place in mid July 1975. But the beginning of the lowland Lao refugee flow into Thailand could be traced earlier to 9 May 1975, when five Coalition Government Ministers and Deputy Ministers had given up their portfolios and fled to Thailand. They had been followed by a number of generals, Lao civil servants and military officers and their families, along with Chinese and Vietnamese merchants and businessmen. Some time before, the media had reported that Prince Bounoum na Champassak had left for Paris from Paksé – the well-known stronghold of the Right.

The Pathet Lao's new radicalism found an impetus in the conviction that the new government was seriously threatened by counter-revolutionary forces. As with many revolutionary movements in the process of consolidation, the PL was inordinately concerned with the threat of destabilization from the outside. Thailand was well known for its virulent anti-communism and had welcomed a number of well-known right-wing civil and military members of the Lao Coalition Government. Nor had the PL forgotten that Thailand had supported the US up to the time of the Vientiane Agreement of February 1973, and perhaps even up to 1975, by providing logistical support to US civilian and military personnel fighting in Vietnam, Laos and Cambodia. It had not forgotten that Thai military units had been active in the anti-communist fight during that period.

However, the immediate cause for the Pathet Lao's change of political line was probably the Thai authorities' decision to close the Thai-Lao border following an episode of shooting across the Mekong river. The incident was followed by an emergency meeting of Pathet Lao leaders at their headquarters in Viengsay, Houaphan province, where the recently launched, tougher approach was being fine-tuned. As the treatment of presumed anti-revolutionaries hardened, ever larger numbers of people were arrested or sent to centres of political reeducation.

I can still travel, even to Southern Laos (20 August, 1975)

As I write these lines, I cannot help being surprised by the freedom of movement I could still enjoy: this was August 1975, long after the communist took power in Phnom Penh and Saigon, and some four months before the Pathet Lao victory in December. A wholly unexpected opportunity to travel to the South came my way when French architect Pierre Clement and his wife, both of them attached to the University of Paris expressed the wish to visit the Khmer ruins of Vat Phou. The couple had learned from Amphay Dore, the Franco-Lao ethnologist and friend, that I had been there before, knew Laos well and could serve as a guide. They offered to include me in their official cultural visit, and arranged all required authorizations.

I jumped at the offer. Upon arrival in Paksé in the early morning, the Clements and I were told to call on the provincial governor. We did not find him at the provincial office and were told to report at the main police station to have our passports and air tickets checked. Once done, we were taken to a large Vietnamese-owned hotel where we waited long hours for the governor. A vivacious man in his mid-thirties, Governor Sisavat, former deputy governor in the previous regime, had recently been appointed to the post. He greeted us in a friendly manner, but pretending to be embarrassed, politely put an end to our Vat Phou plans by saying that our travel authorizations had been mistakenly approved in Vientiane, and were invalid. Security conditions had deteriorated sharply following an assassination attempt against one of the PL leaders by 'Thai-supported reactionaries'. A visit to Vat Phou was out of the question. We were to leave for Vientiane without delay.

I had never come across such attitudes in Luang Phrabang. Why had this happened? I later learned that Pakse and Champassak province were considered serious security risks, and had therefore been placed under the direct control of the Pathet Lao's headquarters at Viengsay. One alleged cause for this special treatment was the supposed political unreliability of the town's large and influential Chinese community. As I heard such rumours, I recalled my impressions of that community during my visit to Paksé in 1972. I had been struck by its size, the apparent wealth of its merchants, its impressive temples, and by the very active Chinese Centre. In a materially more successful manner than the other sizeable non-Lao community – the Vietnamese – the Chinese had consolidated their presence over generations, and become a well-accepted component of the town's ethnic make-up. However, during my first visit, I had learnt that some Chinese merchants had been willing to help the PL by providing them with rice at the height of the fighting. It was likely that the good will which the cooperation of some Chinese merchants had generated among PL cadres had not been extended to the larger Chinese community, let alone to the profiteers who had hoarded rice to sell at inflated prices in town. Like the rich Chinese merchants in other towns, including Luang Phrabang, those in Pakse had indeed been accused of hoarding and selling rice at exorbitant prices, to the detriment of a population already seriously affected by the war. In PL eyes, they were no different to that category of Chinese elsewhere in Laos – they were exploiters of the people. But what probably led the Pathet Lao to approach Pakse's rich Chinese with particular diffidence, was their association with the local elite: this group included prominent members of the Laotian Right, many of whom had connections with anti-communist Thailand at the highest level, or had fled there. Prince Boun Oum Na Champassak was among them.

That association could be especially damning. Not only had the Prince been a prominent actor on the (to the PL) wrong side of politics; he had been a formidable force to reckon with locally - a powerful feudal lord and patron who cemented his influence among ordinary villagers by regularly joining them as principal participant in their annually recurring animistic rituals. Like those I have described for Luang Phrabang, the rituals resonated deeply among the people, at least as much as Buddhist ceremonies. They stood at the centre of a village reality where the individual's well-being, and his very survival required the containment of negative forces by means of offerings and sacrifices, which in this case included the spilling of blood. The Prince never failed to participate every year in the eye-catching Sacrifice of the Buffalo at Vat Phou, a ceremony which confirmed his authority as the uncontested overlord. The orthodox among the Pathet Lao leadership regarded such rituals as old regime superstition which ought to be suppressed, especially when they served to bolster the old social order, keep the feudal lord's authority over the people, and undermine their strategy of village-level political control. The accumulation of right-wing referents, and the presence of forces that harked back to a past which the PL considered reactionary help explain why Champassak was placed under special scrutiny, and why the French architects' and my travel plans were blocked.

I leave Luang Phrabang and follow events from London
(August 1975)

As I followed every step of the Pathet Laos' progress, my personal situation became more uncertain. I was very much attached to Luang Phrabang, but I could see no future there for the time being. Also, after three years in the classroom, I wanted to do something else – teaching had been my first job and I had enjoyed it, but I now needed to move on. Academic research had for some time been a viable alternative, and my fruitful encounter with lowland Lao and Hmong customs had whipped up my appetite for further knowledge. I therefore developed a plan which included a return to Laos: an initial time of study in London, where training in social anthropology and specialized knowledge of Southeast Asia were available, followed by field research in northern Laos. To make plans for the future outside Laos was different from taking steps towards departure, but nevertheless, with much resistance, tremendous hesitation, and second thoughts, I started to make preparations for departure. I fully intended to come back, and said so as part of my farewells.

I left Luang Phrabang in August 1975 and travelled straight to London where I entered the University of London's SOAS (School of Oriental and African Studies). Having enrolled in the Department of Social Anthropology for an M Phil, and been upgraded for a PhD, I selected my line of investigation – the perception of deviant behavior and insanity in rural areas of Northern Laos, in the vicinity of Luang Phrabang.

As this happened, I kept well-informed about developments in Laos, and followed the Pathet Lao's progress towards power. At the end of November, demonstrations in Vientiane called for the dissolution of the Government of National Union and demanded the abolition of the monarchy. On 29 November, Prime Minister Souvannaphoumma, and his half-brother, Pathet Lao leader Prince Souphanouvong asked King Sisavang Vathana to abdicate. Souvannaphoumma then stepped down as Prime Minister, and on 1 and 2 December 1975, a two-day secret session of the National Congress of People's Representatives voted for the establishment of the Lao People's Democratic Republic, with Prince Souphanouvong as President. This was preceded by the decision to abolish the monarchy, thus putting an end to its long-held and much vaunted conciliatory position vis-à-vis the king, and giving an ominous signal as to his fate. By these momentous resolutions, the Pathet Lao had effectively put an end to the old regime. Twenty years after the 1954 Geneva Conference, the movement had gained full political control of what was now a republic.

So many of the questions I had asked were now clarified, but not all. I now knew that King Sisavang Vathana had been unable to play the part of supreme

White cotton strings are tied to my wrists during my farewell *baci*.

conciliator, given the Pathet Lao's unappealable conclusion that as the living symbol of the old society he would be an obstacle to the social transformation to which they were committed, and could be an active instigator of anti-revolutionary forces. But when had this conclusion been reached? What could one make of the Pathet Lao's repeated pronouncements about the monarchy's survival? Had that been a temporary stunt to maximise public support? A smokescreen hiding the real intentions of the dominant radicals? Had the such radicals always intended to put an end to the monarchy? Had Prince Souphanouvong kept giving assurances of the monarchy's survival in the hope that the moderates would prevail, and that the institution would remain? Or had he been a willing party to a calculated manipulation of internal and international opinion? If so, was his wish to abolish the monarchy a matter of ideological conviction? Or was there a strong personal component in it: his resentment as a minor member of the vice-royal branch of the royal family, getting his own back for a lack of prospects, when the PL offered a way to the top?

* * * * * * * * * *

As I asked those questions and followed events from London, I continued to ponder my wish to return to Laos. And then, a host of elements made me reconsider: the hardening of the Vientiane regime, news of widespread bureaucratic control everywhere in the country, letters from my former students spelling out their disappointment at the authorities' increasing authoritarianism, the setting up of reeducation camps, the beginning of a refugee outflow into Thailand, and the alarm of friends recently returned from Vientiane. After much hesitation, I turned back on my intention to go back, and opted instead for the Chiang Mai area of Northern Thailand. The decision to switch to Thailand was not easy. But it proved to be the right one. While still in Luang Phrabang, I had hoped that my former status as a foreign teacher would open all doors under the new regime, and allow me to move as I pleased. But once in London, I realized that if ever I was granted entry, I would be placed under strict control, always seen as someone formerly from the other side. There were too many links that tied me to the pre-revolutionary past, not least my work at schools which catered for members of the former élite, and my friendship with families who had turned out to be Pathet Lao undesirables, had ended up in reeducation camps, or crossed over to Thailand.

The switch of location had many advantages. Northern Thailand was close in language and culture to Northern Laos. I hoped that its relative proximity to the Lao Popular Democratic Republic would make occasional visits there possible. Also, the Chiang Mai area stretched to territories along the Thai-Lao border where camps housed Lao refugees who had fled the new Vientiane regime. From my new place of study, I would be able to visit my former Luang Phrabang students, now turned refugees. Also, Thailand was the political opposite of Laos, the ideal location to gain an understanding of anti-communist politics, a country that defined itself proudly as the effective counter to the three Indochinese revolutions.

Part Two:

Thailand (1977-1979)
Ideological Counter to
the Lao Revolution

8

THE DEMONIZATION OF COMMUNISM

Thailand and Indochina

During the time I lived in London (1975 to 1977), I prepared for my return to Southeast Asia by attending several courses at SOAS. But I also followed developments in and around Indochina. Since my fieldwork would be taking place in Thailand I focused on that country's reactions to its communist neighbours, Laos in particular. Relations between Bangkok and Vientiane were tense, varying with a host of factors, including the relative political weight in each country of hard liners or peace-makers, whether they operated from the capitals, or along the Thai-Lao border. But always at play was an unchanging ideological component which led to continually renewed negative descriptions of the other – strongly anti-communist on the Thai side (with a tendency to blame the Vietnamese as the principal, hidden force); anti-capitalist and anti-American on the Lao side. Provocations came and went across the Mekong, using a similar concoction of objective facts, distorted interpretations, vague accusations of

Thailand's nightmare: the three Indochinese revolutions.

territorial violation and documented instances of cross-border subversive action. Real or trumped-up fears of imminent invasion sometimes followed the incidents, with dramatic consequences. In Laos, forebodings of destabilisation from abroad, Thailand in particular, led to an ever-stricter system of control, to arrests and to confinement in political reeducation camps. Also, a growing concentration of refugees in Thailand's refugee camps further exacerbated the suspicion that a Thai-backed

Opposite page: The instructors of a Village Scout induction session carry a portrait of King Bhumipol. The nation-wide Scout Movement exposed a wide section of the population to intensive courses in anti-communist indoctrination. (photo by M.Muecke)

counter-revolution, allegedly being partly developed in the refugee camps, was under way. In Thailand, the government's concern with Indochinese communism, and with the advance of the Thai Communist Party, led to intolerance, the demonization of dissension, repression, and a massive campaign of anti-communist indoctrination, accompanied by the political manipulation of Buddhism and the monarchy.

In both Thailand and Laos, the image of the threatened nation perpetrated by the hardliners in the government, the army, the police, the security agencies and the state-controlled media resulted in similar excesses of control and repression in the name of a state-promoted ideology of the greater good: in communist Laos, a new socialist order of social justice, freedom, prosperity and national dignity, constructed under the enlightened guidance of the Party; in anti-communist Thailand, the capitalist development of an ever more prosperous nation, sustained by the monarchy and the Buddhist Sangha. In short, Laos and Thailand featured comparable mechanisms of repression and control which contrasting ideologies served to legitimate. This was the political context in which I would be starting my PhD field-work.

*　*　*　*　*　*

I arrived in Thailand in September 1977, registered at the Bangkok-based Thai National Research Council, and, armed with my official authorization, took the train to Chiang Mai. As my planned field of research ('Folk Understandings of the Insane and their Cure') was in some ways medically connected and mainly concerned rural areas, Chiang Mai University advised me to look for support at the Sarapi District Health Centre, just outside town. I was lucky. Inside the Centre, I met the government midwife of a neighbouring sub-district, who was immediately interested in my work, and after a chat offered me the use of an empty house in the

Harvest-time at
Ban Phaya Chompu,
close to Chiang Mai
but rural.

grounds of the Level II Health Centre which she managed. Suchilak (I addressed her as elder sister) said I was more than welcome, and before I knew, I found myself in her car being driven to the Centre, which stood at the edge of Ban Phaya Chompu. Conveniently placed at a short 15 km south of town, the village had retained a strongly rural character, framed as it was by fertile rice fields which were still its main source of sustenance.

I settled well in my house on stilts. Initially, I saw a lot of Suchilak and the children, sharing meals at their insistence. Also, I got to know the villagers and explained my planned study to them, hoping they could help me find suitable informants for my research – 'khon baa' (mentally ill persons) and their families. Everyone was ready to help but, it turned out that there were no disturbed persons in the village. Clearly, the 'khonbaa' I wanted to investigate, would be spread out thinly over the area, perhaps at a rate of one or two per village, if I was lucky. The work was more complicated than I expected, and I felt jealous of the anthropologist who studies one aspect of a single village, where his informants are all village members who gradually get to know him, trust him, and tell him what he wants to know. In my case, I would have to do most of my work outside Ban Phaya Chompu, approaching a new community each time I needed a new informant. That was not going to be easy. Not easy at all. My first step was to secure a means of transport. Having bought a Honda 70, I approached the mayor of a first village, and tried to explain who I was, and what I wanted. 'I am a doctoral student at the University of London studying folk understandings of insanity' No, that would not do. So I tried another line. 'No, I am not a medical doctor, I am doing a study which will be useful to doctors in England who know that the 'baa' are treated effectively in the villages of Chiang Mai, and want to know more'. All this was said in what was still at this stage my hesitant Northern Thai, adapted from my Luang Phrabang Lao. The reaction was on the whole friendly, and I usually ended up talking to my wished-for 'khonbaa', if there was one. But the process each time was a strain. Until one day, the mayor of yet another unexplored village unintentionally provided me with a solution. Taking me for a medical doctor (despite my disclaimers, that is what I was often taken for) he introduced me to Suvet. A former secondary school teacher, this man in his late twenties had lost his eyesight as a result of a motorbike accident. The mayor wondered if I could help him. I said again that I was not a medical doctor, and explained what I was doing, including my visits to healers who treated the insane.

Suvet had been listening carefully, and once the mayor left, we had a long chat. We concluded we could work together to the advantage of both: he could help explain my work whenever I approached a new village, and I would introduce him to the healers with the hope that one of them might find a way to make him see again. The arrangement worked perfectly on my side. Not only were first contacts with villages considerably smoother, but Suvet was soon asking pertinent questions on his own initiative, and filling me in at the end of each interview with what I had missed. But he was not as lucky as I was: he kept being disappointed in his search for an effective healer, never more than during a consultation (described below) with a famous healing monk.

I was ready to start. I had a motorbike, a helpful assistant and the mapping of villages where I would try my luck. And I had Ban Phaya Chompu which remained my base. Though I was often out of the village for the day, I usually visited villages close enough to drive back for the night. In this way, I was still part of the village which, despite all my travels, was home for the next year and seven months.

Initially, I had seen the village in terms of my research – it was a rural community, and its people were close to the land, precisely the social category whose attitudes to mental illness I wanted to grasp. But I soon saw that Ban Phaya Chompu was much

My field assistant Suvet with three anthropologists: Marjorie Muecke (left), Katherine Bowie and myself (below, with Marjorie's assistant Phongsi and her boyfriend)

My home in the grounds of Ban Phaya Chompu Health Station.

My own efforts in the rice fields: separating the rice from the chaff.

Relaxing after a day's work in the fields.

more than a convenient base. The villagers made me discover the ins and outs of their way of life, their proximity to the land, their work in the fields, their concern with the agricultural cycle, their internal solidarity, the solidity of their recurring celebrations and, most of all, their unconditional readiness to take in a foreigner and welcome him. They taught me their values and priorities, those which framed the behaviour of the individuals I would be studying.

A first exposure to anti-communist indoctrination
(October 1977)

Politics and anti-communist nationalist ideology had not initially been part of my work plan, but as I got involved in my subject and interviewed villagers, it was clear that state-level concerns – Cold War fears that Thailand would be the next domino to fall – were having a strong impact on society generally, including on my informants. Anti-communist ideology had developed in response to years of communist militancy in Laos, Cambodia and Vietnam, a reaction to the communist takeover in Indochina after 1975 and to the ever-increasing influence of North Vietnam in the region. But the call for an effective counter-attack also came from political developments inside Thailand – strong criticism of the government by a sizeable number of students, the radicalization of labour and farmers, and the growth of armed activities by the military branch of the Thai Communist Party[1]. In an increasingly polarized environment, the State's resolve to counter and indeed annihilate its perceived enemies ideologically was coupled with vigorous repressive action by the Communist Suppression Operation Command (CSOC)[2], the Thai army and the Border Patrol Police, whose initial role – maintaining the government's presence in the border areas – became increasingly paramilitary. In addition, extreme right-wing groups who were well known for their use of violence were given a free hand[3].

There was another aspect of the offensive against perceived antagonists of the state which added significantly to the dissemination of propaganda: the Village Scout Movement. This I got to know shortly after my arrival in Ban Phaya Chompu, when I was invited to join one of the movement's induction courses in the grounds of a *wat,* in a nearby village. The experience was an eye-opener. I was not invited

---

1   The Thai Communist Party's first Congress took place in 1942; evidence of its military struggle can be traced to 1965; the very tentative estimates of guerrilla fighters range between 14,000 and 18,000 spread over 46 out of 72 provinces, and between 2,000 and 4,000 in Northern Thailand. Irvine 1982: 71.

2   CSOC (Kong banchakan pongkan le prapram comiunit)

3   For an in-depth account of the rise of Thailand's anti-communist ideology and connected developments, see Irvine unpublished PhD thesis 1982: 70-75.

for the duration of five full days, but the two days I attended showed the efficacy of the adopted methods. The group of some two hundred participants was not given a moment's rest. A frenzied succession of events hammered the same exhortations – steadfast loyalty to the monarchy (represented by photographs of the king) and Buddhism (stressed by the presence of monks); absolute rejection of communism. Endless repetition was used to ensure full internalization of the message.

Full acceptance was furthered by the fiction that participants were social equals, members of a group of true nationalists willing to defend the Thai Nation against all odds, under the guidance of the king and queen. Royal patronage was extended to all participants at induction, when all scouts, wearing the same uniform and the same scarf, were transformed into the privileged members of the royally-sponsored patriotic effort. It was understood that equal standing of all under royal protection was an honour which required blind compliance. The participation of monks in the closing ceremony, their chanting, and the delivery of a sermon extolling the merits of the Village Scout movement, placed a lasting seal of approval on the incontestable validity of everything taught during the five days' training.

The activities included humorous sketches and moralistic plays in which the physical punishment of the 'communist traitor', or the reward accorded for an act of Buddhist heroism were acted out and applauded with enthusiasm. During one session of political instruction, the speaker described Thai history as a process in which communism, personified as an evil spirit, had gradually conquered the Thai peoples' original territory, a very extensive area which had at one time incorporated southern China, Laos, Burma, and Cambodia. Using the image of spirit attack, the instructor described the originator of the threat as an aggressive, menacing spirit, a *phii*. He pointed his finger at the map and showed communist Vietnam, Laos and Kampuchea, drawn into the shape of a malevolent such spirit, its gaping mouth ready to ingest the Buddhist Kingdom of Thailand. The message resonated deeply with the villagers. As women and men needed to be protected from evil spirits which made them ill, it was clear that Thailand also had to be shielded from the malevolent spirit of communist Indochina as a whole, without singling out any one of its constituent countries. In his concluding remarks, the instructor strongly urged participants to defend the nation, whatever the cost, and prevent the spirit's entry into Thai territory or forcibly expel it when already present.

At a time of a state-induced concern with the communist threat, it was politically astute to identify an illness-inducing *phii* with communism and to attach fears of illness-producing spirits onto political undesirables labelled 'communists'. It was a highly effective strategy of state defence. Effective and solid, since it identified the communist threat with one of the axiomatic threats of village culture: that posed by the intruding, ill-intentioned *phii*, a being which the culture credits with the power

New recruits receive the distinctive Village Scout scarf before the five-day induction course.
(Photo by M.Muecke)

to undo the precarious health of an individual by upsetting the balance of his four bodily humours.[4] Based on that unquestioned axiom, the link was made between a *phii* and a communist: like a *phii*, a communist enters the Thai nation, but rather than unsettling an individual's humours, it attacks the nation's two sustaining institutions: the monarchy and the Buddhist Sangha.

Once that was established, the Village Scout teacher could apply all the methods used by an exorcist against a *phii* to the different stages of an anti-communist hunt. To begin with, both healers and state ideologues focused on the root cause of the individual's or the state's disturbance (possession by a *phii* or communist penetration) and then decided on the best next step – to weaken or to annihilate. Much as the healer's offensive varied depending on the *phii*'s relative resilience, so could the anti-communist state's approach be soft or aggressive. The healer and the anti-communist state had to operate with extreme caution when their treacherous assailants were cornered, immobilized, confronted and finally defeated. For both *phii* and communist, confrontation could be carried out verbally – by softly cajoling words or insults – or physically, with the help of lethal weapons

---

4   One explanation of illness is that it occurs when the four bodily humours (earth, water, fire and wind) are destabilized by the entry into the body of an evil or angry spirit. For instance, mental disturbance occurs when a spirit causes the wind element to 'blow' in uncontrolled fashion in the direction of the 'mind-heart' (the seat of thought and the emotions) and upsets it.

5   Davis 1974.

(knives or swords for the *phii*, guns for the others). When dealing with relatively benign spirits or communist agents, the weapons could be wielded calmly, but they were used menacingly when the agents of evil were defiant and stood their ground. In general terms, in order to stop the *phii* or communist from attacking again, both healer and the anti-communist state could carry out all stages of the hunt in public. Confronted with the hot pursuit and strict punitive measures that healer or state imposed, it was unlikely that any *phii* or communist would try to play their tricks again.

There were other reasons why the threat of an ill-intentioned spirit had such a strong hold on the imagination, and was such a solid basis for political manipulation. The belief was deeply ingrained in the culture that spirit attack not only threatened a person, but also other entities: a home, a village, a district or a city. When penetrated or negatively affected by a malevolent spirit, such entities also required an exorcism. And in villages or cities that were built on the bank of a river, the expulsion ended dramatically when the evil was loaded onto light bamboo rafts or banana leaf receptacles and was carried down-river, out of sight. As the late anthropologist Richard Davis insisted[5], '*song kho*' ('expel the evil influence') rituals were widespread in Northern Thailand, especially at New Year and during times of extreme hardship, as when an epidemic or a natural catastrophe struck. Such practices continue to be a central feature of Northern Thai culture and are widespread elsewhere in Thailand and beyond, in Indochina (see Part I for a communal ritual of expulsion Luang Phrabang in the 1970s). As an integral part of commonsense reality, the unquestioned assumption has been and continues to be that the person or the community can be cleansed, and strength fully restored.

The solid cultural basis on which the Village Scout teachings were based, go a long way to explain the undoubted appeal and success of their induction sessions.

Village scouts assembled a map of Thailand which they later placed next to an outline of communist Indochina, shaped to resemble a greedy malevolent spirit intending to gobble up its Thai prey. (Photo by M.Muecke)

In a paper on the subject, anthropologist Marjorie Muecke reports that by 1978, some 2.5 million people (5% of the country's population) had participated, had received the anti-communist message and been put in a position to spread it[6].

1976: a year of anti-communist extremism

The political intensity I experienced during the Village Scout induction course of October 1977 showed the Thai state's extreme concern with Indochina's communism. But I only became aware of the full force of the country's response, a veritable anti-communist paranoia, when I delved into the political developments of 1976, and the extreme violence that came with them. Strong anti-communist defensiveness was not a new development in Thailand. Its origin can be traced to the 1950s, when the establishment of strong links with the United States led to the active dissemination of anti-communist ideology. The result, particularly after Marshall Sarit came to power in 1957, was widespread repression on the grounds of 'communist subversion'.[7] What I was witnessing in the 1970s was a new version of well-rehearsed anti-communist practices.

The Thai-Lao border, a feeding ground for nationalist paranoia

The image of the border as a danger point for the country's integrity was not invented by the Village Scout ideologues. It was an image which various dependencies of the Thai state and the media had gradually constructed in the months that followed the 1975 communist takeover of Indochina. The consequent upsurge of anti-communist sentiment was especially virulent in the border areas. When directed against incoming Lao or Cambodian refugees who lived in the confines of well-guarded camps, the sentiment was kept reasonably under control (see below p. 140-144). But it was transformed into hate, and degenerated into episodes of extreme violence when actively directed by the state and the fearmongering media against another target: Thai-based, long-established Vietnamese communities who were alleged to be fifth columns of communist Vietnam[8]. Having reached Thailand in several waves since the 18th century, they had tended to concentrate in the border provinces of the Thai Northeast, and featured the whole range of political opinion: anti-colonialists and nationalists in the 19th century, Ho Chi Minh backers in the 1920s, anti-communists after 1975. The heterogeneous political composition of the communities, some of which showed leftist sympathies, had already led the Thai state to regard the various Vietnamese settlements with a certain caution. But in the febrile post-1975 anti-communist context, mistrust was transformed into frank vindictiveness by certain institutions (the Ministry of the Interior, the border Armed Forces, certain Security Units) and by certain dissatisfied groups of the civilian population. As this happened, a nationwide rumour campaign, initiated in June, portrayed the Vietnamese as the single most dangerous source of national destabilization. Flood[9] describes what happened: verbal abuse led to violent physical assaults on Vietnamese people and property by uncontrollable mobs of technical school students, unemployed hoodlums and organized hate groups that operated in the border northeastern provinces of Nakhon Phanom, Sakhon Nakhon and Udon Thani. This was followed by the arrest without charge of some 16,000 Vietnamese, mostly refugees from the last days of the Saigon regime.

The shrunken penis syndrome

Anti-Vietnamese aggression was followed by accusations of perverse, politically motivated poisoning. Towards the beginning of August 1976, just over a month after anti-Vietnamese violence had broken out, the Thai and English language press (*Thai Rat, Dao Siam, Daily News, Bangkok World, Bangkok Post*) reported, again for the Thai Northeast, that the ingestion of foods allegedly poisoned by the Vietnamese with a 'white powder' was causing a condition of sexual impairment. The foods included noodles, rice, flour, meatballs, salted pork, iced coffee, and soft drinks. Tobacco was also mentioned. Men represented the majority of affected persons, and showed penile shrinkage and sexual impotence, while the minority of women complained of shrinking and itching genitals, withered breasts, frigidity and numbness in the lower abdomen. Patients of both sexes were said to suffer from nausea and dizziness at the outset of the condition. At a later stage, some complained of abdominal aches, facial numbness and headaches. All were beset with a fear of imminent death, to which men added the fear that their sexual organs would be absorbed by their stomachs. In time, complaints spread from the Thai Northeast to other parts of where the Vietnamese had also settled, including Bangkok, and several provinces in the North – a veritable epidemic of sexually connected fears. Reports about the condition continued at least until November 1976.

---

6   Muecke 1980: 407. For an exhaustive analysis of the movement see Muecke's entire article.

7   See Irvine 1982: 445.

8   Vietnamese communities in Thailand are in the main constituted by refugees who have fled political oppression in their country, beginning at the end of the 18th century. During the 19th century they were mainly persecuted religious minorities. Later they comprised opponents to the French Colonial regime. In the first decades of the 20th century, they included increasing numbers of political activists, whose main purpose was the creation of work cooperatives to maintain members' awareness of themselves as patriots fighting for the liberation of Vietnam. Significantly, Ho Chi Minh created the Siamese Communist Party in 1930 in the Thai Northeast as a means of unifying all scattered Viietnamese anti-colonialist, nationalist groups.

9   Flood (1977: 40) quoted in Irvine 1982: 445.

The specialized psychiatric journals provided a mix of serious descriptions and explanations, while the medical profession held a conference on the subject in the southern town of Songkla, focusing on the psychiatric status of the condition and referring to it as the 'shrinking penis syndrome'. Meanwhile, the Ministry of Health categorically denied that the food or the tobacco contained any extraneous chemical substances. But the political scaremongers and scapegoat-hunters argued otherwise. Some denied the validity of the ministry's findings, while adepts of traditional medicine argued that certain herbs (found in Laos and Cambodia) contained substances which could cause impotence and reduce the sexual organs, while remaining undetectable by laboratory methods. And one well-known author of a book on the occult, and founding member of the 'Association of Psychic Research' even claimed that the enemies of the state (the Vietnamese) intended to carry out a political-demographic conquest of Thailand. The intention was to incapacitate Thai men sexually by means of poisonous substances, replace them by Vietnamese males and father a new race who would eventually control Thailand's entire territory. The author noted that the Vietnamese communists had devised a similar strategy of political destabilisation by sexual conquest in Laos.[10]

The shrunken penis syndrome in Laos

While this happened in Thailand, news from Laos reported a sexual affliction almost identical to Thailand's shrunken penis syndrome. Following the ingestion of certain kinds of fruit (papaya and oranges) that had been poisoned with a 'white powder', men suffered impotence or a reduction of the genitals, while Lao women (in contrast to their Thai counterparts), showed increased sexual desire. Also, in an ideological reversal of Thai anti-communist accusations, the use of poisoning powder in Laos was blamed on 'Thai capitalists' or even 'American imperialists'. This occurred at a time when fear of an alleged Thai-supported counter-revolution caused an intensification of security controls, and the arrest and confinement of increasing numbers of alleged 'reactionaries' in so-called political reeducation camps. This was also a time when the number of lowland Lao fleeing the country and seeking asylum in Thailand continued to grow (in 1976 the number rose to just under 20,000, remained the same during 1977 and more than doubled again in 1978 to some 48,000). The presence of anti-LPDR refugees in Thai camps along the Lao border further exacerbated the Lao state's sense of vulnerability and led to

10 Chalo Utakhapat: 1976 in Irvine 1982: 430.
11 Keyes 1971: 155.

even stricter internal controls. In that context, it was not surprising to learn that official statements on Lao radio on January 10, affirmed that the 'capitalist takeover with US support was about to take place' and, in addition, that the Americans were systematically infecting Laotians by injecting a substance into their bodies with 'painless needles'. Dr. Siccart, a French, Vientiane-based medical doctor, reported that the Americans were further accused of carrying out covert attacks against the Lao by means of 'artificial spiders' which they placed in strategic places in the jungle.

Communist Laos and capitalist Thailand were the mirror image of each other's fears, caused by different imagined agents of sexual destabilization. Despite sharp differences in political and economic organization, both states saw an urgent need to fend off alleged destabilizing exterior or interior forces and, if possible, obliterate them. The appearance in both of a similar condition of sexual alteration attested to the dangers to which the nation and its population were exposed, and confirmed the need for punitive action against the alleged originator – in Thailand, the Vietnamese communist, in Laos, the Thai capitalist or the American imperialist.

The paroxysm of verbal and physical anti-communist violence

While the anti-communist fever of 1976 developed into a veritable witch hunt against Vietnamese nationals, it also led to a profound distortion of vision in at least one nationally known member of the Buddhist Sangha: the extreme anti-communist central Thai monk, Phra Khitthivutho. Famous for his incendiary statements, he once affirmed that 'Killing Communists is not a sin (*'khaa komiunit mai baab')*. By tendentious use of rhetoric and misinterpretation of the Buddhist writings, Phra Khitthivutho had argued: 'Communists order people to kill. But if we are to protect our Religion, the Nation and the King, it is necessary to kill communists. Communists are not people, however; they are the devil, impurities and ideology personified, abstractions. It is all right to kill an ideology; the Buddha taught us to do so, and he gave us the Dharmma with which to do it. If defenders of the Buddhist Sangha, and the king use real weapons to kill communists, that is all right because their intention is morally correct. In this way, the merit they gain will be far more than the demerit acquired[11]'. By the time Phra Kitthivutho delivered his speech, he had won the support of significant numbers of low-level government officials, clerks, the urban petit-bourgeoisie, and rural village and commune headmen. Expressed with the authority of the Thai Sangha, one of the pillars of the nation, his outrageous statements not only legitimated past aggressions but encouraged new episodes of violence against supposed enemies of the state. Such actions occurred on October 6, 1976 at Thammassat University – acts of supreme

The culmination of anti-communist fanaticism, Thammassat University, 6 October 1976.
(photo by courtesy of Thongchai Winichakul)

political fanaticism where 'amulets were ripped off the necks of students by people who said the students must be communists, and could not be Buddhists'[12]. Some students were dragged by the neck until their necks snapped, while others were hanged and, once dead, were viciously battered. The horrifying scenes shocked the nation. Reports filled the main newspapers worldwide, including in London where I read the blood-chilling descriptions of the massacre[13],[14].

The students were accused of being the carriers of communism, I could well have said 'carriers of the spirit of communism', to keep in tune with the widespread understanding at the time that the students had been possessed by an evil spirit that had to be expelled. Acting in the spirit of Phra Khittivutho's statements that communists are not human, the hate-filled crowds unleashed their uncontrolled fury against the corpses. As was consistent with the exorcistic model, the killings at Thammassat were followed by a cleansing ritual reminiscent of the purification and strengthening of a patient after the expulsion of an illness-producing spirit.

---

12 Turton 1977: 1A.

13 See Anderson 1977 for an exhaustive account. Anderson provides an analysis of the factors which explain the emergence of a new kind of violence of which October 6 is the most blood-stained example. Quoted in Irvine 1982 Unpublished PhD thesis.

14 For an analysis of the attempt to cancel the memory of the events, see Thongchai Winichakul 2020.

I give an offering to a healer to reciprocate for his teaching. As I got to know him, I realized that his politics were close to the nationalist ideology being promoted by the state, as were those of all other healers.

Political conservatism among the healers

Having learned about the intensity of anti-communist violence in 1976, and participated in a Village Scout induction course, I was not surprised to find that the healers I met as part of my PhD research stood politically with the *status quo*. Some of the healers were 'spirit specialists' (*'mo phii'*) who mainly talked to me about their methods of diagnosis and cure. But they did not fail to spell out where they stood politically. They were Buddhists, supporters of the monarchy and committed anti-communists. To add to their political respectability, they claimed that for all actions, curative and political, they counted on the support of the highest echelons of the military, prominent members of the economic elite and even, in some cases, the royal court in Bangkok. They were more than just medical practitioners; they were active political players who had fully absorbed the prevailing political ideology, energetically spread its central messages among patients and loyal followers, and enjoyed the resulting benefit to their reputations and prestige.

The well-known spirit specialist and healer, Mɔ Suvan, sits next to various skulls, one source of his magical power. (photo M. Muecke)

Mo Suvan demonstrates the efficacy of his magic. The point of his sword does not pierce the skin of a client who has just been tattooed for invulnerability (Photo M.Muecke).

Within this group I found a committed nationalist, royalist and Buddhist in the person of the well-known 'specialist' or 'Dr' Mo Suvan. He was known for his skillful activation of various kinds of magic and for his healing skills. His receiving room was crowded with Buddha images, showed a photograph of himself as a monk, and several mementoes of the royal family such as a photograph of the king's daughter, HRH Princess Maha Sirindthorn. Everything in the room proclaimed he was a frontline supporter of the Thai nation, the Buddhist Sangha, and the king.

The heavily charged atmosphere was the background against which he carried out his highly dramatic curative practices, approaching each patient as a vulnerable entity recently attacked and unsettled by a malevolent spirit (the same model as the state was applying to the country as a whole). Mo Suvan

Suvan points a sword at a mentally affected patient to expel the illness-inducing spirit (photo M. Muecke).

approached the illness-producing spirit inside the patient with strong verbal threats, and by brandishing a pointed instrument (a sword or a knife) which in the most resistant cases he pressed hard against the patient, usually the arm. But there was more: before the event, Suvan maximized the instrument's exorcistic efficacy by dipping it into magically treated water (*nam mon*), which had been transformed into a spirit repellent by speaking the syllables of a mantra into it. Thus equipped for battle, Suvan was almost always victorious, even against the most tenacious of enemies. And once the spirit was expelled, the patient followed a detailed recovery treatment:

Inscribing invulnerability tattoos.

several sessions of pressure massage combined with a strict diet. This ensured that humoural balance was re-established, and that resilience against future spirit attack was restored.

The same approach (strengthening against the potential assault of negative forces) was also applied on the political/military front, just the kind of thing the Village Scout training sessions described. In the context of the anti-communist fight, Suvan boasted that soldiers and officers of the Thai Army regularly approached him to be protected by means of amulets or tattoos into which invulnerability magic was infused. He even claimed that an American GI soldier had sought him out for this purpose before going to the front in Vietnam.

Another dramatic demonstration of invulnerability magic. As blood oozes from a client's recently tattoed back, Suvan runs the sword's edge down the skin, which remains uncut.

I could never confirm this, but I did witness his tattooing sessions. He applied the designs on chests and backs, incorporating magico-religious symbols which offered protection from physical attack, including those carried out with life-threatening instruments such as knives, swords or guns. The tattooed young men included a wide range of characters – local glamour boys wishing to enhance their appeal, local thugs, or just ordinary men from all walks of life wishing to increase their personal resilience.

Suvan demonstrated the tattoos' efficacy by carrying out a test. The client had requested invisible inking, perhaps because he feared that a visible tattoo could bar him from entering certain occupations, the state bureaucracy, for instance. In the absence of ink, Suvan's pointed instrument was pressed against the skin, causing the tattoo to appear momentarily in red, the combined result of a slight irritation of the skin and some oozing of blood. For the test, Mo Suvan ran the blade of a sword with some pressure along his client's back. The skin was not pierced, showing only a path of clear skin where the blade had moved.

The tattooed clients had been made invulnerable to assault by sharp weapons, just as the state ideologues hoped the nation would become immune to communist aggression thanks to the concerted actions of individuals, villages and the state.

Anti-communism among the mediums

Fifty-two spirit mediums, who operated in Chiang Mai town and its immediate vicinity were, like the *mo phii*, central to my study in their role as healers, although they also acted as counsellors of the heart, or as instruments of good fortune who predicted the number of a winning lottery-ticket. Like the *mo phii*, they were also strong defenders of the status quo, some of them active anti-communists.

Spirit mediums being possessed.

But while the *mo phii* (who were men) claimed full credit for their powers, the mediums (most of them women) said that their skills (curative or otherwise) were the attribute of their possessing spirits, insisting that they themselves were merely the spirits' passive instruments.

The spirits were superior beings who had honoured them by making them into their permanent mounts (*maa khii* – horses to ride), into human intermediaries to be used for the benefit of mankind. Crucially for my study, many of the mediums claimed that the spirits had first helped them recover from a serious mental disturbance. I soon came to the conclusion that spirit mediumship had operated as a coping mechanism which allowed afflicted persons to act out aspects of their internal conflicts through the identity of a possessing spirit. Many of the older mediums, who had suffered mental disturbance in their adolescence and young adulthood, had been able to move gradually towards self-control by such enactments, and reach a level of balance.

Mediums claimed to have several spirits (up to 8 or 10) who would possess them separately, in succession. When possessed, the medium would adopt a new persona which fitted her description of each possessing spirit – its name, character, manner and style of dress. The construction of the spirits' identities could reveal mediums' psychological make-up and inner contradictions, but it also brought to light their political convictions. For although some of their spirits' features came from the mediums' imagination and deep internal needs, the spirits' full identities were developed with elements which the mediums took from the prevailing, highly politicized environment – from the current stock of available nationalist symbols, including those connected with the defensive anti-communist nationalism that was promoted by the state. The spirits were thus described as famous heroes of the past and credited with patriotic virtues, such as unflinching courage and superior military ability in the defence of the kingdom's integrity. Some spirits were even identified with kings or princely warriors of the past, national heroes who had been killed in battle when resisting a well-known historical enemy such as the Burmese. According to this logic, one medium displayed an antique sword in her receiving room as tangible proof of one of her spirits' royal lineage and nationalist valour.

The same medium gave another of her spirits the identity of a more recent king, namely King Chulalongkorn, the revered monarch who preserved the country's independence in the face of European efforts to colonize the region in the late 19th century, and placed Thailand on the road to modernization at the beginning of the 20th. The medium showed me a locket with King Chulalongkorn's portrait as proof of her claim.

A medium's multiple identities as human being and mount of several spirits gave her a relative advantage over healers such as the *mo phii* in terms of political

A medium holds an antique sword belonging to one of her possessing sprits – a defender of the nation and a hero.

respectability. For she could multiply her loyalty to the nation, the Buddhist Sangha, and the king by the number of spirits possessing her. When the spirits spoke through her, they stressed their own personal deeds of heroism, their Buddhist devotion, their royal ancestry or their anti-communist fervour. As for the medium herself, when not possessed, she could express her ideological conviction by decorating her receiving room according to the latest nationalist fashion. For instance, she could fill it with a plethora of Buddha statues, incense sticks, candles and flower offerings, or photographs of famous meditating monks, or photographs of King Bhumiphol and his daughter Princess Maha Chakri Sirinthorn. At one point, it became all the rage to place a new kind of ornament in the receiving room – one metre high plastic statues that portrayed well-known kings.

A medium shows a locket portrait of King Chulalongkorn whom she claimed as one of her possessing spirits.

With such indicators of political and religious conviction, mediums as a group found an additional way of attracting clients, over and above the appeal of their professional competence. The political indicators were also used to compete against each other, adding to other markers of superiority – the size of consulting rooms, the wealth of clients, or the number of patients they had cured. All this was combined with endless attempts to discredit others by means of insidious accusations – as inveterate liars who had never been possessed by any spirit of note, as mediocrities who were possessed by karmically low-level beings, as charlatans who could not cure, or as tricksters who wore dark glasses to hide their dishonesty.

This contest for status found its fullest expression during the celebratory

A leading Chiang Mai medium (3d from right) poses with her subordinates at her annual Teacher Spirits celebration.

events which each medium organized annually to honour her possessing spirits and (to further complicate matters) to pay respect to a higher level of spirit – the possessing spirits' own teachers: the Teacher Spirits. Since the circle of mediums comprised some fifty members, there were in a single year many opportunities for intense competition and mutual evaluation of relative worth. The system worked like a cocktail party circuit, where each hostess competed by the number of guests, the quality of invitations (printed out by the richest), the amount of drink (abundant), and the quality of the music (played loudly and non-stop on traditional instruments). Each event offered a perfect opportunity to show off, all participants boasting about their possessing spirits' attributes, including their historical-political status.

Each event began in total seriousness. To understand the proceedings, I was told to focus on the possessing spirit (not on the medium). Placed at centre stage, the possessing spirit invited its own highly revered Teacher Spirits to settle on a circular lacquer offering-platter, which had been bedecked for the occasion with a collection of fruit, cakes, areca nuts, candles, beer and other offerings. Once the Teacher Spirits had been lured by the irresistible delicacies, the medium (possessed by the 'pupil' possessing spirit) would lift the bedecked platter with the Teacher Spirits, carry and place it on an elevated altar, the highest, most sacred location in the room. The ritual was aptly called 'the Ceremony of the Raising of the Teachers' (*pithi yok khuu*).

A medium and neighbour at Ban Phaya Chompu gets help to lift the Teacher Spirits and their offerings and place them on the elevated altar.

A male medium, lifted by his assistant, has just placed the Teacher Spirits on the elevated altar.

Once the Teacher Spirits had been appropriately placed, the possessing spirit would leave the medium's body. She was then free to focus on the party and take care of the guests. As everyone changed gear into party mode, a frankly hedonistic atmosphere developed and all manner of horseplay and excesses was unleashed. The behaviour confirmed what I had noticed in other ways – many of the mediums were eccentric marginals, for whom the medium world offered a framework within which various kinds of off-beat characteristics could be dealt with and occasionally expressed. From the angle of sexual orientation, for instance, the mediums' parties showed some same-sex flirting. The women would act out their attraction to other women when allegedly possessed by a male possessing spirit, and act accordingly. As for the small minority of male mediums, many of whom had transvestite leanings sometimes combined with same-sex interests, the party also provided a chance for self-expression. But while the medium role offered both genders an opportunity to play out their respective differences, the release could unfortunately be only momentary, as the orientation tended to be denied once the medium was no longer possessed and became his or her 'normal' self.

The parties that followed the 'Raising of the Teachers' ritual ceremony were always great fun, occasions where everyone became chatty and would willingly joke and gossip, encouraged by the high-pitched music, the dancing, the drink and the intense heat which in the hot season, could rise to 40°. But despite the rowdiness, the most distinguished were cold-headed enough to indicate by a look, a snub or a disparaging remark, who was high and who was low within the hierarchy; whose possessing spirit was a more devout Buddhist, was more royal or more of a national hero. From my side, my credentials were those of a student and a foreigner, who by writing about the mediums, confirmed their value, and satisfied their vanity. Also, I became the mediums' self-styled photographer, giving copies to those who wanted them – a way for them to remember where in the hierarchy they stood, and for me to thank them for letting me in.

Among the elite group, Mother S. was regularly possessed by a spirit who was famous for his curative powers (the Magical Prince of Seven Colours), while another of her spirits was known for his divinatory ability to foretell lottery ticket winning numbers. Based on such solid reputations, Mother S. enjoyed uncontested dominance at the top of the pile. But she found an additional basis for her supremacy by being a strong supporter of the Buddhist Sangha, one of the pillars of the state. In a conspicuous display of Buddhist devotion, she organized a '*kan thood pha pa*' (literally 'presentation of forest clothes'), a merit-making practice whereby a group of laymen presents gifts to a monastery, such as new robes for the monks, food and money. In 1978, Mother S. sponsored the first ever medium-sponsored *pha pa,* with contributions from her closest medium friends. The procession to the *wat* was a sight to be seen. Performed in the grand style, it was led by a double row of traditional dancers, with a group of clients taking up the rear. At the centre, it featured a pick-up vehicle where Mother S. and her fellow co-sponsors stood next to a 'money tree' to which they had attached a large number of bills (the tree was a bamboo stem of 1.50m tall with thin pieces of wood as its branches). Following the event, such donation rallies became increasingly popular among the wealthier

I became a regular participant of the spirit mediums' festivities.

Confirming her Buddhist commitment, the organizer of a pha paa and her apprentices are about to be driven to the wat (top photo). As they approach the wat, the serious religious objective is combined with joyful dancing (bottom photo).

mediums – an effective way of demonstrating dominant status, wealth, Buddhist devotion and faultless reliability as a pillar of national stability.

The *pha pa* showed that the wealth of clients ultimately sustained the entire spirit mediums' edifice. Their donations, given in reciprocation of service, could be substantial: in the case of Mother S., for instance, they consisted of a large teak house in Chiang Mai, a motor car and small diamond earrings. The financial support of important clients decided where mediums stood within the hierarchy: those at the top being patronized by members of the Chiang Mai and even Bangkok military, economic and political elites – powerful men who usually shied away from making consultations in public, and obtained the advice they required through their wives. The generally pro-state political orientation of such clients provided an additional reason for mediums to identify with nationalist politics, and to make a show of their ideological preference. As mentioned, their reputations were linked to a variety of non-political skills, which were completed by a battery of associations with the status quo. On occasion, their ideological armour was supplemented by frankly political interventions in politically charged contexts such as the Thai-Lao border. One medium's account showed her visiting the Mekong bank opposite communist Laos as a matter of professional routine. She quoted the case of soldiers who more than physical injuries showed signs of 'disturbances of the mind-heart' her term for a whole range of psychological upsets. Her diagnosis in the case of a 'disturbed' soldier was: 'attack by a malevolent spirit'. It was politically revealing that the malevolent agent was said to be a communist *phii*. I was not surprised. I had been to the Village Scout training, where such an occurrence would have appeared as just another run-of-the-mill expression of the communist threat.

Anti-communism among healing monks

Monks counted a small minority of healers. They were often generalists, but I managed to find some who specialized in the insane. One such practitioner was Phra Som, whose methods relied on the power of magically charged water and incantations rather than severe words, or the use of pointed instruments. He was known for his gentle application of the 'cleansing by exorcism' model.

Like Phra Som, most healing monks I met liked to keep a low profile, and kept

Phra Som infuses special potency into the water in preparation for an exorcism, Mae Hong Son 1978.

their clientele small, but some had become highly visible, based on a reputation for exceptional curative powers which transcended the immediate vicinity and attracted very high numbers. Such was the case of the highly influential Khuubaa Thammachai – the Revered Thammachai – widely known in Northern Thailand and beyond. His reputation rested on his Buddhist devotion, his mental powers, ample knowledge of traditional medicine, ability to cure serious illness including cancer, and politically, his strong anti-communist stand.

Vat Thung Luang, of which the Khuubaa was the abbot, was some 35 km. north of Chiang Mai. It was a well-known centre of Buddhist devotion, but mainly operated as a lavishly endowed centre of traditional medicine with a variety of facilities – an ornate cement structure of labyrinths and grottoes for lay meditation practice, medicinal steam-bath facilities, a production unit of herbal-based medicaments and a separate building for seriously ill patients. The monastery had been created thanks to the merit-making generosity of wealthy patrons from the Chiang Mai and Bangkok elite. On either side of the road which led to the main temple, numerous life-size Buddha images attested to the patrons' religious zeal.

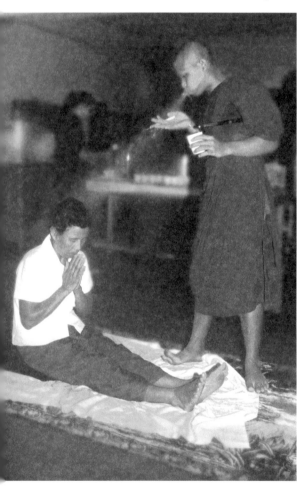

The expulsion model being applied in Central Thailand. (Samnak Pu Savaan Bangkok)

I visited Vat Thung Luang on 30 September 1978. The Khuubaa willingly spoke about the medical but also political application of his psychic power. This, he said, rested mainly on his mental energy or 'psychic flow' (*khasee chit*) which he had strengthened and learned to control during years of intense meditation practice. Medically, the 'psychic flow' enabled him to diagnose illness. The diagnosis was followed by a standard exorcism ritual. In addition, to complete the treatment at the post-exorcism stage and restore humoural balance, the Khuubaa encouraged patients to remain in the *wat*, and meditate. He also recommended specific doses of traditional medicine which could be bought at the monastery from the nuns.

One of the Khuubaa's assistants, a middle-aged monk added that the same approach of diagnosis and cure was followed for victims of bad spirits, including malevolent Lao spirits who crossed over from communist Laos. The Khuubaa came across such spirit-affected patients when visiting the border. For instance, he once treated a soldier who was possessed by a Laotian *phii dud leuad* a Laotian blood-sucking spirit who liked to suck the blood of Thai soldiers, and then gave it to wounded Lao soldiers who needed it for their recovery. The monk explained that the Khuubaa had got rid of the spirit by pronouncing incantations infused with the power of aggressive animals. The Khuubaa was asked to visit the border to treat specific patients, but also, more generally to boost the morale of the army, the Border Patrol Police and other police forces deployed there. My guide added that the Khuubaa also used his psychic energy to determine which villages were most contaminated by communism. When visiting areas which were vulnerable to enemy attack, he sprinkled blessed water over the fighting men and distributed amulets cast in his own image to make them invulnerable. This was not as extreme as Phra Khitthivuto, but nonetheless the Khuubaa's political engagement was clear.

9

LAO REFUGEES IN THE BORDER CAMPS IDEOLOGICAL ALLIES OR COMMUNIST FOES?

I kept coming across different aspects of anti-communist ideology. One was the notion that Thailand's borders with Indochina was where communist aggression was at its most threatening. I had seen the idea being developed in the Village Scout sessions, illustrated by the violent treatment of Vietnamese border communities, and reinforced by the occasional political interventions along the border by spirit doctors, mediums and monks. As with the Thai-Kampuchean border, that with Laos ran along highly vulnerable areas where the Thai state needed to be most on the defensive. I was keenly aware that Lao refugee camps had been set up precisely there, and I feared that the explosive cumulative effect of extreme political sensitivity, the concentration of security forces and an enhanced state of vigilance could negatively affect the refugees. I could not forget that I counted some of my former Luang Phrabang students among them. Like the Thai-based Vietnamese, would the refugees be regarded with suspicion, as communist infiltrators masquerading as anti-communists?

Lowland Lao refugees at Nong Khai Refugee Camp

Ever since I left Laos in August 1975, I had corresponded with my former students, writing from London, and later, from Ban Phaya Chompu. The letters I received were bitter, filled with complaints of bad food, claustrophobic accommodation and chronic inactivity. But it was a lack of viable options for the future that filled them with despair – getting to desirable destinations such as France or the United States was a complicated and long process, while in Thailand, the authorities refused them the right to work. I had followed their stories from Ban Phaya Chompu, but that soon proved insufficient, and before long, I travelled by bus to one of the refugee camps, close to Nong Khai. Across the Mekong, the town faced Vientiane, the Laotian capital, a seemingly inoffensive point of departure for Lao asylum seekers who continued to brave the treacherous river and vigilant Thai officials to reach the Thai bank.

Foreign visitors to the Lao refugee camp were subjected to strict security, and access required written authorization. To get a pass, I presented my researcher's identity card at the mayor's office. A police officer confirmed that tight security measures had been imposed in Nong Khai, but that Lao refugees were not a concern – they were, after all, Thailand's younger brothers. The problem was the Vietnamese communists (ah! that sounded familiar). Yes, the Vietnamese were everywhere in

Laos. They controlled the country and infiltrated incoming refugee groups. The camps had to be carefully guarded and controlled. He apologised for not processing my camp pass himself, and directed me to the Provincial Office where I spent what remained of the morning requesting the document. I had to wait until the following morning for the governor's signature.

I was staying at the Prachak Hotel. Walking through the lobby that afternoon, I came across a group of acquaintances from Luang Phrabang. They had travelled to Vientiane, and from there, had crossed the river into Thailand. Rather than keeping them in the camp, the police had allowed them to move freely in Nong Khai, giving them preferential treatment, I knew, because of pre-1975 personal connections with the authorities, or money, or both. Narong, a former student at the Luang Phrabang Lycée greeted me. His father, a Luang Phrabang representative at the Lao National Assembly in Vientiane, had been sent away for political 'reeducation' some months before. Narong did not know when he would be released, and fearing the worse, had decided to flee. Escaping from Luang Phrabang with a close relative, he had reached Vientiane by road and one night had crossed over by boat to Nong Khai.

I collected my pass on the following morning. As was consistent with the security-conscious environment, it was issued for a single entry. I headed towards the camp, passed the gate and found a friendly refugee, the owner of a three-wheel bicycle-taxi. For a small fee, he took me to the far end of the camp where I found Nyai, my Luang Phrabang next-door neighbour who had asked me by letter to visit. He was living in a bamboo long-house which seemed spacious by camp standards. Seventeen people lived there, all top-level civil servants from Vientiane, a fact, which more than their number, explained their relatively comfortable living arrangements. I had lunch with them. They totally rejected the new Lao regime and criticized it bitterly, blaming it, among other grudges, for interfering constantly with their daily lives. At the beginning, the Pathet Lao had forbidden buying and selling in the market, then they had allowed it, but there had never been anything worth buying, no nice food to eat – no black sweet rice with coconut milk, no savoury *miang'* (pork meat rolled with peanuts into a lettuce leaf). Also, the number of animals which families could keep had been strictly controlled. Though each family had eventually been allowed to keep ten chickens and two pigs, slaughtering any number of them had required permission from a local official – the local spy. Everything, absolutely everything, had been controlled. Nyai added that each province was being subjected to different levels of control, He was convinced that Luang Phrabang was worse than Vientiane. Everywhere in the country, people were afraid, afraid of being lectured on trivial matters, of being arrested, of being sent away for so-called political reeducation and of being kept there for indefinite periods of time, perhaps permanently.

Nyai was indignant. The son of a deceased civil servant in the royal palace, and a former technician in the UK-financed Luang Phrabang Radio Station, he had had a tough time. Everything had changed after the Pathet Lao took over. Early that year, he was fired by the radio station because, his boss said, his programmes had a pro-western bias and were interspersed with western music. Nyai appealed to the radio station director, but that led nowhere. In Vientiane, he managed to get an appointment with the Minister of Communications. The minister said he could not reverse the Radio Station's decision and promised to find him a job in Vientiane, but that never materialized. After a time, the minister advised him to fly back to Luang Phrabang and wait. Back there, he was arrested and locked up.

He was placed in solitary confinement, in a tiny dark cell for two months, and given terrible food. He was allowed out only once a day for fifteen minutes. In time, however, his situation changed – he was transferred to a larger cell which he shared with other prisoners. When his father died, he was given special permission to attend the cremation. Then, conditions got worse again when news reached his family and the authorities that his younger brother had died in France where the boy had been travelling with his French teacher. The news emphasized the family's connections with the West and soon, another family member – Nyai's middle brother – was sent away for political reeducation. Only the mother and sister remained at home, coping with all the house chores, and with Sombath, the mentally retarded older brother. After many months in detention, Nyai managed to escape with the help of a guard. He travelled to Vientiane soon after where friends – the well-placed civil servants I had just met – invited him to cross over to Thailand. He joined them, and once the group safely reached Nong Khai, he stayed with them.

Nyai told me about the counter-revolutionary resistance which operated in the camp. Its proximity to the river border – the Mekong – favoured the presence of anti-Pathet Lao activists. They used the refugee centre as a safe haven, and as a point of recruitment for new freedom fighters. They were about five hundred strong in Nong Khai, while Udon refugee camp further south had almost five thousand. The men trained every day, with Thai tacit approval, and although their incursions into Laos were dangerous, they persevered. They were determined to get rid of the Pathet Lao, and regain control. Nyai was not interested – he would not join. All he wanted was to leave the camp, leave Thailand and find his way to Europe. He wanted to escape the resistance and its continual pressures, his forced confinement and his lack of freedom. He was tired of the sharp differences between rich and poor refugees, tired of how refugees with cash and high status could buy occasional outings into town, better food and even better living spaces. In fact, the old social order had been reproduced in the different camp sections.

Nyai was tired of thanking the group of *phuu nyai* – 'big people' – who had helped him leave.

Back at the Prachak Hotel, I thought about Nyai's comments. In the eyes of the Thai authorities, the Lao elite did not pose any security risks – their anti-regime position was unquestioned. Also, as I knew was the case with Narong, the son of a well-known politician, and with Nyai's influential hosts, the rich and powerful could afford to be generous and have access to special perks and more flexible conditions.

It was still true, however, that refugees in Nong Khai who were almost entirely Lao lowlanders, benefitted as a group from the closeness between Lao and Thai culture. The fact clearly encouraged the Thai authorities to be relatively lenient elder brothers to their Laotian younger brothers, even when not especially rich or socially well-placed. That became clear when I visited Sopthuang, a camp that housed refugees from highland Laos. Being perceived by the Thai authorities in the same light as their own hill peoples, the refugees were considered as an ethnically and culturally different people, to be approached with a certain social distance. But there were other reasons for separating the highland from the lowland refugees. These I would discover at Sopthuang.

Sopthuang: a separate refugee camp for Laotian hill peoples

Several refugee camps had been set up especially for highlanders, among them Ban Vinay, Namyao, Chiengham and Sopthuang. I decided to visit Sopthuang and found a way of going there when Marjorie Muecke – a fellow social anthropologist working in Chiang Mai – offered to drive there in her Volkswagen. We drove to the border, towards the third week of December 1977, hoping to visit all hilltribe camps. We ended up concentrating on Sopthuang camp which included a large component of Hmong refugees, and where I wanted to visit Khampaeng, a former Khmu' Luang Phrabang student.

We drove straight to the capital of Nan province. Being aware that the Thai authorities in the camps worked closely with the United Nations High Commission for Refugees (UNHCR), we approached the organization's representative as soon as we arrived. Jacques Mouchet, a small, jovial, friendly Frenchman welcomed us warmly, gave us a drink and talked at length about the camp. Official Thai scrutiny, he said, was very tight at Sopthuang. He confirmed that the camp housed only hill peoples – Hmong, Yao and Khmu'. That, he said, should not surprise us. The division of refugee camps along ethnic lines reflected the sharp distinction which prevailed both in Laos and Thailand between a dominant group of lowlanders and the mountain dwelling peoples, who were relegated to the bottom of the social scale. That was one reason for placing them in separate facilities such as Sopthuang.

However, there was another reason for the separate camps: the well-known anti-Pathet Lao belligerence for which some of the hill folks were famous, particularly the anti-communist Hmong and some of the Yao. The belligerence required tighter security and army control. Although carefully watched, some among the refugees continued to organize political-military initiatives against the LPDR, using the camps as their base. While some lower-level Thai officials sympathized with the anti-communist militancy, and could turn a blind eye, the higher echelons disapproved, as the camp-based resistance movement's sporadic forays into Lao territory were potential sources of diplomatic or even military conflict with Laos. They could also provoke Pathet Lao retaliation close to the camp fences, and in some cases inside them. In fact, PL forces regularly entered the camps in the sections closest to the border, and kept a small permanent presence there. Jacques contrasted conditions at Sopthuang to those in Nong Khai: like the Nong Khai camp, the Nan one bordered Laos on its eastern side, but was separated from it by a mountainous land border. And this was more porous, more vulnerable to uncontrolled movements than the precisely delineated, more easily monitored Mekong. Also, the camp site was located in a remote area. The Nong Khai camp was close to the provincial capital, but Sopthuang was very far from Nan town.

As Jacques spoke, Marjorie and I looked at each other, wondering whether we would ever be able to enter the camp. It had been a struggle for me to get a day camp pass for Nong Khai camp, and we feared it would impossible to get one for Sopthuang. We had no official reason to justify a visit – we could only say we were

Hmong couples face each other at New Year to play catch, a form of courtship, Sopthuang Refugee Camp.

visiting some of my former Luang Phrabang students. Jacques agreed, it would not be easy, but, he said, we had chosen the best time to come – the end of the year. We could take advantage of the relative laxity in security arrangements, and try to enter the camp without a pass.

A difficult road led us towards the site. The area was sparsely dotted with poverty-stricken villages which contrasted sharply with the comparative affluence of Nan town. We caught sight of the camp's bamboo fence which led to the main gate. We had expected to find Thai villagers selling food, soap and other necessities to supplement the refugees' limited camp rations, as existed outside the camp in Nong Khai. But we saw no vendors – the villagers had not set up even the most precarious stalls. This was indeed an isolated, poverty-stricken area.

Having no camp pass, we had to keep a low profile. Marjorie parked the Volkswagen some distance away from the main entrance. As Jacques had anticipated, we found no security personnel on duty that day – December 30. As we entered, some Hmong refugees, dressed in their New Year finery, welcomed us, and immediately invited us to the camp section where the Hmong New Year festivities were in full swing.

With vivid memories of the Hmong New Year festivities I had witnessed in Laos, I felt my stomach tighten. Standing in parallel rows within the confinement of the camp, Hmong young men and women were playing the traditional courtship ball game in strict confinement – a far cry from the scenes I had seen in the free spaces with spectacular views in the highest mountains of Laos.

Hmong refugees sacrifice a cock to decide whether to return to Laos. (Photo by M. Muecke)

We stayed for a while and talked. Hmong families were preoccupied by the unresolved question of whether to return to Laos, or remain in the camp. They would have preferred to be resettled, preferably in the United States, but they knew that the visit to Sopthuang of some Western embassy who might select them was only a remote possibility. As for returning to Laos, the LPDR's policies put them off. For instance, there was a policy which encouraged abandoning from slash-and-burn agriculture and poppy cultivation in the mountains, in favour of irrigated rice cultivation in the lowlands. More off-putting still was the rumour that low Hmong participation in the proposed program had led the authorities to resort to military force. This approach, I could say, closely paralleled the Thai state's policy vis-à-vis the Hmong in the 1970s, although this had been imposed to counter communist engagement, rather than anti-communist activism, which was the concern in Laos.

Marjorie and I would have been more than happy to stay with the Hmong, but I had committed myself to meet Khampaeng, my Khmu' student who had written some weeks before to invite me to his wedding. He had arrived at Sopthuang with his girlfriend's family earlier that year, leaving his parents and siblings in Laos. After a few inquiries, we found him not far from the edge of the Hmong section. He and I were glad to meet as teacher and pupil after more than two years. The wedding would be taking place in the evening, in the Khmu' section. Khampaeng decided to show us the exact spot just then, a long walk away, on the far side of the camp, at its very edge, facing Laos.

Back home in Laos, Khampaeng's people lived on the mid-level slopes of mountainous areas, below the highest locations where the Hmong settled. The Khmu' were known by the lowland Lao as 'Kha', which means slave, a name which placed them at the bottom of the ethnic hierarchy. At Sopthuang, their status, and their relatively small number, had led to their being placed in the most exposed section of the camp, where the Pathet Lao's occasional incursions hit first. The Thai authorities had placed them where the Lao social order placed them, at the bottom of the pile. Despite this new expression of the old system of discrimination, Khampaeng felt that relationships among ethnic groups in the camps were better than in pre-revolutionary Laos. Before the revolution, the complicated puzzle of mountain peoples had often been marked by mutual suspicion and occasional rivalry. By contrast, the pressures to which all groups were exposed at Sopthuang weakened competition, and encouraged solidarity and cooperation. In this congenial context, Black Tai, Hmong, Khmu' and Akha interacted freely.

Khampaeng and Boua's wedding ceremony started as planned. The bride and groom, their families and friends sat cross-legged on the small bamboo verandah, surrounding a low table covered with fruit, sticky rice, strong rice alcohol, and

The long path leading to the Khmu' section.

Inter-ethnic solidarity in Sopthuang camp: a Black Tai woman visits her Hmong neighbours.

banana leaf-cones filled with flowers and small candles. The Master of Ceremonies, an elderly man, was there to strengthen the couple before they entered a new life as man and wife. In a carefully performed ceremony – the *baci* – he called the spirits of Khampaeng's and Boua's thirty-two bodily parts, reintegrating them into the young couple's bodies, after luring them there by means of cajoling words, food and drink. The Master then made sure the spirits remained in place by tying white cotton strings around the bride and groom's wrists. The guests then tied more strings until the couple's wrists became thick with white bracelets which ensured that the spirits would not escape and would preserve the couple's strength. They symbolized the guests' sincere friendship.

The wedding *baci* was held in the most exposed section of the camp. (photo by M. Muecke)

I was glad for the new married couple, but again, as with the Hmong, I felt heavy-hearted at the sight of a ceremony being carried out so modestly, in such difficult circumstances. I had seen it performed an infinite number of times in Luang Phrabang, where any significant occasion in a person's life had been a reason for organizing one. It had been at the heart of my Luang Phrabang life, an all-purpose energy-booster to face each and every challenge – a long journey, an examination, an illness, a birthday, a wedding, the birth of a child.

These thoughts, the tying of the cotton strings, the pungent drink, the group's good wishes, all came abruptly to a stop when several strong blasts exploded close by – a new Pathet Lao incursion. Everyone stood up. Marjorie and I did not know where to turn, but Khampaeng took over. Marjorie was taken to the bride's family's house, and I was told not to move and stay with Khampaeng. It was dead quiet, and though we heard no new bangs, the expectation that the Pathet Lao might act again kept us awake. The wedding's festive atmosphere and the Hmong New Year celebrations we had seen upon arrival had hidden the mood of palpable anxiety which now prevailed. I wondered what would have happened if the camp authorities had been there, with full military presence in the barracks. Would the Pathet Lao intruders have been spotted, and the fear we had experienced been avoided? Kampaeng's answer was no – life in the Khmu' section of Sopthuang was lived in a permanent state of insecure expectation.

The following morning was 1 January, the day the camp staff and guards were expected back. There was no time to linger over the night's events. We thanked everyone and left. Back in the Volkwagen, Marjorie and I tried to digest what we had seen – the confinement, the rudimentary facilities, the isolation and sense of abandonment in this remote, poverty-stricken, inhospitable place. The camp's military regime was an added concern, as was the high number of pressures that came from all sides – from the Thai authorities, from the Pathet Lao and from the active resistance movement which tried to convince the young men to join.

As we drove to Chiang Mai, we felt discouraged, but at least we had plenty of time to share our thoughts. During my Luang Phrabang days, there had been widespread belief in the Pathet Lao's generous intentions, and many of my students had backed them. Disappointment had come later, and many had fled, ending up in camps where despite the differences we had seen, refugees were caught between a reality they were fleeing, and one that rejected them, between a new communist order with which they could not live, and a Thai Buddhist kingdom that kept them in confinement, while the one solution which offered a way out – resettlement in a First World country – was increasingly out of reach, perhaps more so at Sopthuang than Nong Khai.

Marjorie and I drove back to Chiang Mai leaving the refugees to their uncertain future. There was nothing we could do but promise to keep in touch.

A Thai military barracks (on the hill at the back) dominates Sopthuang camp.

10

I COMPLETE MY Ph.D FIELDWORK AND MOVE ON

Back to Ban Phaya Chompu, I went back to village life and to my research. My interviews of patients and healers had borne fruit, and information was piling up, but as it never seemed sufficient and I kept prolonging, I ended up staying until my SOAS grant had almost run out. That was it! I had to start packing up my notes, recordings and photographs. I had stayed a full year and seven months and there were lots of farewells; elder sister Phi Suchilak and her family, who had adopted me at the health station; my friends in the village who had welcomed me and taken me into their homes and taught me how to work in the rice fields; my fellow anthropologist, Marjorie Muecke, and my field assistant Suvet. As for the people I had met as part of my study: monks, mediums, healers, patients, I did not know then that good bye would not be as definite as I thought, for I would meet them again at the time of writing. Each of them would find their way into some page or paragraph of my thesis.

My farewell *baisi* (the equivalent of the Lao *baci*) was organized at the local school at Ban Phaya Chompu. It differed from Khampaeng and Boua's wedding *baci* at Sopthuang by being celebrated without danger, of course, and by taking place around a more elaborate offering bowl than the one in the camp. But the substance was the same: the village officiant lured my 32 souls onto the offering bowl and ensured that they remain with me and give me strength for my journey to London. All the guests tied my wrists with white cotton strings to keep the spirits inside me, symbols of friendship which remained until they fell apart of their own accord, disintegrating long after I had left Ban Phaya Chompu.

I flew straight to London from Bangkok, and settled one block away from the School of Oriental and African Studies. Three years of quiet reflection on Northern Thai ideas of insanity and on Thai politics awaited me, until I completed my thesis in 1982. As I was finishing the writing, I approached the Office of the United Nations High Commissioner for Refugees (UNHCR) for employment, aiming specifically at a post in the Lao refugee camps in Thailand. The move made sense – it offered some continuity with my years in Laos and with the thesis I had just completed. But there was a hitch – there were no vacancies in the camps. So instead of Thailand, I was offered a post on the other side of the globe – in Argentina – with the title 'Coordinator of the Lao Refugee Integration Programme'. It took a little time before I could digest the offer and picture myself in Buenos Aires rather than Nong Khai. But of course, I said yes.

The Argentina programme turned out to be more varied ethnically than its title implied. It comprised a majority of lowland Lao, but also a few Lao Hmong and some Cambodians. It was a unique situation, one in which a group of Southeast Asian refugees was attempting to integrate in the most adverse conditions, responding to the challenges of a radically different South American environment.

My farewell *baisi*: I bow before my 32 souls which the officiant has lured onto the offering bowl.

Part Three:

Lao Refugees in Argentina (1982-1984)

11
UNDER THE DICTATORSHIP

I arrive in a country facing the Falkland/ Malvinas war

By 1981, the settlement of Lao refugees in Argentina had run into difficulties. Many refugees had refused to adapt, and some had even become rebellious. As a result, two successive programme coordinators, an Italian Roman Catholic priest with many years in Laos, and a Laotian woman with training in social work, had given up and left. The post had become vacant just as I was job hunting at UNHCR, and, following an interview in Geneva, I was offered the complicated job, thanks essentially to a happy coincidence between the job's specific requirements and my credentials: knowledge of Lao culture and language, following three years in Luang Phrabang, and, as a Mexican national, fluency in Spanish. My expertise as a fully certified social anthropologist, with a brand-new PhD from the School of Oriental and African Studies, was probably another reason for recruiting me: the knowledge I had recently acquired in Northern Thailand about village culture (close to Lao village culture) would help me explain Lao refugees' beliefs and attitudes to the Argentinians, and vice-versa.

I was enthusiastic: not only did my PhD thesis have academic value, it would also have practical application once I reached Argentina, a rare occurrence for social anthropological work, which tends to remain in the rarified atmosphere of research institutes and universities. However, like my two predecessors, the job required me to join the UNHCR bureaucracy as 'Coordinator' of a fourteen-person team of social workers. From UNHCR Geneva's stand-point, my principal task was to make sure that the refugees' negative attitudes were reversed, not only for their sake, but also to restore the credibility of UNHCR, and its Geneva-based Americas Bureau, who were ultimately responsible for the venture. The Indochinese Refugee Programme had to be salvaged. My job was to make it function.

I was due to arrive in Buenos Aires in early 1982, but my double Mexican/British nationality complicated the move. Diplomatic relations had been deteriorating between Argentina and the UK over the Falkland/Malvinas islands, in a process which would eventually lead, on 2 April 1982, to a declaration of war. UNHCR Headquarters had recruited me as a Mexican, and confirmed my appointment before that, in late 1981. But in the context of the mounting Anglo-Argentinian conflict, and as anti-British sentiment in Argentina grew, my British/Mexican

Opposite page: Lao refugees at Jujuy Refugee Centre Argentina.

Thatcher is worse than Hitler but Haig is Dracula.

double nationality and my surname (Irvine) raised the issue of my security. The UNHCR office in Buenos Aires saw no problem when the government confirmed my appointment, but the Americas Bureau thought differently, and travel to Buenos Aires kept being postponed until Geneva was finally convinced that there was no risk.

I landed in Buenos Aires on 25 April 1982, the day the British fleet attacked the Georgia islands. Strong nationalism was in the air, as the capital tried to develop a new South American persona despite its strong identification with Europe. Public opinion condemned the UK, and was indignant at what it considered imperialistic aggression. 'British Square' became 'Argentinian Air Force' Square, and proud posters, exhibited everywhere on café fronts, buildings and dilapidated walls, reiterated the message that 'the Malvinas had been, were and would always remain Argentinian'. National flags were sold everywhere in the streets, headbands bearing the words 'Argentinian Sovereignty' became all the rage, while Argentina's resistance to the first English invasion of 1806 was repeatedly referred to in the media. But the main targets of public outrage were the British Government and its American ally. Anti-Thatcher and anti-Haig posters were seen everywhere in town, and on the front pages of newspapers and magazines.

Margaret Thatcher was unanimously condemned. Serious political analysis was combined with the satire of unforgiving cartoons which vied against each other in biting criticism. But no one objected to the presence of individual British people, nor to that of a Mexican-British national like myself. I was never the target of animosity, as UNHCR headquarters had feared, not even in the most difficult moments of the conflict when anti-British feelings were at their peak. As a Mexican national with a British name, I was welcomed like any newcomer, and at the UNHCR office, all the staff bent over backwards to make me feel at home, including some Argentinian nationals who had British surnames like myself. They took me under their wing, and made sure I was properly installed in a flat, close to the office, in central Buenos Aires. From the angle of work, the UNHCR Representative and other staff welcomed me as the awaited-for 'Laos expert', who was expected to 'free them' from the Laotian problem. 'Free them' because, to them, the Laotians were a problematic, rebellious and, in the end, incomprehensible group.

I moved from a wooden house on stilts in Thailand, to a small bedsit in London, to a high-rise building in central Buenos Aires.

How did the Lao refugees end up in Argentina?

In 1979, a mass of Indochinese refugees from Vietnam, Laos and Cambodia had poured into neighbouring countries. Faced with the unprecedented refugee flow, the international community responded immediately, and in July, a gathering of some sixty countries discussed the issue in Geneva. Out of these, thirty offered to assist, among them Argentina, who offered to welcome up to 1,000 refugee families from Laos. At the time, thousands of refugees had been stranded in a number of Southeast Asian countries, where they were tolerated rather than welcomed, being confined in closed camps, without work or meaningful activities, or prospects for the future. The refugees' overarching wish was to escape the stifling environment, to be resettled out of the camps, and indeed out of Southeast Asia, into the imagined panacea of first-world countries – the United Kingdom, France, Australia or the USA. But as the resettlement quotas among these countries diminished, and the desired solution became feasible for only small numbers, refugees were offered other options.

In the autumn of 1979, a Refugee Selection Committee from the Buenos Aires Ministry of the Interior visited Thailand's refugee camps, on the Thai side of the Thai-Lao border. The attractive resettlement package it offered drew the attention of refugees like a magnet – rapid processing of individual applications (that of other countries was notoriously slow), a monthly 300 US dollars per family, individual housing, health and educational support. The offer was accompanied by engaging descriptions of the country's natural beauty, and by the screening of a film (made for the 1978 Football World Cup) which featured images of some of the country's most impressive sights – the spectacular Iguazu waterfalls on the Argentine-Brazilian border, and the rich woodlands and snow-covered peaks bordering Chile. As information about the proposal spread, one irresistible but specious rumour circulated (perhaps on the initiative of unrealistic, over-optimistic refugees) that Argentina was just next door to the United States, making the South American country into an imaginary springboard to that most-wished-for destination.

The Selection Committee limited its recruitment efforts to young couples with experience in agricultural work, promising them a future of prosperity in exchange for hard work. Although some potential candidates were put off by the exclusion of the elderly (the Argentinian authorities saw them as a potential burden) and of single individuals (who could be problematic since they were without a family's control), many were convinced, volunteered and were processed for departure. All selected families came from Laos and spoke Lao, with the exception of four Cambodian families, who had managed to enter the Laotian camp, and could speak a mixture of Thai and Lao. Otherwise, the group comprised a majority of urban lowland Lao, some urban Lao-Vietnamese and a group of mountain-dwelling, Hmong families. I refer to the group as 'Lao refugees', except when specific ethnic components are relevant.

* * * * * * *

When the first group of Laotians arrived in 1979, the military dictatorship stood largely unchallenged inside Argentina, although discontent had been mounting, and some of its critics had started to speak out. In 1982, however, in a textbook example of outside threats bringing about internal cohesion, the conflict over the Falklands/Malvinas Islands generated strong government support. As Argentina's armed forces stood to defend the islands, and the government and the media built up the issue as a matter of humiliated national pride, so did public opinion rally around the government. Conditions were ripe for the regime to construct a virtuous image of itself. For instance, General Reynaldo Bignone, the last general in power before the democratic government was confirmed in October 1983, did what he could to whitewash the past. Concerning the regime's persecution of supposed communists and '*subversivos*', the General gave the regime's executioners the benefit of the doubt. He described them as '*presumed perpetrators*' of the regime's '*supposed excesses*', and exonerated them from any legal process, by leaving judgment as to their guilt to the highest of arbiters – *to God and His Tribunal*. But the '*supposed excesses*' included the kidnapping of alleged subversive individuals, who were tortured and murdered, their corpses disposed of by different means, sometimes by being thrown from helicopters into the sea. Despite the authorities' denial of the dictatorship's sinister methods, and their new war-related lease on power, some anti-government sentiment, which had been voiced for a time, continued to be expressed. For instance, at weekly gatherings staged in front of Government House (Casa Rosada), the mothers of abducted persons (Madres de la Plaza de Mayo) continued to demand that the government give back their sons or daughters, some of whom had been pregnant when kidnapped.

Mothers of abducted victims demonstrated each Thursday in front of the Casa Rosada (Government House).

12

THE SOCIAL WORKERS' ACCOUNT OF THE PAST

Disastrous beginnings

28 April 1982. I walked into the main meeting room at the Buenos Aires UNHCR office. Fourteen social workers were ready to tell all they knew about the refuges, starting with their arrival in 1979. The group coordinator, Norma Rodriguez, got the ball rolling, and before inviting everyone to have their say, she generalized that the refugees, including those who were coming to terms with their lot, were dissatisfied. Some were critical of their new environment, many rejected it, while a very vocal minority had become aggressive and even violent. She insisted, however, that the refugees could not be blamed. Theirs was simply a response to badly paid jobs, bad housing, and the callous attitudes of a slow, insensitive bureaucracy, who often approached them with the duress of the military.

Each account added another layer of detail to a story whose ill-fated beginnings, in a highly militarized context, and without adequate preparations, had determined subsequent difficulties. The government's various refugee directives, implemented by a Directorate in the Ministry of the Interior, had been a disaster. One in particular decreed that families should be scattered in small units, based on the idea that Laotians living together in large groups would tend to stay among themselves rather than integrate. Other agencies of the state, radicals in the ministry, the army and the police, had backed the approach from the angle of national security. Choosing to ignore the refugees' reason for leaving Laos (rejection of the communist regime), they regarded them as potential communists! They actually believed that before leaving Laos, the refugees had been infected by the 'communist virus', that this lay dormant inside them, and could be easily reactivated and spread. The refugees were a potential source of communist contagion which had to be contained.

The authorities regarded the Laotians with distrust for another reason. They were associated with UNHCR, which they regarded with suspicion, characterizing its staff as a group of 'lefties', who not only worked for the ideologically suspicious Laotian group, but also gave support to potentially destabilizing 'left-wing' Latin American refugees, specifically Chileans, who had fled the Pinochet regime. Also, UNHCR was openly supportive of the Madres de Plaza de Mayo who were, for the authorities, the mothers of dangerous 'subversivos'.

The social workers' account continued: Argentina being a military dictatorship, the refugees had been treated in military style as soon as they had landed. Their new Argentinian life began at the airport, with a formal ceremony which centred on the Argentinian flag, and included a strong nationalist speech which exhorted the newcomers, in Spanish (a language they had not yet learnt), to fulfill 'all responsibilities towards generous Argentina', and 'behave'. They were later taken to a reception centre at Ezeiza, in the suburbs of Buenos Aires, where they were given a crash course in Spanish and local customs. Once that was completed, the refugees were separated and sent to ten different provinces, away from the capital: Santa Fé, Entre Rios, Cordoba, Rio Negro, Mendoza, la Pampa, Misiones, Salta, Jujuy and Buenos Aires Province. In this way, the national authorities in Buenos Aires handed over responsibility for the refugees to the local authorities. But these in turn entrusted the families to private landowners who provided them with jobs and accommodation, based on prevailing practices for the recruitment of cheap labour. Accordingly, the families were settled in private estates, the men generally working as peons, the women as servants in the main house. According to the government's directive to keep families separate, the estates usually recruited a single family, though there were exceptions, the number sometimes increasing to a maximum of three.

The main house.

The women of three families in the same estate.

The discrepancy between the authorities' promises and actual conditions surprised the refugees, particularly since what was offered was unlike anything they had known in Laos. The families were being asked to fit into a (to them) totally unfamiliar system of large estates and landless dependents, in which their lot seemed limited to the bare necessities, with few prospects of progress. A sense of hopelessness took hold of the families, some even giving into despair, until a few of the more badly affected decided to take things into their own hands, abandon their settlements, and travel to Buenos Aires. Despite their isolation, the families had managed to coordinate their escape plan by means of recorded tapes, which they sent each other by mail. Once in the capital, they staged a demonstration in front of the US embassy during which they demanded, loudly and clearly, to be resettled in the United States.

I listened to the blood-chilling account of what happened next, hanging on to each and every one of Roberto Rodriguez's words, the UNHCR Deputy Representative, who had joined our meeting to describe the nightmarish moments that followed the demonstration.

'The police appeared on the scene, and threatened to bus the refugees back to the provinces. The refugees escaped, and went straight to one of the neglected hotels in central Buenos Aires, the home of other Laotians who had previously escaped their settlements, and were surviving independently. The hotel, a decrepit, run-down affair, comprised three stories built around a patio. From the patio's centre, a flight of stairs spiraled to the top, around the shaft of an old-style lift. Roberto clarified: 'Until that point, I had not been involved. I was working at my desk at the UNHCR office, only a few blocks away. But I rushed over as soon as someone from the hotel told me on the phone that a police raid was taking place. At the hotel, some uniformed policemen were standing by the entrance. I pushed my way into the hall, and once inside, I could hear a fight going on upstairs. On the third floor, the police could not get the Laotian men to walk downstairs, although they had pushed several couples out of their rooms, and into the corridor. The police officers held the men by their arms and legs, and dragged them to the top of the stairs, while the women were pulled by the arm, and forced downstairs. Meanwhile, some of the younger refugees ran frantically along the corridors, trying to get away. The women shouted loudly, and the children were in tears, terrified. In the midst of this chaos, I walked down to the hotel entrance which was now crowded with the families. They had no choice but to obey. By then, they seemed resigned. Just outside, a bus waited for them to board.

'I asked who was in charge. A policeman spoke up. He said the refugees were to be taken out of Buenos Aires, and back to Santa Fe. The refugees' mutiny had been a disaster, he said, and had caused an accident – a baby had been badly hurt, and was in hospital. He said nothing else. Eager to know more, I entered the bus, where five or six refugees were already sitting, ready to leave. After some hesitation, they told me – the baby was dead. The mother had held it in her arms as she ran away from the police, and entered the lift. It isn't clear what exactly happened next. In a moment of panic the mother pressed herself and the baby against one side of the lift – an old-fashioned model, open at the side – and as the lift moved down, the baby's head had hit the side hard, and was badly mangled.' (Beyond Roberto's account, the rumour circulated later among the social workers that the child's head had been severed). Roberto continued: 'Having heard this terrible thing, I immediately asked the police officer in charge to contact the Interior Ministry, and demand that the operation be immediately stopped. I waited in vain for an answer, the raid continued, and within fifteen minutes, all the refugees had been forced onto the bus. I felt I could not leave them in the hands of the police, and proceeded to get on. The official tried to bar the way, but I pushed myself inside the bus, lying that the Ministry wanted UNHCR to go with the group. I had to go – anything could happen, I thought, and my presence would perhaps prevent further violence. In the end, the refugees were quiet all the way. But once they reached Santa Fe, they refused point blank to return to their settlements, and stood their ground for as long as they could, until the next day, when faced with lack of food and a place to stay, they gave in.'

The social workers completed Roberto's account. Having been sent back to their settlements, and been quiet for a time, the refugees had fled again. One large group of families categorically rejected Argentina. They refused to accept any further help from the authorities' or UNHCR; they feared that by accepting their support, they would be permanently tied to the country, and would never be able to leave. They accused the government of lying to them in Thailand, and blamed UNHCR for deceiving them and taking them to Argentina under false pretenses. They demanded repeatedly that UNHCR take them out of Argentina, to France, to the US. Faced with such insistence, the social workers explained in all ways possible that the move was not possible – UNHCR could not resettle refugees more than once. This was to no avail. The refugees continued to insist, until the time came when, having faced repeated refusals, they opted for a desperate, last-resort alternative: to return voluntarily to Laos, the country from which they had fled. UNHCR Buenos Aires sent the repatriation forms to the Laotian capital as requested. UNHCR Vientiane first confirmed that the return to Laos was safe – refugees who had returned recently from Thailand had done so without reprisals. But the communist authorities would not hear of accepting anyone from Argentina. Some of the men were known to have been in the military, so that the entire group was considered a security risk. Despite all efforts from UNHCR Vientiane, no exceptions could be made.

With repatriation blocked, the families felt trapped. But one thing was clear to them. They would keep refusing the hacienda option. Accordingly, many abandoned the estates and settled as best they could in Buenos Aires, just surviving.

A new panacea: the Permanent Solution package

The social worker's account now turned to the time when the Interior Ministry, faced with the failure of its 'hacienda refugee' approach, came up with a new, urban-based solution. The municipalities, rather than private persons, would henceforth be given full responsibility for the refugees as job and accommodation providers. The ministry issued the relevant instructions, but these did not always go down well. Many local authorities resisted, pointing to their scarce resources, and to their own population's needs. Also, once implementation began, the refugees themselves were critical of the approach, and although some did accept the jobs, housing, schooling and medical care that was offered, a very visible minority, who combined past resentments with high expectations, rejected everything and refused to work, constraining the municipality to feed and house them in special refugee centres. In certain locations, refugee rejections had provoked some animosity among the population and the local bureaucracy, which in turn generated negative attitudes among municipal staff vis-à-vis families who were willing to engage.

Facing what seemed a never-ending string of unresolved problems, UNHCR Buenos Aires decided to bombard Headquarters with a succession of reports

Refugees work as municipal gardeners in Villaguay Entre Rios Province.

written by the social workers, which documented all the difficulties, and requested adequate resources to launch a new, more dynamic approach to complement the authorities' efforts. It recommended a final joint UNHCR/Ministry initiative which would lead to the settlement of the vast majority of refugees, and finally permit the definite closure of the programme. The reports gave rise to a fruitful exchange of proposals and counter-proposals between Buenos Aires, Geneva and the Ministry of the Interior which at last led to a momentous agreement: the UNHCR budget was to be expanded, so that each refugee family could be provided with a uniform sustainable solution which UNHCR and the government would provide jointly. Specifically, a house would be provided by UNHCR, and the government would guarantee that each family head had access to a municipal job. The package was baptized 'Permanent Solution'.

My first contact with the social workers, and each of their detailed accounts showed me the difficulties they had been facing in their respective areas of responsibility, and pointed to the truly extraordinary challenge that awaited me. Fortunately, however, I would be armed with the budget that covered UNHCR's component of the Permanent Solution package, and would be able to count on the social workers' remarkable competence. The highly motivated group had been in close contact with the refugees since their arrival in 1979. Their accumulated knowledge, and their familiarity with the refugees' mentality, equipped them well for this new, hopefully more successful stage.

The team of social workers and myself (front row), Buenos Aires 1982.

13
I GET TO KNOW THE REFUGEES

The hard reality of hacienda refugees

In an effort to see what had gone wrong with the hacienda refugees, I called on Mr. Alessandro, a former refugee employer. A genial Italian and prosperous wine-producer, he had employed two refugee families in 1980. Despite all his efforts to make them happy, they had left the estate and fled to Buenos Aires within a year of their arrival. Showing signs of sadness, Mr. Alessandro pointed to a small wooden model of a Laotian house-on-stilts, which stood on his mantelpiece as decoration. He sounded genuinely disappointed when he said that his 'Lao children' had abandoned him. He had treated them well, like members of his own family. They had been asked to work for a reasonable number of hours, had been fed and housed and provided with a good wage. They had even been promised a small plot of land as an eventual reward for hard work.

Mr. Alessandro was clearly well meaning and a good sort. But his was the attitude of an all-powerful proprietor being paternalistically considerate towards his absolute subordinates. He was convinced of his own generosity, and as I listened, I knew that from his point of view, the deal he had offered as a landlord-father to those he regarded as his refugee-sons and refugee-daughters *had* been generous. But the refugees could not have operated within such a model. They had wanted more benefits immediately, and I could imagine, despite Mr. Alessandro's evident good intentions, that they had found the peon regime oppressive. In Laos, I remembered, such a system was unknown, and all but the very destitute were the owners of a house plot and some agricultural land. It was not clear what specific circumstances had triggered the refugees' decision to leave, but all the same, Mr. Alessandro had been disappointed when the conditions he had offered in good faith had been rejected for the precarious living conditions of Buenos Aires.

Mr. Alessandro's case showed that even in the best of cases, the discrepant expectations of landlords and refugees could easily lead to a break in their relationship. And when landlords were not gentle paternalists like him, the link could be broken even more easily. Among many refugee employers, the ethic of hard work for future benefits had been combined with quasi-military conceptions of obedience to authority, which were well tuned to the regime's methods, and gave the refugees little breathing space. Also, the average pay had been low, consisting in some cases only of food for work, with some pocket money, while housing had been basic, often sub standard. If two families had fled the wine-producer's well-intentioned treatment, others with less accommodating masters had found even more reasons to abscond.

A measure of the refugees' isolation: social workers stranded between refugee settlements, La Pampa Province.

Regardless of how their employers treated them, another negative aspect which the refugees had to face was their isolation from other fellow Laotians. According to Ministry of the Interior directives, they had been settled inside large estates, in remote locations where they had few opportunities to communicate. They could make the occasional telephone call, but this depended on a landlord's permission. Also, the considerable distance between settlements – 300 to 400 km or more – seriously limited face-to-face meetings which, again, depended on a landlord's willingness. Nor could the social workers' or my own visits be frequent. In order to meet the refugees, we had to travel very long distances between settlements, and in my case, when travelling from my office in Buenos Aires to the most distant provinces, the first leg of the visit required a flight before long hours on the road.

Given such conditions, most 'hacienda refugees' had abandoned the estates. Those who stayed on were paragons of perseverance who gained my full admiration. In an interesting example of ethnic differentiation, these were mostly Hmong, not Laotian. Back home in Laos, the Hmong had known the tough, semi-nomadic existence of slash-and-burn agricultural work, on the highest altitudes of Laos. When still in their home environment, their resistance to adverse conditions, their tenacity for work, and their loyalty to the clan and to a political cause (e.g. anti-communism) had been proverbial. In Argentina, these qualities were translated into a dogged determination to create acceptable conditions for their families, albeit in the lowlands, and under a system of land tenure which, as with the ethnic Lao, was disconcerting. In their painfully acquired Spanish, they found ways of communicating with estate landlords and administrators who, learning to appreciate and trust them, taught them to use mechanized agricultural methods. There is no doubt that their new life in the flat lowlands of Argentina, with a different climate, people, language and diet, was infinitely challenging, not least when such conditions were coupled with substandard accommodation. In one case, I was shocked to find a family living in a former warehouse, dingy and unprotected from freezing winter temperatures. But the Hmong family persevered regardless, and remained.

Norma Rodriguez and I visit a Hmong 'hacienda refugee' at home (above). This was inside a former ware house. Below: Realico, La Pampa.

Out of the haciendas, what next?

The refugees who had escaped from the isolation of remote rural areas, and had demonstrated noisily in front of the American Embassy, continued to resist the authorities' determination to make them return to the private estates. Some escaped more than once and, refusing to go back, managed to live in locations of their own choice.

In Buenos Aires, they became what I now called 'hotel refugees', a group that faced a difficult, hand-to-mouth existence in single rooms. The men were the breadwinners, and went into town to make a living, while the women mostly stayed in their rooms with the children. One notable exception, however, was a self-appointed leader in her thirties, who proudly supported her husband and family by selling secondhand clothes. Becoming a model for others, she discovered through her newly found Argentinian friends, that the northernmost province of Misiones, bordering Brazil and Paraguay, offered ample opportunities for petty trading. These she learned to exploit to the full, travelling regularly to the north, where she bought cheaply the material she sold in the capital at a profit.

While this exceptional woman made her business prosper, the fleeing hacienda refugees who had reached the big city found it difficult to survive. Rarely managing to make ends meet, many of them ended up in a new kind of dependency: they contacted Buenos Aires-based NGOs (including the Comision Catolica or Caritas) who provided them with emergency handouts for as long as was necessary. In fact, UNHCR subsidized these agencies and footed the bill, but this had not been made public, for fear that the authorities insist that UNHCR cover the needs of all families whose government-provided solution had collapsed. According to the division of responsibilities between UNHCR and the Interior Ministry, such families had to be dealt with by the ministry. But the Argentinian side argued that its part of the deal had been met: they had provided a solution (hacienda settlement). That this had been rejected by the refugees did not alter the fact. The ministry considered that it could legitimately disengage, and pass on the burden to the UN.

For the authorities, the hotel refugees were an economic and logistical problem. It had also become a political and public image issue, as the media had been informing the public of the refugees' situation. They reported on the refugees' discontent, focusing on the most depressed groups, and the worst living conditions – those in the run-down Buenos Aires hotels, for instance. Together with the ministry, UNHCR was of course also blamed, the highly critical narrative urging both institutions to find dignified, long-term solutions which would meet refugee expectations. Concerning the central government, I hoped that the media's reports would make it ensure that the provinces were more proactive in identifying municipal jobs for the refugees. To the extent that the media succeeded in that respect, the reporting

Refugee life in a Buenos Aires Hotel. (Foto by Cherep)

benefitted the refugees. I was concerned, however, that the media's one-sided focus on the worst situations, with no mention of the more positive cases, was feeding into public prejudice. On the whole, the reports *did* reflect conditions, but the social workers had reported occasional episodes of anti-refugee sentiment which, we all felt, the reporting could easily exacerbate. Of course, that was something we had to live with, except when the reporting was demonstrably false (one article made the scandalous claim that in the insalubrious environment they inhabited, it was not uncommon for the refugees to be feeding on rats).

In any case, the reports did not tell us anything we did not know and, for the time being, we continued to ensure that the angry, exhausted and demoralized group was provided with emergency handouts. My team of social workers kept encouraging them to adopt a more positive attitude to their Argentinian environment, while I reminded my counterpart at the Interior Ministry of the urgent need to develop more adequate responses.

* * * * * * *

Some of the former 'hacienda refugees' ended up in the provincial capitals, sometimes near to their former workplaces where they were offered jobs and accommodation. But they were firm in their refusal to engage. In Cordoba Province, the local authorities faced an especially determined group who refused all contact with Argentina. The adults turned down all offers of municipal jobs and Spanish-language training, and rejected schooling for the children. They were determined to remain entirely Lao, and acted as if they feared being infected by contact with anything or anybody Argentinian. As for the local officials, having seen all their employment and housing offers rejected, they remained remarkably cool-headed, did what they could, housed the refugees in an unused local government building (Villa de Soto), and backed them in their wish to create a farm in which they intended to live as they had in Laos. The families cultivated their own vegetables, raised their own chickens, and reduced contact with the outside world to a minimum by designating certain adults to communicate with officials. This they did as seldom as possible.

I reached the centre in mid-morning. The life they had chosen went together with an evident unconcern for their living arrangements and personal appearance. Clearly depressed, they looked rundown, but they were cordial, chatted in a friendly manner, and were glad to pose for a group photograph. They welcomed me as their elder brother – after all, I could speak to them about Laos in their own language. Some of the men surprised me. Those with a military past had heard about the so-called '*Reservistas 2 de Abril*' – Argentinian army volunteers. Responding to the

Families determined to remain Lao live as they would back home, 'Villa de Soto' Centre Cordoba.

all-pervasive anti-British nationalism, and anxious to do more than just cultivate vegetables for their daily needs, they said half-jokingly that they wanted to enroll, defend the Malvinas and get rid of the British. I could see they wanted to be liked. But their social worker, Ana Maria Molina, told me that they were not always easygoing – they could be difficult, and often vented their accumulated anger by making aggressive demands to both local officials and to her. They always repeated the same wish – to leave Argentina and to be resettled in the US. Clearly, Anna Maria said, they wanted my support for their plans by talking softly to me, as the Buenos Aires 'elder brother' and 'UNHCR boss'. I concluded that they were more desperate than other groups, more in need of support – they had stood their ground valiantly against all odds, and now found themselves against a wall.

* * * * * *

My next visit was to a group who had also ended up in an unused building, this time in Jujuy Province. As in Cordoba, the refugees had refused to work, and depended entirely on the municipality's handouts. But they had been taking care of themselves, and the centre did not have the other's air of defeat. It was clean and well ordered, a truly congenial environment. The families were well dressed and well groomed, and seemed on the whole to have come to terms with their lot, although they kept saying that their life in Argentina was only temporary.

Another group of estate escapees had ended up in Salta Province, in an unused hospital. The place was run down, but this did not depress them; many among them were good weavers, and this allowed them to move forward. The group had refused all offers of municipal work, but had convinced the authorities to give them wood and tools to make rudimentary looms.

By the time I called, they had linked up commercially with the local people, and as regular demand developed for the woven materials, a batch of these was placed in consignment with the market merchants each week.

But the care they put into weaving and selling was out of gear with their grim living conditions – the place reminded me of Cordoba, or the Buenos Aires hotels at their worst. The dormitories seemed abandoned, the mattresses on the floor were barely covered, and in the absence of storage space, clothes hung from mosquito-net railings, and pots and cups were everywhere. And yet, the uninterrupted work on the looms generated an atmosphere of hopeful activism. It was as if the refugees and their children were saying: 'We're keeping busy but we're ready to pack our bags right now, and go'.

The more positive atmosphere of Jujuy Centre.

Above and below left: In Salta, the refugees' run-down dormitories inside an abandoned hospital featured functional weaving-looms.

Above: The finished product sold well at the market.

Grim surroundings at the former Salta hospital.

14

UNDER THE DEMOCRATIC GOVERNMENT

Demonstrations celebrate the end of the dictatorship, 'No amnesty, no forgetting, JUSTICE'.

The new democratic government coldshoulders the refugees

My work had started under the military dictatorship, and progressed within the framework of its limitations. With the arrival of democracy in 1983, an electric sense of liberation was everywhere, and with it, a certainty that the sombre days were over – Argentina had reached a time of new beginnings. I hoped the refugees would also benefit, although on this count, events would prove me wrong. For the time being, however, I chose to push the refugees to the back of my mind and joined the crowds, camera in hand, determined to catch the unique historical moment, the demonstrations and the surrounding political euphoria. Past abductions and assassinations were in everyone's mind, while the repressed anger of many years exploded each time more loudly. The victims' mothers marched as a group, showed photographs of their abducted children, displayed their names on banners, and demanded to see them again in clear, loud voices.

At the foot of the city's famous Obelisk, on Avenida 9 de Julio, a unique tribute was paid to the 30,000 people who had been abducted and never been found. Young women and men knelt over large sheets of paper which they had placed

'May our children be found alive'.

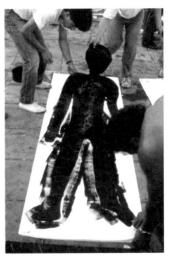

A named poster was made for each abducted person.

before them, on the ground. Armed with black paint, brushes and a life-size silhouette, they drew the outline of a man or woman on each sheet, which became a poster, with the person's name.

Two students were responsible for the victims' name lists. They crossed out the names of all completed posters, which other students would later affix on walls and fences, and the fronts of houses. No longer hidden, the 30,000 victims haunted Buenos Aires by their presence, and demanded justice.

Posters of the 30,000 abducted persons covered the walls of Buenos Aires, each with a name.

Amid the pervasive collective euphoria, I wondered how the democratic government would treat the Lao. The dictatorship had been ousted, and I expected that the democratic authorities would embrace the refugees, not perhaps as warmly as they did the Chileans who were fleeing the abhorred Pinochet regime, but at least with some of the openness that seemed to be everywhere one turned. I was wrong. Against all expectations, the desired support was not immediately forthcoming. Alfonsin's government was clear: Southeast Asian refugees were the defeated dictatorship's creation. The military regime's supposed humanitarian gesture of inviting them had been a ploy to gain international legitimacy, and the democratic government could not be held accountable for the generals' manipulation of international opinion. In the language of diplomacy: in the collapsed state of the economy and given current high levels of unemployment, the integration of Laotians was not a priority.

We had a glimmer of hope, however, when on November 1, 1984, President Alfonsin approved a law which lifted the so-called 'geographic limitation'. This specified that Argentina agreed to grant asylum to European refugees, and to European refugees only. By Alfonsin's modification, Argentina was in principle opening its doors to refugees from all continents. But in contradiction with the generous spirit of the measure, Indochinese refugees continued to be seen, first and foremost, as the unwanted legacy of a superseded Argentinian authoritarian past. Only as a after thought, were they regarded as people with rights. In addition to this chilling response, we feared that the attitudes and methods of the dictatorship would persist among former government officials who remained in place. It was clear that time was needed before democratic methods could take root, and replace those which had prevailed. In fact, the small dose of optimism which I still retained, was seriously undermined when I encountered more than one skeptic who, facing the economy's sharp decline, despite Alfonsin's promises, believed that the country's recovery could only be ensured by a firm hand, as firm as that shown by the previous government.

The new government gives in

Although the new authorities had little sympathy for the Lao refugees, and considered them an economic and political nuisance, they could not deny the reality of their presence. The refugees had been invited by a legitimate Argentinian government (however abhorred), had been brought in with the participation of the UN Refugee Agency, and were here to stay. And having continued to face complaints of lack of support from the provincial authorities, and continual visits from UNHCR, the new national authorities had to take responsibility for the unwanted group, and reluctantly agreed to participate in the previously agreed UNHCR/government venture which had been agreed – the 'permanent solution' program.

Delivering the solution, however, turned out to be more difficult than expected. For instance, catastrophic economic conditions affected our ability to provide each refugee family with a house of comparable quality. Galloping inflation and an unfavorable exchange rate reduced the purchase value of the amount provided and, as a result, families whose houses had been bought last, complained bitterly about their homes' poor standards, compared to those purchased first. To add to our difficulties, funds from UNHCR Headquarters did not always reach Buenos Aires according to schedule, the consequent delays in delivery causing frustration among the social workers, and unmanageable anger among the refugees.

A further problem was that not all families wanted the permanent solution. For good reason: opting for the package meant foregoing any further assistance from the government and UNHCR. It meant that all family expenses (including water and electricity) would be shouldered by the family head's meagre salary. Also, there was a fear of losing the psychological support that the institutions provided. A dependence had developed on both types of help and, although refugees never ceased to complain and always demanded more, relinquishing their rights to being subsidized and counselled was something, which on the brink of losing them, they wished to avoid at all costs.

Their attachment to UNHCR was particularly strong. It was also ambiguous. On the one hand, it was described as the benevolent 'UNHCR father and mother'. But it was also seen as the all-powerful but faulty UN Refugee Agency, the source of all their evils who had brought them to this, their Argentinian dead end. Accordingly, my team and I were required to fill a kind of parental role, but also, the organizational protection role which UNHCR's mandate proclaimed. The refugees felt that the agency's protection was an unmovable benefit, due to them as a permanent right, and were distressed to learn that once the Argentinian authorities had regularized their legal status (one aspect of the 'package') which would eventually lead to their acquiring Argentinian nationality, they would cease to come under the UNHCR's protection umbrella.

The agonizing decision, which the families faced before taking the plunge, was exacerbated when we had to announce UNHCR Geneva's warning that the Permanent Solution Programme would not be indefinitely available, and could be terminated in the very near future. The real dilemma facing each family, therefore, was between self-reliance with a house and a very small income, or procrastinating, and running the risk of missing the solution, and ending up with nothing.

Faced with these facts, even some of the remaining hardliners in the Cordoba, Salta and Jujuy centres, and those who had ended up in the Buenos Aires hotels as petty traders, gradually came to accept the support they had so strongly resisted. Most of these more recalcitrant families agreed to receive the standard package, while some particularly resourceful families, who had proved to have the stamina and the skill to survive, and even prosper under their own steam in Buenos Aires, received a personalized solution. In their package, the UNHCR housing money was used to set up a small business appropriate to their proven skills, a beauty parlour, a photocopying centre, a fast food/takeaway or a restaurant, each of which was designed by a business expert who ensured its sustainability and its capacity to generate enough income to cover all expenses.

With notable exceptions, the majority of packages were delivered according to the refugees' wishes, in an urban setting, thus reversing the original programme's rural orientation. Some, however, did remain rural, among them four extraordinarily hardy and persistent Hmong families. They had decided to keep their jobs as agricultural hands in a large hacienda, despite terrible conditions: substandard housing (a small, slightly refurbished former horse stall) which offered deficient insulation, in the winter months particularly, when they faced temperatures approaching zero and high levels of humidity, with minimal heating. But they had gained something which they valued even more than a decent home: the trust of their employers – in one case being given the responsibility of driving one of the estate tractors. Their choice for the future was therefore a package in which the UNHCR home was combined nicely with their hacienda job.

The four cases eventually achieved success after long years of dogged resistance to hardship. But one family, it should be admitted, had the additional challenge of having to face one of UNHCR's occasional administrative bottlenecks. As the family head prepared to sign for his new home, he got the shock of his life when he learnt that the funds from UNHCR Geneva for his anxiously awaited home had been delayed. Maria Angelica Forte, the family's social worker, had to muster all her courage to break the news and face the family's dramatic reaction. In a textbook example of frustrated hope of improvement leading to rebellion, the previously humble Hmong family lost its cool, and vented its full indignation. Maria Angelica tried all arguments to calm them down, promised that the money would be arriving soon, blamed Geneva, blamed Buenos Aires, I know not what else. To no avail. To crown it all, the family discovered a further bureaucratic mix-up: that the money had been made available for the purchase of a house for another Hmong family, who lived in another province, and was behind them in the queue... Maria Angelica had to put up with strong recriminations over the phone, followed by visits to her office which allowed the wife to complain face-to-face and the husband to threaten. Only when Maria Angelica was able eventually to invite the family to sign all papers, more than a month later, did the family go back to being their reasonable, conciliatory selves.

A Hmong refugee shows the tractor for which he is responsible to a visiting Geneva colleague, Angelo Rasanayagam, April 1983.

A Hmong's family's 'permanent solution': a house in Rio Negro Province.

Misiones Province, a haven for the independent-minded

Some of the more resourceful independent-minded families, who were among the last to resist taking the package, found a way out in the northernmost province of Misiones, adjacent to Paraguay and Brazil. They travelled there following the trail of the adventurous and dynamic refugee women, already known to the reader, who having discovered the area's trade opportunities, had combined life in the rundown Buenos Aires hotels with occasional trips to the north. The newcomers reached Misiones, liked it, and picking up on their predecessors' contacts, got into the petty trading business, eventually generating enough income to make ends meet. Showing real business acumen, they entered the profitable retail clothes trade, and learnt to take advantage of the rates of exchange when moving across the Paranà river into Paraguay or Brazil. They, of course, kept repeating that they would one day leave Argentina, but after a while, they started enjoying Posadas, the provincial capital. As they made good money, learnt Spanish, and developed a network of local friends, they felt increasingly comfortable, and ended up fitting into this Argentina of their own making.

News of their success circulated among other reluctant families, including among some of those still living in the now-almost-empty refugee centres. They also followed the pull of the Misiones magnet which, with its hot climate, intense vegetation, red earth and blue skies seemed almost Laotian, as was the welcoming attitude and the physical appearance of the local people.

It was a pleasure to see the last of the confined families gradually being drawn there, away from the grim, claustrophobic refugee centres, able to establish a semi-urban, independent life, similar in many ways to what they had left back home. Having been rewarded by a measure of success, many such families did not want to take a single cent from UNHCR, nor sought employment from the government. They wanted to remain free.

Others gradually became package-takers. But having their own views, they resisted the orthodox one-family solution, being interested instead in a communal

The people of Misiones welcomed the Laotians.

approach. They proposed to plan their future according to a model we had not originally envisaged. This they developed with Elsa Guerrero, the German-Argentinian social worker for the province. Jovial and relaxed, she epitomized the casual atmosphere of the area, giving advice as a friendly gesture, in a way that was well suited to the refugees' relaxed ways and independent spirit, and to their still unresolved resentment of the authority they had rebelled against in the haciendas. Elsa found that this group's dislike of hacienda life was not a dislike of rural living – what they had fled was not the countryside, but enforced isolation from other Lao families, and subordination to an all-powerful employer.

Elsa helped twenty families develop an agricultural cooperative *cum* housing estate. The families' permanent solution money was merged to fund the project, while the local authorities agreed to deal with the venture's legal aspects. In a miracle of coordination, the families learned to abandon their narrow self-interests for those of the group, while Elsa helped resolve the inevitable petty squabbles, negotiated the necessary division of tasks with the family heads, and managed to harmonize their views with heroic patience. Everything seemed to have been smoothed out. But some members still worried that the community's interests would make them lose out, and travelled all the way to my Buenos Aires office to discuss the issue. Individualism and personal advantage as a priority kept being a concern. This was a clear reminder, I believed, of the kinds of difficulties which the Lao communist regime had faced during its initial, hardline agricultural collectivization phase.

Talking to me and to Elsa seemed to have ironed out such concerns, but on inauguration day, came an unexpected surprise which a furious Elsa described in a note. 'I invited everybody to the inauguration, including the municipality officials who were looking forward to seeing the completed project – the houses, and the chickens and the pigs, which we had carefully selected. But when, early that morning, I checked that everything was in order, all I could see were the twenty houses, and nothing else. No pigs, no chickens. This is why: some days before the inauguration, having made sure that I was not there, the family heads had a meeting. As had happened before, they had a huge row about how to share the profits from the sale of the piglets and the eggs, and never reached an agreement. They decided to dump the livestock business. Opting for ready cash, they sold all the pigs and the chickens, and kept the money, now determined to use it to get into the clothes business'.

Elsa was bitterly disappointed. The Itaembé Agricultural Venture – mixed agriculture cooperative and housing estate, and largest refugee project ever attempted in Argentina and Elsa's magnificent five-star project, had been dumped. All that effort for nothing! But sitting in Buenos Aires, I felt that something important had been achieved. For these twenty families, the umbilical cord had finally been severed, and they had become self-reliant. It didn't matter that in the end, they had followed their individualistic bent, and opted for the clothes business. What mattered was that the project functioned.

* * * * * *

While Misiones' special environment had enabled even the most reluctant Laotian families to come to terms with Argentina, it also offered an option to those determined to leave Argentina at all costs. Its borders with Paraguay or Brazil represented a possible route of escape to freedom, and many tried it. Elsa was well placed to describe these desperate attempts, some of them breakneck adventures that involved thousands of kilometres of perilous travel and ended in disaster and forced return.

In Elsa's own words: 'One group of fifteen families left Misiones for French Guyana. They crossed into Brazil, stopped at the Foz de Iguazù, and then decided on the route to follow – 6,000km! When they eventually reached French Guyana (I still don't understand how they made it), it took some time before they were allowed entry. Once inside, they didn't like what they saw, and requested the immigration authorities for travel documents to go to France. They didn't get them. Out of the fifteen families, only four were allowed to stay, I don't quite know why. The others were deported back to Argentina. Some were put on a charter flight direct from Cayenne to Buenos Aires, others were sent to various points on the Guyana border with Brazil from where they had to face the return journey.' Once back in Posadas, the refugees recognized they would never be able to leave, and finally requested a 'permanent solution'. But some time later, another group made a new attempt. This time, the objective was to reach the US. The refugees managed to cross through Bolivia and reached Peru, but were blocked there and forcefully sent back. Back in Misiones, however, they remained undeterred and planned to make another attempt.

I was reminded of the sorry fact that when in 1979, the Argentinian Selection Committee offered to resettle Lao refugees, the rumour had circulated among potential recruits that Argentina was close to the United States, and could be used as a springboard to get there. Even before leaving the refugee camps, Argentina's imagined proximity to the US encouraged many to sign up. The dream had survived prolonged exposure to Argentinian reality, but despite all efforts, it had to be dropped.

15
MENTAL COLLAPSE AND AGGRESSION - SOME EXTREME REFUGEE RESPONSES

Exposure to Argentina seriously challenged the adaptive capacities of all Lao refugee families. Whether in the haciendas or in the municipalities, in the rundown hotels or in the refugee centres, whether settling in Misiones, or waiting to escape, the range of cases all faced major obstacles. But one common feature allowed these to be conquered: an unexpectedly solid inner strength, which refugees were able to tap into from the depths of the self at a moment of crisis. When this was coupled with the outside support of family members, or friends, or a social worker, they were able to survive episodes in which disappointment, frustration, anger and depression freely mingled.

But for those who lacked that inner capacity to recover, and could not find a reason for moving forward, the way out was to block out reality and lock themselves hermetically inside themselves. These individuals were statistically a small minority within the refugee group, but their stories are a reminder that the sustained efforts required to adapt are not available to all. There were some ten such cases, of which I give a few examples below.

Bounthong and violated personal space

An urgent telephone call from a municipality just outside Buenos Aires asked me to get in touch as a matter of urgency. The problem was Bounthong. He was acting strangely. Perhaps I could help by talking to him in Lao, before a psychologist was consulted? His family had been one of the first to receive the permanent solution, and was considered a success story. He and his wife had been happy with their new home, and Bounthong's job as a member of the municipal cleaning brigade seemed to be going smoothly. That morning, however, his wife told the municipality that Bounthong would not be going to work; he was sitting in his bedroom, immobile and in silence. For some time, he had been getting into a strange mood, did not talk to anyone at work, and sat at home in a corner without saying a word. He had been frequently late for work, and that morning, he had just sat at home. His wife could not get a word out of him.

I went to visit, confident of my role as the older brother who can offer protection. He greeted me with respect, raising his joined hands to his forehead. But he would not talk, he just looked blankly beyond me. Only on a second visit, some days later, did he speak a little – he felt tired and would not go back to work. '*Bo muan*' he said. 'I don't enjoy the work. I won't go back'.

I needed to get his fellow workers' version of the story. Carlos was the most willing and told me. Bounthong, with his small size and ready smiles, had become the group's plaything, a kind of reluctant clown. Carlos thought that Bounthong had enjoyed that, but as we talked, it was clear that there had been a lot of rough horseplay and pushing around, and many jokes at Bounthong's expense.

I agreed with the municipality. We needed to organize a meeting with the cleaning brigade to explain how Lao people interacted. We met a fortnight later. With a slide-projector and a screen, I talked through a small collection of slides which I had taken in Laos before the revolution. The striking beauty of Luang Phrabang, its temples and royal palace captured the brigade's attention, and they were all ears when I explained the huge gap that separated Argentinians from the Laotians. The Lao, I said, regarded their bodies as if enclosed in an invisible aura, a protective cushion of vital space which had to be respected. They experienced any trespassing of that space as a kind of violation. By contrast, Argentinians welcomed physical contact. To the Lao, the head was an especially sensitive area, believed to be the place of habitation of a person's thirty-two souls, one for each part of the body. To touch it, as was the Argentinian custom when greeting a child, or when playing around with a man like Bounthong, was not a good idea, and had to be avoided.

In contrast to Argentina's egalitarian ways among persons of the same social class, the Lao were very hierarchical in all interpersonal relationships. They approached all others as older or younger siblings according to their age, treating them and expected to be treated by them with appropriate deference. A person's age was the first thing a Lao person wanted to know when making a new acquaintance. At this point, I showed a slide of the king of Laos. I explained that in pre-revolutionary Laos, the hierarchy started at the top of society with the monarch, who was revered like a sacred being. The people honoured him at New Year by pouring blessed water over him as a sign of respect, in the same way as they poured water over Buddha images which were considered sacred. The king and the Buddha were approached with reverence, much like a crucifix or a statue of the Madonna was by Roman Catholics. Though of course ordinary Lao persons were not approached with such high regard, a measure of respect for their age and their space was expected for all. This was alien to Argentinians' greater tendency to touch, and had to be considered when dealing with a Lao person like Bounthong.

As I talked, I could see the cleaning brigade listening carefully, and when I finished, Carlos and two others approached me. They had understood the message. 'How could we have known? When we hit Bounthong on the shoulder and pushed him around, we did so affectionately, as good friends. We never thought he would be insulted'.

I explain Lao customs to the municipality's cleaning team (at the back) and staff.

The slides and the explanations were not enough to end Bounthong's condition. But the apologies he received from his fellow workers paved the way for his eventual return to work. That happened after many sessions with Mario, a professional psychologist who had been recruited to help problem cases. With patience and perseverance Mario established a good relationship with Bounthong and his wife, despite their rudimentary Spanish and Mario's even more rudimentary Lao. Somehow, they managed to communicate.

Nantavet and the piercing effect of an Argentinian voice
Nantavet belonged to one of the more intransigent families. For no apparent reason, he had one day stopped participating in group activities, opting to live in autistic isolation next to his bed, in the refugee centre dormitory where his wife and children also slept. He entered Mario's office calmly, together with the social worker. But he bolted as soon as he heard Mario talk. He would not say a word. He told me the reason later: he could not tolerate Mario's voice. As with all Argentinians, he said, Mario's voice was like a needle that went into his ear, and threatened to pierce his eardrum.

Hmong exorcism
Mario's methods could not work when odd behavior was attributed to spirit possession. In Laos, such a case would have been addressed by a medium, or by a

traditional healer of sorts. But the Argentinian delegation, who had travelled to the Thai camps in 1979 to select refugees had excluded the elderly – the very people who could have played the medium role. By mistake, however, Brietu, an elderly Hmong man, had been approved by the Selection Committee, together with his son and daughter-in-law. Once in Argentina, they were sent to La Pampa Province. All Hmong families in the programme knew where Brietu lived, relieved that someone with his knowledge could be available in an emergency. When a young man fell prey to extended periods of fever, thousands of miles away in the southern province of Rio Negro, his social worker Maria Angelica got worried. Medication and several consultations with a local doctor had not worked. Maria Angelica and I decided that a traditional Hmong treatment could possibly do the trick, and so, with funds from the Indochinese Refugee Budget, old Brietu flew from La Pampa to exorcise the illness-producing spirit. Once the young man recovered, Brietu flew back home.

I become the target of collective aggression

Mental collapse was the refugees' most extreme reaction to a toxic accumulation of stress, frustration and anger, a form of escape for the minority who had been most negatively affected by Argentina's environment. Another, more common response was aggression, which could be acted out in a variety of ways, some more threatening than others. Anger and aggression focused on the municipalities' staff and on UNHCR's social worker team. But in time, I also became a target – from being a kind of saviour, I became, for some of the angrier refugees, a double-crosser, a traitor to their cause. Soon after I reached Buenos Aires in 1982, my credentials (life in Laos, knowledge of the culture and the language) had made me into the group's long-awaited 'elder brother' who would put everything right. Also, an increase in UNHCR funds, which coincided with my arrival, was attributed to my influence, making me seem, in addition, the all-powerful controller of inexhaustible resources. Based on this exaggerated perception of my own importance, I was well placed to manage the programme. But with the passage of time, when unrealistic expectations were set against some of my decisions, hope turned to disappointment, and to increasingly vocal expressions of rejection. I was being exposed to the same process of deterioration which had confronted the two people who had preceded me as coordinators: a process in which excessively high expectations turn into disappointment, threats and aggression. Both my predecessors had felt forced to leave. Would I, also, need to do that?

On July 15, 1984 the mechanism of deferred aggression was activated by Bounthieme. Based on his past experience in managing a restaurant in Vientiane, and eager to make good in Buenos Aires, he had proposed to set up a business with his family's permanent solution money. He wanted to enter a partnership with a Korean immigrant and long-time Buenos Aires resident, who owned a restaurant. Alberto, our UNHCR business consultant, carried out a careful feasibility study, approved the proposal, and helped implement it. Initially, the joint venture worked well – a good relationship developed with the Korean, and Bounthieme, his wife and their two children were more than satisfied. They showed this by frequent friendly visits to my office, where they described their success.

But in time, we heard that the two partners no longer got on, until, one day, the business collapsed. The Korean turned out to be a crook, and disappeared with all the ready cash, leaving a mountain of debts behind him. Despite all efforts, the restaurant had to be liquidated, leaving Bounthieme and family with just enough money to cover basic expenses. Looking for a way out, Bounthieme came to see me. He argued that the bankruptcy was not his fault but the Korean's, and asked me, as his elder brother, to give him a second chance, repay the Korean's debts, and put the restaurant back on its feet. He said everybody knew I was free to use the UNHCR money as I pleased. If I did not help, his family would starve…

It was not possible to do what Bounthieme wanted. Even if the Korean's defection argued in his favour, to provide a second package to his family was simply not an option. The budget had been calculated to cover the exact number of families in the progamme, and requesting an additional amount from Headquarters for a special case was a no-go. Also, the amount destined for each refugee family in Argentina was very high compared to other resettlement programmes, and the strong criticism it had provoked inside UNHCR excluded a doubling-up for even one family. And even if approved, doubling a single family's benefit would have led to a Pandora's box of requests by others, and created an unmanageable situation. There was only one solution. Bounthieme had to lower his expectations drastically, take a municipal job which the local authorities would provide, and count on an occasional emergency top-up until he became self-sufficient.

Bounthieme persisted, was given the same negative response, but again and again. Unable to take no for an answer, he became increasingly aggressive, until he became unmanageable. I decided not to see him until he calmed down, but he insisted, and telephoned my assistant several times a day. Initially, he spoke politely to her, but when he threatened her and used offensive language, I tried something else: I invited him and his wife to a meet with Norma, the social worker, Alberto, the business expert, and myself, hoping that we could make him see reason.

The meeting promised to be tempestuous. Bounthieme and his wife came into the meeting room, and were asked to sit on two chairs, while I sat on a low sofa opposite them, together with Norma and Alberto. A policeman stood by the doorway, ready to intervene, in case the meeting got out of hand (this was a practice that had been introduced by the office after a number of aggressive refugees, some of them Chileans, had become difficult with other colleagues). Speaking in a neutral voice, Bounthieme started by complaining in a normal tone about our response, but as he progressed in his argument, he gradually raised his voice and, speaking more quickly and more loudly, blamed all three of us angrily for making him pay for the Korean's swindle – we were deliberately starving his family, we were lying about the lack of money, and he knew we had pocketed some of it, as everyone knew. While he almost shouted, I tried to speak as quietly and as slowly as I could, but we embarked on a difficult exchange all the same, until his wife, who until then had kept quiet, turned to Bounthieme and shrieked at the top of her voice 'It's time to put an end to all this'. She seized a kitchen knife, which she had kept hidden on her lap under a rolled-up newspaper, and gave it to him. He jumped to his feet, rushed towards me and pointed the knife straight at me. I was sitting low on the sofa, so all I could do was turn my body sideways towards Alberto. I am not sure that Bounthieme wanted to do more than frighten me and the others, but fortunately, the policeman leapt forward instantly, grabbed him by the shoulders, held his right arm and twisted it to make him drop the knife.

The municipal authorities were called, Bounthieme was arrested and his wife allowed to go home. We were pretty shaken, disappointed at our failed attempt, and dismayed to see how affected the couple was. The next thing we knew was that within a few hours, the police released Bounthieme on the grounds that 'the authorities could not arrest a refugee who was under United Nations protection'. We were not sure what Bounthieme would do next. We let things lie for a time. Norma started calling on the family again, until they had to accept that the restaurant dream was out of reach.

* * * * * *

The Bounthieme incident had left Norma, Albert and I alarmed that the anger that had been brewing under the surface in Bounthieme's family could emerge and explode elsewhere. And it provided firm evidence that my standing among the refugees was collapsing, having remained quite stable for over two years.

I say 'quite stable' because Bounthieme's incident in June, had been preceded by an earlier sign of disaffection in March. At that time, three social workers from our team, based in three provinces, had reported that a largish group had been talking against me – seven family heads from Misiones province, ten from Cordoba and six from Salta and Jujuy had accused me of being a traitor, blaming me for doing nothing for them, and for siding with the authorities against them. The women had even threatened to come to the Buenos Aires UNHCR office and disfigure me with acid… In fact, the same words of intimidation were delivered to me personally soon after, in August. As I was walking out of the lift on the ground floor of the UNHCR office, I came face to face with a group of Lao women who said: 'Be careful when you go down into the underground. One of these days we will wait for you and throw acid at you'.

Getting ready to leave

The threats and aggression I experienced made me stop and reflect. I felt a good deal of affection for the group – they came from a country which had marked me deeply, and they had faced a succession of extraordinarily challenging situations. I kept repeating to myself that those who had turned against me were a minority whose behaviour was entirely understandable, but whose trust I had lost. Was there a way to regain it? What other approach should I have taken? After much brooding, it was clear that I had reached the end of the road. One thing I had learnt during my time in Luang Phrabang: that in a Lao relationship, when one of the partners violates the other's subjectively defined line of tolerance, the relationship breaks down, without hope of being mended. In Argentina, the line of tolerance among the angrier refugees seemed unreasonable, but that was not the point, the point was that for some in the group, I had crossed that line and reached a point where there was no turning back. The conclusion was unavoidable, it was time to leave.

The Argentina job was not yet completed, though, and was further complicated by a new difficulty. The flow of funds from UNHCR Geneva had become increasingly erratic, a disastrous trend that was badly affecting our speed of delivery, making refugees ever more anxious. Things got even worse when Geneva made the serious announcement, which had previously been made as an empty threat, of the programme's imminent closure. Faced with the news that permanent solutions would cease and that the social worker team would be dismantled, refugees panicked, lost all hesitation about being tied to Argentina, and now demanded their permanent solution. As for the team and for me, the news sounded a bell of alarm. We needed to deliver solutions for 82 outstanding families before closure. The social workers and I were caught in that uncomfortable middle-ground between the refugees' anxieties and Geneva's slow delivery.

However, a lot had been achieved. We had managed to find solutions for 211 out of 293 families. They comprised a minority of individual family successes: some tenacious Hmong 'hacienda refugees', the Misiones independent-minded group, and a solid body of 'municipals' who had come to terms with life in small towns with their own house and a modest job. As for the most recalcitrant, even they had gradually capitulated, goaded by the spectacle of increasing

The children of many families
at the Salta Hospital Reception
Centre (Foto by Cherep).

numbers of permanent solution takers, and by the pull exerted by their own children who drew them towards increased interaction with the environment. I took my cue from a September 1983 official figure of 600 new births (an average of 2.05 per family), thereby enabling the prediction that a sizeable group of well-adapted Lao families would be a permanent feature of Argentina's demographic structure.

My last days in Buenos Aires saw me busy writing a concluding report which spelt out all the difficulties and outstanding issues, and pleaded for the postponement of the programme's closure. I left Argentina without a response, but I was soon glad to hear that in addition to my arguments, the unrelenting pressure exerted by the families through the social workers, and the many reports which the team sent to Geneva through the UNHCR Representative, succeeded in prolonging the programme for two more years.

* * * * * *

By the time I heard the news, I was back in Southeast Asia, taking up a new UNHCR job in Hanoi. I had stopped in Geneva to report on my mission, looking forward to discussing the lessons that could be extracted from the Lao Argentinian experience, and their preventive applicability to similar operations in the future. However, I found that apart from a few exceptions, there was little interest. In the sea of needs at the centre, where UNHCR sometimes dealt with hundreds of thousands of refugees, many of whom had been vegetating in camps for decades, there was little time for the small Laotian group. Fair enough. But regardless of refugee numbers, I could see that the practice of reflecting on, and identifying the weaknesses of completed interventions was not on the whole in the agency's culture: the agency moved on inexorably from one operation to the next, without taking the time to analyze outcomes and their impact on individuals.

One question remained in my mind. How had it been at all possible for such a programme to be approved? Despite the reservations which my intimate knowledge of the facts maintained, I concluded that UNHCR's acceptance of Argentina's offer to resettle Lao families 1979, is explained, but not justified by the facts of the Indochinese refugee crisis: an unprecedented number of refugees pouring out of Vietnam, Laos and Cambodia, the scarcity of resettlement options, and the accumulation of refugees in the futureless confinement of rudimentary camps. Also, the offer had not been taken up without considerable soul-searching. It had given rise to a strong internal debate in which those against had opposed acceptance as a matter of principle, as they repeated that Argentina's offer was the self-interested, legitimating gesture of a military dictatorship that was well known for its violation of human rights. But faced with the intractable fact of mounting numbers, and the Americas Bureau's interest in placing some of the Indochinese refugees in Latin America, arguments of principle foundered, in favour of the process, often faced by the agency, in which an intractable dilemma is resolved pragmatically.

I had to recognize, however, that once the programme's difficulties had become evident, the Americas Bureau in Geneva had admitted its mistake, and tried to correct it. It had made extraordinary funds available for sustainable solutions, and placed fourteen social workers and a coordinator in a position to accompany the group through its difficulties. Those inputs did help. On the other hand, despite Geneva's good intentions, and all our efforts, it was not possible to make up for the long period of extreme disorientation which the refugees had been forced to endure. They had entered Argentina entirely on the wrong footing, were left without cultural and language preparation for too long, were exposed to military discipline that was too strict, and developed negative feelings that ran too deep.

As I write these lines today, the information I have been able to access tells us that many families have come to terms with their lot. But that result has been achieved at a very high price. If one focuses only on the small number of casualties – those who suffered mental collapse – the cynical view is that any resettled group of refugees includes those who fail to adapt and cannot cope, the supposedly normal casualties of any refugee group, the expected victims of statistical inevitability. But what number of casualties is acceptable? I prefer to think that even one individual case of collapse is one too many, and indicates deficiencies in planning or a mistaken choice in the country of resettlement, or both[1]. The mental conditions I have described were extreme expressions of the anxieties which all families experienced, which many voiced with anger, rather than with intransigent rejection or mental collapse. Though each family responded differently, the group's collective gut reaction showed that the challenges posed by Argentina were excessive. The gap between what Argentina could offer and what the refugees needed was too wide. The few success stories, and the gradual adaptation of most families in the very long run are a tribute to their endurance, and to the dedication of those individuals, officials, social workers and ordinary citizens who each contributed to correct an initially defective undertaking.

* * * * * * *

Once I completed my Buenos Aires job, I could say that I had experienced several radically different political realities: the end of the monarchy and revolution in Laos, obsessive anti-communism in Thailand and the transition from anti-communist military dictatorship to democracy in Argentina. But I had never tasted life under a communist regime. My new job in Hanoi offered that opportunity. By September 1985, I was back in Southeast Asia, dealing with Kampuchean refugees in communist Vietnam. A year later I was active along the Thai-Lao border coordinating a protection programme for incoming asylum seekers from communist Laos. I do not deal with those two experiences in this book, but jump instead in Part Four to 1987, when I was appointed Head of Mission in Kampuchea.

---

1   Placing the Argentinian experience of Lao refugees against Lao resettlement programmes elsewhere (including in the US, Australia, France and the UK) is beyond the scope of this book. It is clear however, that the experience of the refugees in Argentina was among the most challenging, given the isolation to which family units were subjected upon arrival, without the element of peer group support to help ease their gradual entry into a radically alien environment. For an account of the disturbing anxieties that can face a refugee in his first encounter with a foreign land, see Lemoine and Mougne 1983. In the context of the USA, the culturally specific images of terror in the minds of a group of Hmong men, and their exacerbation in the new environment, are shown to have been one of a number of factors which struck the weak constitutions of a number of male individuals suffering congenital heart malformation, and led to their death.

Part Four:

Kampuchea
Repatriation to a Devastated
Revisionist State (1987-1990)

16

NEW BEGINNINGS IN THE POPULAR REPUBLIC OF KAMPUCHEA (PRK)

Kampuchea, an out-of-the-way destination

Nakhon Phanom, September 1987. Having completed my third UNHCR refugee job, I was busy preparing to move to Kampuchea where I had just been appointed Head of the UNHCR Office in Phnom Penh. I was glad. The move to a city that stood by the Mekong satisfied my need for continuity. It linked my immediate future to my 1972 Southeast Asian beginnings on the banks of the same river in Laos, and to my present work location, on the right bank of the Mekong, in the Thai Northeast.

On the map, the Khmer capital seemed close enough, and easily accessible by way of the Mekong. The unrealistic idea of travelling there by boat had taken my fancy, but, of course, there were intractable obstacles which stood in the way – impassable stretches of water, intransigent officials at the land border, and probable blockages in areas still under Khmer Rouge control. The only way to reach the destination was by air, but even that turned out to be difficult in the complicated international situation in which Kampuchea found itself. It had suffered the stigma of being Vietnam's puppet ever since that country invaded it in 1979, and after the West and China strongly condemned Hanoi's move, the Phnom Penh regime was regarded by those powers as an international pariah state. From then on, travel to the Kampuchean capital from the West became difficult, and once Thailand aligned itself with all other PRK opponents, the most practicable and direct access from Bangkok was blocked. My only way of reaching Phnom Penh, therefore, was through the roundabout route via Vietnam.

On 11 December 1987, I boarded the Air France flight from Bangkok to Ho Chi Minh City. Than Son Nhut airport awaited me there, with its fussy bureaucracy and interminable checking of documents. Given the rudimentary facilities, travelers had to take their bags from the conveyor belt, drag them all the way to the departure area, and place them on a departing flight cart. I did the same, and when I finally boarded the Phnom Penh flight, it was with a sense of foreboding – Kampuchea was proving difficult to reach, and leaving it was unlikely to be easy. That guess turned out to be exactly right. Flights into and out of Phnom Penh proved to be consistently unreliable, and subject to last-minute cancellations.

Opposite page: A soldier from the Popular Republic of Kampuchea at Angkor Wat, 1988.

Settling in Phnom Penh

The long route to Kampuchea: south from Bangkok over the Gulf of Thailand, NE to Ho Chi Minh City and finally, west to Phnom Penh.

Jean Claude Concolato, whose job I was about to take over, asked me for drinks. He lived in the grounds of the former Hotel Le Royal, which the communist authorities had renamed Samaki (Solidarity). His bungalow, which was to be mine as soon as he left, was one of many in the hotel compound, and had housed the heads of the UNHCR office for years. It had the faint flavour of the French-colonial 1930s, which remained untouched in the main building, with the splendid dereliction of its very high ceilings, slightly soiled wooden doors, and lusterless but solid interior staircase. Before I entered the bungalow, I pointed to the swimming pool, which seemed to offer a welcome spot of freshness, but my enthusiasm was soon deflated when I was told that chronic shortages of chemicals made swimming possible only when the murky green liquid that filled it was replaced by clean water... In short, the Samaki had seen better days. But it was the height of comfort compared to the general dereliction I had seen in town.

Over drinks, Jean Claude told me not to be misled by the hotel's appearance of comfort. The colonial aura, the gardens and the comfortable bungalows were a smokescreen. The hotel compound was a carefully guarded ghetto for westerners, governed by rules which sealed off the real Kampuchea outside. The rules barred entry to all Khmer visitors other than government officials, thus limiting social life in the bungalows to non-Cambodians. There was a huge difference between the way westerners and the Eastern Bloc lived. The Soviets and the Cubans, whether diplomats or development workers, mostly lived in separate houses, and though they were watched by the authorities, they circulated more freely than westerners ever could.

At this point, Robyn Blake walked in. A New Zealander, she was the office secretary, who was to remain with me after Jean Claude left. Well informed on the ins and outs of life in Phnom Penh, she did not hesitate to add the odd comment to his account. After just over a year in Phnom Penh, Jean Claude seemed tired. It was not his style to complain, but he made his meaning clear in his pointed description of difficulties, and when he stressed the fact that UNHCR contracts allowed a week off every three months, the periodic travel out of Phnom Penh being a safety valve which was needed to keep sane.

Having worked in Vietnam, where I lived in another foreigners' ghetto in 1984, I knew exactly what he meant. I remembered my own sense of isolation during my time with UNHCR in Hanoi, and the relief provided by mandatory seven-day breaks. However, I would soon discover that my days in Hanoi provided a standard against which conditions in Kampuchea seemed more manageable. It was possible in Phnom Penh to move about town on foot, by car, or by cyclo and, language limitations allowing, to talk to anyone one happened to come across, shopkeepers and cyclo-drivers or food vendors. There was no rule against talking to people who went to the same restaurants, or against developing something resembling friendship as a spillover of official business, during working meals or after official meetings.

* * * * * * *

The Samaki Hotel: the main building and my bungalow Phnom Penh, 1987.

On the following day, I called on Jean Claude and Robyn at the two-room UNHCR office in the rundown Monorom Hotel. Standing two blocks away from the Samaki, it had the signs of prolonged abandonment: cracked flooring and slight humidity stains which showed under a recent coat of paint. Sitting at his desk, and surrounded by dusty copies of *Le Monde* which rose in piles from the floor, Jean Claude picked up where we had left off the evening before. I learned that all foreigners' movements were followed by a network of informers everywhere they went. I had expected this, but the news nonetheless dashed my hope that the Monorom would be my oasis of freedom. I had fantasized that it would offer a daily route of escape from the Samaki's confinement, transported there by Sam, the friendly Kampuchean driver who had welcomed me at the airport upon arrival. To make things worse, I learned that Sam was a government employee, and although UNHCR paid his salary, it was the Ministry of the Interior who defined his two sole tasks: to keep an eye on the Head of UNHCR, drive him inside Phnom Penh and outside, on occasional field trips, and take him every day from the Samaki to the Monorom. Sam was not a UNHCR person, and so was not allowed to enter the hotel, let alone come up to the office on the first floor – his spying job concerned outside movements only. In time, I discovered that on Saturday mornings, he regularly attended an Interior Ministry meeting where he had to report on UNHCR's movements.

The spying system was not entirely unexpected, nor seemed especially draconian compared to the stricter, more oppressive approach I had experienced in Hanoi. The Vietnamese system had kept westerners under watch in the office and at home; it had forbidden access to most cafés and restaurants, and barred contact with the man in the street. However, understanding the logic behind the measures, I remembered, had helped me come to terms with the imposed limitations. I therefore looked for the reasons behind the Kampuchean system. They boiled down to the idea, persuasive in a context of international isolation and political and military vulnerability, that we westerners were all politically one with 'the enemy' (the western powers led by the US and China). We were potential agents of subversion whose ideas and contacts had to be carefully followed. Our whereabouts had to be known at all times. As in Vietnam, where the system probably originated, we could not be trusted. And to make matters worse, in my case, as a UNHCR official, I was identified with that other enemy, the United Nations, the organization who had kept the Khmer Rouge in the UN Cambodia seat until 1983, and continued to think of the PRK as an illegitimate Vietnamese creation. UNHCR shared with all UN staff a common aura of unreliability.

Still, there were good political and economic reasons why the PRK tolerated our presence. First, it believed (unrealistically) that UNHCR could encourage the

United Nations to recognize the PRK as one of its legitimate members. Secondly, it welcomed UNHCR's longstanding funding of projects for displaced persons: people fleeing US bombings as a spillover of the Vietnam war in the 1960s, victims of the Khmer Rouge in the 1970s, villagers escaping military confrontations between the PRK and the Thailand-based coalition. Being confronted with some 150,000 such persons (1993 UN figure), the authorities wished to see that UNHCR's support continue, even if it only covered a fraction of the needs.

Polarising politics and the working environment

The ambiguity with which UNHCR was regarded was clear to me at my very first contact with the authorities. This took place as soon as I reached Phnom Penh, as part of a tight schedule of introductory meetings which Jean Claude had prepared. I was of course welcomed as per the usual diplomatic courtesy, but it was immediately evident that the government wanted to keep us at arms' length, and minimize direct contact with our small office. The message was that our main interlocutor was to be the Kampuchean Red Cross, and only in very special occasions the Foreign Ministry.

Accordingly, Jean Claude Concolato's official farewell dinner was organized by the KRC whose President, Madame Plech Pirun, and her staff dominated the event, while only two or three officials from the Ministry of Foreign Affairs attended. This was in all respects a KRC show, and at dinner, Jean Claude and I were placed across the table from the evening's undisputed figure of authority, our Red Cross hostess.

The KRC's primacy in UNHCR's linkage with the authorities was again evident the following morning at the KRC's office, during Jean Claude Concolato's last working session. Plech Pirun presided, while Jean Claude made a nicely worded speech, gave a farewell gift in the form of a Buddha image, and raised an issue which he had been following fruitlessly for months: the expansion of the two-staff UNHCR office by one person. The government had continued to refuse approval, and refused again on that day. The ambiguous answer which Madame Plech Pirun gave, essentially another no, showed the KRC for what it was: a humanitarian agency in name, but in fact a government agency which played the double role of ally to our cause, and loyal government adjunct. Rather than admitting to the government's politically motivated unwillingness to expand the presence of a UN agency, Plech Pirun talked vaguely about the government's difficulties in approving the entry of more foreigners into Kampuchea. I could see that the KRC's friendly attitude was not incompatible with a net refusal, however veiled.

* * * * * * * *

Politics were to be central to my relationship with the government. They would also colour my contacts with NGOs and other humanitarian agencies, for it turned out that interrelationships hinged partly on relative political proximity to the PRK. Agencies who were unconditional PRK supporters sided against those who, by mandate and by policy, had to be neutral; these included my office, the other UN agencies (UNICEF and the World Food Programme), the International Red Cross and some NGOs. During my first Head of Agencies meeting, taken by Jean Claude Concolato, discussions were harmonious enough. Only later did the weekly information sharing prove to be a forum for political alignment and occasional confrontation. Basing their political weight on the size of their programs, some of the more influential among the PRK-backers did not lose a single opportunity to show their political preference. This was reciprocated by strong official support and, in the absence of any western diplomatic representation, by being accorded quasi-ambassadorial status and evident preferential treatment. On 31 December 1987, less than a month after my arrival, I saw an example of this when Hun Sen, Prime Minister since 1985, stressed in a speech delivered during an end-of-the-year official reception, the importance of those agencies' contributions and thanked them profusely. Significantly, this event was held in the former French Administration's Government House, and was attended by the government and (eastern) diplomatic corps in full.

However, despite the political divide among agencies, strong solidarity and professional cooperation linked many of the individuals who worked in them, particularly junior staff who did not feel obliged, as some senior managers, to keep a high ideological profile. After all, whether PRK backers or not, the humanitarians were all in the same boat. Despite differing relationships with the authorities, we faced similar difficulties of daily living and of work: the suspicion of the authorities, their surveillance practices and bureaucratic blockages, the limits which they placed on our movements. Conversations about the pervasive spying system were an especially strong basis for bonding, though I soon saw that such talk could lead to exaggerated fears of continual scrutiny, and had to be resisted for the sake of our sanity. In any case, the ongoing dialogue among some humanitarian agency personnel was a welcome palliative to our confinement. I saw a good example of it only ten days after my arrival when I found myself on board a large cargo boat which was docked by a pier, on the Tonle Sap. It was December 20, 1987. The authorities had organized a large Christmas party on board to which all humanitarian agencies were invited. The event's high point was the dancing of the *ramvong*, where partners from different agencies moved to the sound of the loudspeakers which blared out their Khmer music at top volume. The gathering showed that we could be friends, even if some considered themselves political rivals.

Persisting logistical difficulties in 1988: a ferry carries its heavy load across the river.

Relationships among the UN agencies was a separate issue. I soon found out that a level of ambiguity existed between us and UNICEF, the largest UN agency in Kampuchea. And I would learn to smile with irony at the hierarchy of precedence which the head of that agency tried to impose, from the height of his well-staffed office at the Samaki, on our own two Monorom rooms, and on the World Food Programme's equally unimpressive premises. It had to be admitted, however, that there was an objective basis for UNICEF's institutional pride: it had been the first UN agency to enter Kampuchea in the post-Khmer Rouge period when, together with the International Committee of the Red Cross, it had provided humanitarian aid throughout the country, despite almost insurmountable logistical difficulties. Some of these persisted in my time and continued to raise considerable obstacles to internal travel.

17

DEVASTATED KAMPUCHEA – A DIFFICULT ENVIRONMENT FOR RETURNS

The legacy of the past

Phnom Penh was slowly emerging from a succession of devastations. Some of these had taken place even before the Khmer Rouge catastrophe. In the early 1970s, the capital had witnessed unprecedented demographic growth (from 600,000 in 1968 to 1.5 million in 1974) following Marshal Lon Nol and his American patrons' use of all available military means to destroy the then insurgent Khmer Rouge movement. As the Cambodian army and US bombing battered the countryside, thousands of terrorized villagers sought refuge in Phnom Penh, and as the new-comers joined the ranks of the urban poor, the city's services came to near breaking point. The population increase and the generalized brutality and corruption which an overwhelming military presence generated, left their ugly deforming mark on the capital.

Further major disasters took place after 1975 under the Khmer Rouge. Following the radical reduction of its population to 10,000 by means of forced expulsions, the city was transformed to fit the regime's new ideology. Animals were put to pasture in the gardens of abandoned villas, vegetables were grown in the Royal Palace grounds, the National Bank was dynamited, the use of money was banned, the names of streets, restaurants and hospitals were erased. Also, the use of running water and electricity was limited to a few government buildings and eight embassies, while more than half of the National Library's collections were pillaged or destroyed, together with the General Archive of Cambodian History. As for Buddhism, the then Khmer Rouge Minister of Culture, Yun Yat, affirmed that Buddhist practice was incompatible with socialist revolution, since historic materialism affirmed that Buddhism was a lie. As a result, monks were forced to disrobe and were shot when they failed to comply[1].

The physical and psychological scars left behind by that difficult past were a heavy burden which Phnom Penh still carried, even eight years after the Khmer Rouge demise. But as I moved around, it was clear that the government was trying hard to put the city back on its feet – the wider boulevards had been paved anew, and some of the city's main landmarks, such as the former Royal Palace and the Museum of Archeology were being restored. However, these pockets of renewal seemed out of

---

1   See Perez Gay 2004: 21-22; Strangio 2014: 266; Elizabeth Becker 1998: 164-174.

Persisting urban decay 1987-8.

gear with the rest of town, where derelict buildings and pothole-ridden side-streets persisted as evidence of war damage and prolonged abandonment.

Phnom Penh's rundown condition in 1987 shocked me, but this was a far cry from previous state which had given rise to a succession of damning judgments. In March 1977, for instance, Yugoslav Television had carried out the first-ever media coverage of Khmer Rouge Kampuchea and said: 'The capital is destroyed, deserted and deep in darkness, as if following a massive bombing campaign'. Nor was the city I got to know 'something between a refugee camp and a mammoth rubbish dump' as Phnom Penh was described in the early 1980s[2]. My Phnom Penh showed signs of hope – rather than dejected, people seemed determined to struggle. As already noted, many came from the countryside, and had entered Phnom Penh after the Khmer Rouge were ousted, attracted by the mirage of urban wealth. Though their expectations had not been met, they had found a place to live – former bourgeois flats or villas, or abandoned and rundown luxury hotels which widespread looting had reduced to empty shells. The country people's outdoor living, their cooking arrangements on the sidewalks, their chickens, pigs and dogs, and their approach to hygiene reflected their village ways. These remained unchanged despite the threat of illness to which children were especially vulnerable.

2   Brian Eads quoted by Strangio 2014: 32.

With troops of children, drying of clothes and washing of dishes by the main entrance, the former Grand Hotel was now home to the urban poor.

Conditions could have improved more than they had, but that would have required stricter measures which, from the political angle, would have been difficult to implement. As Vickery notes, the authorities could have pooled human and financial resources more than they did, or imposed stricter licensing and heavier taxes, or organized the under-employed into labour groups to help address the city's deficient hygiene, and the rundown, chaotic environment[3]. But the drastic measures of the Khmer Rouge had not been forgotten, and the municipality willingly avoided all measures that could be associated with them. The result was a city where a few impeccably renovated areas contrasted sharply with continued decay.

The effects of the ongoing military conflict

To the disfiguring effect of past catastrophes, I had to add the impact of current fighting. The war had not come near Phnom Penh, let alone touched it. But evidence of the fighting was there in the high number of war victims, disabled men on crutches, or in wheelchairs. They gathered at the morning market, smoking with a defiant air, waiting for the odd scrap of food, a cigarette or a bank note. They stood there jobless, without an income, surviving by begging. I was sure that deep down, people felt sorry for them, but I soon discovered that they avoided them. They did not want to be reminded that their soldier sons, brothers or husbands could also be

---

3   See Vickery 1984: 240.

maimed. And there was fear. For these were angry men, who could throw a grenade when least expected. It was awful to say, but such things did happen.

The authorities did what they could for them, acting jointly with agencies such as Handicap International, the Kampuchean Red Cross, the French Red Cross, the Cuban medical team, and others. But the problem was huge. Millions of landmines had been and continued to be planted. In the countryside, civilian men, women and children still risked hitting one every day of their lives, in their fields, in the market, when they took the children to school.[4]

We knew that the war was claiming casualties each day along the distant frontline, close to the Thai border, and sometimes closer to town, during occasional sporadic confrontations. With such generalized insecurity, how could refugee returns take place? I knew the necessary conditions were far from satisfied, not only from the evidence provided by the victims, and the occasional reports on the war, but also from my own observations.

War victims in Phnom Penh, 1988.

---

4   During my visit to Cambodia in 2016, the issue of unexploded ordinance had only been partly addressed. There appeared to be no comprehensive countrywide support system for war casualties. However, a number of NGOs had been responding, including one associated with a small war victims museum which I happened to spot on the way to Ta Phrom. The museum showed photographs of war casualties, and introduced the Cambodian Self-Help Demining (CSHD), an all-Khmer NGO who had been operating since 2008 with inputs from ex child-soldiers, the parents of victims and university graduates. Later, by the side of the path that led to the Ta Phrom archeological site, I came across a small traditional Khmer orchestra. The musicians were landmine victims. They played without stopping, and waited for tourists to drop a coin or buy one of their CDs.

Military escort on the way to Svei Rieng Province, 1988.

Such observations were gathered each time I left the protected environment of Phnom Penh on occasional monitoring trips to UNHCR-funded projects. For each trip, I had to be cleared for security, and the authorities insisted on providing military protection. As we drove towards the projects, the AK-47s and rockets which our escorts strapped to their backs, kept reminding us that perhaps the Khmer Rouge were close. I often wondered whether the arrangements would offer protection if the case arose. The escorts seemed young and inexperienced, and had probably been given this relatively risk-free job in lieu of older men, who were needed at the frontline. All the same, I was glad they were there, for there was a lingering doubt in my mind whether, in the unlikely case of an attack, the Khmer Rouge would respect the UNHCR stickers on our vehicles, or those of the Kampuchean Red Cross, who always came with us. In many cases, escorts were clearly superfluous, but when we drove through the more insecure areas, their presence was welcome.

Our Red Cross partners kept reminding us of the need to be cautious, and added to the grim reality we were facing by taking us to sites where evidence of past Khmer Rouge atrocities kept our escorts' warnings alive. In one location, we were confronted by the macabre spectacle of skulls, neatly arranged in rows along the top of low stone walls, or in pits. Such places were objective evidence of Khmer Rouge horrors, and although, as we will see, the PRK was manipulating them for their own advantage, the sites were reminders that the Khmer Rouge were still fighting the PRK, perhaps in areas much closer than we suspected.

The persisting memory of the Khmer Rouge

Eight long years had elapsed since Vietnam's invading forces had decimated the Khmer Rouge, but the memory of Pol Pot's devastating policies was still alive. Only three weeks after my arrival, I had my first, extraordinarily vivid firsthand account of what had happened.

Together with the Kampuchean Red Cross, we drove to Svei Rieng where we visited and checked on the management of the medical dispensary, one of UNHCR's projects for displaced persons. At lunch time, the conversation turned to the past. Monsieur Puy's memory remained sharp: after the Khmer Rouge take-over in 1975, he had been pushed out of Phnom Penh with his wife and three children, and forced onto the road to Battambang. There they remained until 1979. Speaking in French, Puy explained: 'The camp chief was the kind of man who liked to frighten us by boasting about his murderous exploits. One day, he proudly claimed to have killed 99 people. "Just one more", he bragged, "and I will complete 100". Some days later, the trouble began. At lunch time, the camp chief did not sit down, but instead remained standing, and watched us with his superior supervisor's look. Among us, there was a man whose wife had just died, probably from exhaustion and bad food. He had been badly affected, and occasionally got into fits of uncontrollable anger. The camp chief had singled him out as a trouble-maker, and was always picking on him. On that day, the chief stared at him in a provocative way, until the man reacted, crying out at the top of his voice: "we can't eat this soup, we can't eat it". He took hold of his soup bowl, and aiming at the cook and at the two men who had been serving, he hurled it across the room with full force. The camp chief then went straight at him, forced him to the ground and in front of us all, some fifty people, he kicked him in the head, caught hold of a knife, and holding it menacingly, stabbed him. He cut him open, reached for his liver, extracted it and kept it, intending to eat it later.'

The horrific scene seemed to be the nightmarish product of a sick mind. To better understand what had happened, I later looked at the specialized literature which analyses various forms of extreme behaviour in Cambodia. It confirmed that Khmer culture considers it legitimate to resort to extreme episodes of violence under certain circumstances, such as when a man is confronted by a dangerous enemy. Puy's camp chief followed Khmer Rouge ideology in thinking that all town dwellers and intellectuals were mortal enemies. Clearly a fanatic, he considered all camp inmates in that light. The man who had mocked his authority had been transformed by that act into his arch-enemy, a man to be destroyed. When he extracted the man's liver, the camp chief imposed the punitive measure which the culture permitted.

The Mexican historian Perez Gay has found several examples of the practice in Cambodia's remote past. In a letter dated 1296, Zhou Daguan, Chinese Ambassador to King Jayawarman VII, notes that a collection of human livers was customarily offered to the king each year. He further specifies: 'A recently extracted liver, which the Khmer believe to be the seat of courage, is mixed with wine and drunk in a religious ritual. It is sometimes used to wash the heads of the monarch's elephants. The liver must always be extracted from the body of a living man, never from a corpse.' A further report of the same practice is provided in the 19th century by a French missionary who affirms that episodes of revenge focused on the enemy's liver. We are further told that in the 1960s, under Sihanouk, attacks on enemies that focused on the liver were not unknown among the government's military and left-wing opponents[5]. Another specialist, Vickery, has also looked at the issue[6]. Among other comments, he refers to a book published in 1973 by one Bun Chan Mol. This former leader of the Free Khmer (the Khmer Issarak) was responsible for executing spies suspected of working with the French Colonial Administration. The book describes episodes of extraordinary cruelty which 'were considered normal by his underlings as a way of dealing with their enemies'. The extraction of the liver from living men, or from very fresh corpses, was a practice that was known in past centuries, and also, as Monsieur Puy showed, in the 1970s. In all cases, the extreme practice stood within the parameters of what was permissible.

Monsieur Puy's account had left me open mouthed. It was evident that the telling had transported him mentally to the past, for after a pause, he continued to talk about the period, this time focusing on his son. The boy was ten years old at the time. 'I often saw him crying, out of hunger. He was always looking for food, and would eat anything he could find. I was afraid for his health, and needed to stop him. I followed him whenever I could, though I was very weak then, and walked like an old man, with the help of a long stick, a kind of pole. He also, was very weak, you see, and could not walk – he moved on all fours, trying to escape from me, but when I caught up with him, I would hit him hard to stop his rummaging, stop him from eating rubbish. I was so afraid, so afraid he would get sick and die'.

That evening as we drove back to Phnom Penh, there was no more talk. I tried to absorb what had been said, while my mind's eye kept seeing Monsieur Puy's empty look during the telling, as if in a kind of trance. I could not understand. I just looked out of the window at the thickets of pencil-thin palm trees.

* * * * * * *

5 Perez Gay 2004.
6 See Vickery 1984: 7-8.

Some months later, we were back in Svei Rieng celebrating prize-day at a UNHCR project school. This time, our party included the vivacious Dr. My Samedi, Dean of the Faculty of Medicine and Secretary General of the Red Cross.

The event was followed by lunch. I sat next to the doctor, and as the meal progressed, he talked about his days under the Khmer Rouge: 'I was forcibly evacuated to Kompong Thom; like everybody else, I worked in the rice fields. They knew I was a doctor. Initially, that made no difference, until one day the baby daughter of the District Chief developed a fever, and everything changed. The chief told me that I just *had* to cure her, by whatever means. He indicated a storeroom where I could find medicines – western medicines, he specified. I never imagined that the Khmer Rouge could have such a rich supply of pills and other western medical stuff, when their ideology favoured the use of traditional medicine. I looked around in the storeroom, and found what I needed.

The infant recovered, and I was no longer regarded as just another suspicious former city dweller, fit only to be reformed. I was a doctor who could cure. My life was transformed: I no longer had to work in the fields, and my food improved. Like the Khmer Rouge officials, I was fed on chicken and an abundance of vegetables. But this improvement was short lived. It came to an end when a political purge directed against the District Chief resulted in his death. His wife, his family and the baby I had saved were also killed. It was horrific. Soon after, things got bad again with the arrival of a new Chief Officer, who imposed the strictest discipline, work from sunrise to dawn, and small food rations. But for some unknown reason – perhaps my being a doctor – the new chief treated me with some leniency. He did not allow me to practice as a doctor, but I was not forced back to the rice fields, I had more food, and my new job, carrying water in buckets to water the vegetable gardens, kept me at work for less hours. This went on until the Vietnamese reached the area, and made the Khmer Rouge cadres take to their heels. By this time, my regime of work and little food, though relatively less demanding than that of others, had taken its toll. I had lost a lot of weight, and was very weak. I stayed in Kompong Thom with a group of survivors until we recovered our strength, and were able finally to take to the road back to Phnom Penh. The new authorities knew who I was and welcomed me, and soon I was back working at the Faculty of Medicine. There was a big job to do: Phnom Penh was devastated.'

Dr. My Samedi's words and those of Monsieur Puy led me into the dark hole of their past. But before them, others had done the same by means of an involuntary gesture, an empty expression, or a momentary terrified look. This happened one day with Madame Plech Pirun, the President of the Red Cross who had welcomed me upon arrival. During one meeting which she chaired, she interrupted her comments and, sitting in silence with a blank face, she started to wring her hands,

Dr. Mi Samedi at Svei Rieng with his staff and Robyn Blake (UNHCR).

looking at them intently, in a flash recollection of the work the Khmer Rouge had forced her to do. The moment of silence seemed to stretch. She said nothing, just looked at her hands, transported despite herself to those terrible days. Then she took hold of herself, and picked up the discussion where she had left it.

* * * * * * *

As Monsieur Puy's recollections had done before, Dr. My Samedi's memories and Madame Plech Pirun's flashback put squarely before me the dilemma they had faced in 1979, when Vietnamese forces had just put an end to the Khmer Rouge genocide. Were the Vietnamese liberators, or invaders? When the new Popular Republic of Kampuchea was created under Vietnamese protection, what should they have done? Stayed or left? All three decided to stay. For Monsieur Puy, the alternative had been to become a refugee in Thailand; for Madame Plech Pirun and My Samedi, both members of the Phnom Penh élite, it was exile in France. The decision to stay had not been easy, for there were many historical examples of Vietnam's intention to control and even conquer the country, and for many Khmer, the Vietnamese were the traditional enemy. They knew that Vietnam's invasion had been self-seeking, its primary objective to protect its own borders from Khmer Rouge aggression, rather than save Kampucheans from the Khmer Rouge. Also, to leave the country would have meant joining the tripartite coalition that was fighting Phnom Penh with full Khmer Rouge participation, as one of its powerful military components. This fact was in itself a sufficient reason to remain, and to insist, when all was said and done, that Vietnam's intervention had freed them from a living hell.

The stayers had been condemned by those who had fled for playing into Vietnam's ambitions. But they found some comfort when they learned that Prince Sihanouk himself had felt for their difficult dilemma. Having endured three years of house arrest under the Khmer Rouge in Phnom Penh, and the loss of fourteen members of his family, the Prince knew the Khmer Rouge for what they were, and could understand those who had stayed. Such understanding mattered, coming from the man most Khmer considered the Father of the Nation and who could, in that role, transcend the extreme factionalism which divided it.

In his book, *Prisonnier des Khmers Rouges*[7], Prince Sihanouk referred to the people I have just mentioned, and wrote: 'I ask myself today if it makes sense to blame honorable personalities such as Dr. My Samedi and Madame Plech Pirun (former Head of the Red Cross under Lon Nol) for collaborating with the Vietnamese'[8]. Sihanouk also mentioned on the same page his own personal hesitations, conceding that at a moment of near despair, he had wondered whether the time had come for a 'foreign country (i.e Vietnam) to intervene'. For the prince to have admitted to such soul searching and hesitations had been a balm to those who stayed with the PRK.

However, Sihanouk's doubts were short lived. They were followed by the unshakeable resolve to fight the PRK, and expel the Vietnamese. On January 6, 1979, as the Vietnamese army advanced towards Phnom Penh, the Khmer Rouge leaders Pol Pot and Ieng Sary, who had kept Sihanouk prisoner in Phnom Penh, organized for him to be flown to Beijing. They hoped that the Chinese leadership, who fully backed them, would convince Sihanouk to condemn the Vietnamese invasion internationally, and stand behind their Democratic Kampuchea (DK) as the country's legitimate government. As Elizabeth Becker has described, everything happened according to plan. By January 11, 1979, China had arranged for the prince to reach New York, in time to speak at the United Nations. There, he denounced Vietnam's military occupation in the strongest terms, reinforcing China's strong push in favour of their Khmer Rouge client, and against the Soviet Union and Vietnam. In a lamentable, politically manipulated debate, mention of Khmer Rouge atrocities was avoided, while the discussion focused on Vietnam's violation of the country's sovereignty. The UN General Assembly condemned the invasion, and gave into China's strong pressure in favour of the Khmer Rouge: their presence at the UN as holders of the Cambodia seat was approved by a vote of 71 nations in favour, 35 against and 43 abstentions[9].

By this decision, the scene was set for an extended conflict between Khmer and Khmer. On the anti-Phnom Penh side, the CGDK (Coalition Government of Democratic Kampuchea) was set up in July 1982 with the backing of China, the US

---

7 Norodom, Sihanouk 1986: 312.

8 My translation from the original French.

9 For a detailed account, see Becker 1998: 444-445.

and the West. Highly unstable, because constituted by three rival factions (Footnote), the conflict-strewn coalition was held together thanks to the skillful leadership of Prince Sihanouk. As for the opposing side, it was guided from Phnom Penh by the PRK regime and its Vietnamese ally, with Soviet support. The prince's New York intervention, which had confirmed his role as the highest leader of Cambodia, was decisive in according legitimacy to the Khmer Rouge, and helped relegate the newly established Phnom Penh government to international pariah status. To make things worse, the animosity between the opposing camps was exacerbated by highly aggressive propaganda campaigns, the PRK focusing on Khmer Rouge crimes and exalting Vietnam, the Coalition bombarding their dependent populations with virulent anti-PRK and anti-Vietnamese attacks. On either side, the propaganda was almost indestructible because partly based on fact. It raised a formidable obstacle of contrasting meanings to reconciliation.

Faced with such intractable facts, I asked myself the question whether hundreds of thousands of Kampucheans in Thailand could be expected to consider return, when they continued to be bombarded with relentless anti-Vietnamese and anti-PRK propaganda? Would they retract their hate of the PRK and the Vietnamese invader, when demonization of the regime and Vietnam was key to their own personal justifications for fleeing, and to the international arguments that backed them? Could the population inside Kampuchea be expected to welcome them, having been continually exposed to the idea that the abhorred Khmer Rouge were part of the Thailand-based anti-PRK coalition, and that some of the camps were inhabited by Khmer Rouge sympathisers who were determined to come back? If political realities and propaganda made it unlikely that people would want to return, and raised formidable obstacles to an eventual understanding between the two sides, what was the point of trying so hard to convince Phnom Penh to allow single individuals to return?

The political manipulation of Khmer Rouge atrocities

Khmer Rouge atrocities were key to the PRK's propaganda machinery. More than other elements, they served to justify the creation of a new Kampuchean state under Vietnamese protection, and helped consolidate the state's self-image as the only effective bulwark against a possible Khmer Rouge comeback. The state, therefore, had good reasons for maintaining the collective odium for the Khmer Rouge. It sought to reinvigorate it by way of periodic, carefully organized rituals of ideological reinforcement. One such ritual, the Day of Hate, had taken place each year on May 20, since 1984.

In 1988, the event was organized at Tuol Sleng. This former high school had been transformed by the Khmer Rouge into an extermination centre, called 'S-21', which witnessed the incarceration, torture and assassination of at least 12,900 supposed enemies of the state. Their memory was preserved for posterity by a meticulous system of recording which was developed by the assassins themselves. Despite the historical evidence confirming the murderous acts, Tuol Sleng was a subject of heated debate and political controversy, being regarded by critics of the regime as a mere Vietnamese/PRK propaganda stunt, which exaggerated or even invented the centre's macabre activities. However, although the evidence that confirmed the existence of the assassination machinery was able to dispel the most extreme negationist claims, it did not put a stop to criticism concerning the political use of Tuol Sleng crimes. In so far as the criticism focused on the PRK's self-interested manipulations of suffering, it was of course legitimate. But it had its downside. For it was often accompanied by statements that reduced the scale of Khmer Rouge human rights violations, belittling them beyond recognition. Negating the full horror of events between 1975 and 1979 resulted in invalidating the experience of the victims, and prevented both them and the collectivity from coming to terms with a deep psychological trauma which needed to be faced and fully recognized before being resolved.

The issue reminded me of the debate surrounding the Holocaust Museum in Jerusalem which has sometimes been seen primarily as serving to justify the militaristic, anti-Palestinian policies of the Israeli state. But well-documented horrors cannot be dismissed as exaggerated or even invented versions of reality, however much they might be actively manipulated to serve a political agenda. Significantly, the objective reality of the bloodcurdling events that occurred at Tuol Sleng was eventually fully confirmed, after careful scrutiny by the Extraordinary Chambers in the Courts of Cambodia (ECCC). Known informally as the Khmer Rouge, or Cambodia Tribunal, it was created in 2001 to try serious crimes committed during the Khmer Rouge period. The mixed Cambodian/International body confirmed the veracity of accusations, and eventually tried the Director of Tuol Sleng, Comrade Duich, alongside four prominent members of the leadership, Nuon Chea, Khieu Samphan, Ieng Sary and Ieng Thirith.

* * * * * * * *

The PRK leadership attached considerable importance to Day of Hate celebrations. The careful planning which preceded the 1988 event showed this, as did the status of the participants: the President of the PRK and the Foreign Affairs and Interior Ministers; the highest levels of the diplomatic corps, international organisations and humanitarian agencies. To these was added a large number of very senior monks, an early indication of the PRK's developing openness to Buddhism, which would

Day of Hate 1988 President Heng Samrin leads the way, Ministers Chea Sim and Hun Sen follow.

find its full expression one year later, as an effective and consciously used instrument of legitimation.[10] To give the event the full weight it merited, the victims were commemorated by a large memorial where the principal guests, headed by the PRK leadership and the ambassadors, were invited to present lavish flower offerings.

A series of performances were organized for maximum effect, each re-enacting Khmer Rouge atrocities and their devastating consequences for individuals, while the loud notes of a choir echoed a pervading sense of bitterness and resentment. One actress could

Below: Guests present flower wreaths to honour Khmer Rouge victims.

not control her emotions and at the end of the performance, she ended up crying, as she leant against a man who played the part of a victorious, anti-Khmer Rouge fighter. Other actors showed the entry of Vietnamese forces into Kampuchea on 7 January 1979, and described, according to the official script, how Vietnam had liberated the Kampuchean people from Khmer Rouge tyranny, and enabled the foundation of the PRK. The version of history which the PRK leadership promoted required a strong pro-Vietnamese, and anti-Khmer Rouge narrative as a priority.

Guests tried to give their full attention to the various performances, but the length of the event, and the torrid midday heat resulted in visible somnolence, even among the most prominent. Also, there were several distractions on the side: two Australian cameramen, incongruously dressed in clinging shorts, the collars of their short-sleeved shirts pulled up at the back, walked casually among the crowd,

---

10 See p. 236-239 below.

searching single-mindedly for dramatic shots, oblivious of the day's solemnity, and neglectful of the surrounding crowd. A Japanese television crew did the same, bringing their cameras close to their subjects – a spectator's tear-covered face, a group of female soldiers, a group of Eastern Bloc ambassadors sweating profusely under the ferocious sun, a middle-aged woman describing the massacre of her entire family, President Heng Samrin in tears.

A group of stone-faced Muslim Chams squatted in a small circle, their sombre expressions reflecting the persecution which the Khmer Rouge had inflicted on them. It is not certain that all Chams were subjected to systematic oppression, but at least some had suffered discrimination and exclusion, even before the Khmer Rouge took over. On the other hand, we know that Cham men were sought for their fighting skills: in Cold War Cambodia, in the early seventies, some had been welcomed in Phnom Penh by the anti-communist Lon Nol regime, who incorporated them into the armed forces. Later, the Chams' association with anti-communists, and the fact that some among them had refused to fight with the Khmer Rouge when invited, provoked unprecedented Khmer Rouge retaliation in some areas, including the massacre of entire communities. There were therefore good reasons for the Cham to take pride of place during the Day of Hate.

The expressions of grief, the repeated rejection of the Khmer Rouge past, and the occasional explosions of feeling, mirrored the psychological state of many participants, but also that of thousands of men, women and children who were not present, but had also been Khmer Rouge victims. At certain moments, the utterances reached a paroxysm of sentiment, and became a liberating collective catharsis. The denunciation of past crimes expressed a long-repressed, but viscerally felt demand for justice.

At certain moments, I was deeply touched. In others, I was irritated by the way horrific events of the past were being used. This was not the first time I was confronted with similar instances of political manipulation, nor the first time I reacted with comparable ambivalence – first with empathy for the victims, later with anger against the propagandists. I had come across one similar instance of in Takeo where, driving along a road, I caught sight of various propaganda panels showing Khmer Rouge cruelty. The panels had been placed by the road, like commercial advertisements, except that the images were rooted in well-known events, and had, like the Day of Hate's theatrical performances, a strong emotional appeal. They were effective pieces of propaganda.

Day of Hate 1988: the Muslim Cham remember Khmer Rouge oppression.

Anti-Khmer Rouge panels showing Khmer Rouge atrocities, Takeo 1988.

Nine years had elapsed since the collapse of the Khmer Rouge, but the PRK authorities continued to manipulate their past depredations at every possible occasion. However, the PRK's accusations against the Khmer Rouge and other pieces of propaganda, did not seem able to divert attention from its own shortcomings – its authoritarianism, intolerance of criticism, and human rights violations. These had provoked negative reactions internationally and inside Kampuchea, noticeably in Phnom Penh, where disaffection with the regime had been growing. Political manipulation could not dispel the accumulation of evidence concerning corruption, nepotism, inefficiency, abuse of power, and the disconcerting news, that despite the authorities' condemnation of the Khmer Rouge, the PRK was recruiting former Khmer Rouge cadres at all levels of the bureaucracy.

The scale of PRK deficiencies was bad news for my repatriation job. Although it was difficult to assess their actual impact on potential returnees, they were likely to influence perceptions of the PRK, and discourage returns. To make matters worse, there were rumours in town that the regime's authoritarianism, and general conditions of poverty, were pushing people to hit the road towards Thailand and into the camps. In such circumstances, who indeed among the hundreds of thousands of displaced Kampucheans in Thailand would be willing to return?

18

A DIFFICULT REPATRIATION DISCUSSION
(1987/1988)

The PRK's inflexible opposition to refugee returns

Mr. Uch was my counterpart at the Ministry of Foreign Affairs. I started to visit him concerning repatriation soon after my arrival, the first of many meetings which took place whenever political conditions for the returns improved. In the prevailing polarized context, we approached the issue from opposing points of view, our well-worn arguments moving, at each encounter, from one side of the table to the other, and ending invariably with Mr. Uch's conclusion that repatriation could not take place.

His reasoning was simple. Many of the Khmer displaced persons in Thailand had joined anti-PRK resistance groups. If a repatriation movement ever got going, resistance fighters could easily infiltrate returnee groups, enter the country, and carry out destabilizing activities. There was some basis for Mr. Uch's concern; many of the camps were anti-PRK strongholds which functioned under ruthless military commanders as recruitment and rest-and-recreation centres for fighting men. Such commanders seemed to be operating with little interference from Thailand's military and border authorities, and even benefitted from their encouragement, since Thai officers tended to share the Khmer commanders' strong anti-communist and anti-PRK views. More than that, the Thai authorities' own Vietnam-centred version of the communist threat served to validate the strong pronouncements which the various anti-PRK factions were making against Phnom Penh. Conveniently for the Khmer resistance, the areas bordering communist Kampuchea were precisely those where Thailand's own anti-communist strategy was applied with particular vigour. It was where Thai nationalist defensiveness was strongest.

Mr. Uch's intransigence was probably increased by additional factors which he never discussed, but were surely common knowledge in Phnom Penh at the time. Western-bloc donors and China had been benefitting the camps with massive quantities of international aid which was keeping the anti-PRK resistance alive, while the needs of impoverished Kampuchea were being given insufficient attention. I could imagine Mr. Uch asking the question: under those conditions, why should the PRK comply with UNHCR's requests? From his and the PRK's point of view, UNHCR was financed by a hypocritical West who argued on humanitarian grounds for the repatriation of those who wished to go home, whilst supporting a policy which kept the displaced population in the camps (and the potential returnees it included) for as long as the political objectives of anti-PRK forces required it. The policy, considered perverse by Phnom Penh, was to maintain the camps indefinitely in place as a power base for the Royalist, Republican and Khmer Rouge components of the anti-PRK Coalition, until such a time as the PRK was blown out of existence by political and military means.

As I later was able to confirm, between 1982 and 1991, unprecedented amounts of international aid (US$ 200 million in cash contributions and US$ 230 million in kind) were channeled to one border agency alone, the United Nations Border Relief Operation – UNBRO. The aid had not only helped sustain the resistance, it had also ensured that the camps enjoyed standards of accommodation, food, water, education and medical care that were markedly superior to those which rural and even urban Kampuchea could offer. To the PRK, the superior material conditions in the camps were a blatant example of politically motivated, internationally sanctioned injustice, at a time when the country was still recovering from the Khmer Rouge disaster, and was fighting Thai-based coalition forces. The aid had effectively transformed the camps into permanent magnets that served to attract a steady number of Kampucheans out of the country, thereby weakening the PRK's population base. Of course, there were many reasons explaining an individual's decision to leave Kampuchea, but the superior conditions in the camps were certainly a factor behind the constant flow of departures to Thailand.

It is not difficult to see why the high profile which the UN had accorded to UNBRO could provoke bitter criticism in Phnom Penh. The agency functioned under a very high-profile UN official, the Special Representative of the Secretary General (SRSG), who reported to the UN Secretary General in New York and who carried, in the PRK's view, an excessively wide range of responsibilities: the control of *all* international assistance available to the Khmer, *both* on the border *and* inside Kampuchea. The SRSG was seen as the power through whom the decision had been made to channel the largest slice of aid available for Cambodia to the camps, precisely those locations which Phnom Penh considered enemy strongholds. To make things worse, even that smaller part of the aid which Kampuchea had received, had been discontinued in 1983, on the grounds that the post-Khmer Rouge emergency had ended. The PRK placed the responsibility for all such decisions partly on the powers that were behind the coalition, but also on the highest UN authorities. From their point of view, it was the UN who had been the main voice and implementor of the anti-PRK policy, and spoke for the US, and the US-led western powers who acted under the propelling influence of China.

Such views about UNBRO obviated the undeniable fact that the agency had probably saved thousands of lives from generalized violence and starvation. Also, its staff and the NGOs had shown single-minded dedication in a very difficult working environment. But the Phnom Penh authorities did not wish to recognize this. Nor did they know at that time (nor did I, for that matter) that UNBRO had consistently sought to counter the political pressures exerted on the camps' population. They did not know that UNBRO had struggled, since its creation, to put an end to the military and political use of the camps, and had repeatedly denounced the practice to the Thai authorities and the Thai Supreme Command[11]. However, even if the PRK had known, its negative perception of the agency would not have changed. In the PRK's view, the verdict was simple – UNBRO's one essential task was, and continued to be, to keep the population base of its enemies in indefinite confinement in Thailand.

UNHCR Thailand was regarded by Phnom Penh as yet another active sustainer of the border area's anti-PRK *status quo*. However, it was seen more favourably than UNBRO, as it had made a name for itself internationally by responding effectively to the Khmer population influx in 1979. It had set up the Khao-I-Dang refugee camp in record time, an achievement of almost heroic proportions, given the adverse political and logistical conditions that prevailed at the time[12]. Also, UNHCR insisted that Khao-I-Dang only housed registered refugees, who were protected in that camp from the insistent pressures of the resistance. They were not, therefore, anti-PRK activists. Also, having access, as refugees, to resettlement opportunities, persons confined to Khao-I-Dang geared all their efforts to satisfy the acceptance criteria of receiving countries (the UK, France, Germany, the US), and avoided, UNHCR was convinced, any kind of involvement in anti-PRK activities which would have excluded them from being selected.

Whatever the arguments, I made little headway with Mr. Uch. Specifically about Khao-I-Dang, he wondered whether even that camp had not been infiltrated by the resistance. In any case, he doubted that a single person would ever volunteer to return, given the continual bombardment of anti-PRK propaganda to which the population of all camps was subjected. It did not help that in mid-1987, UNHCR Thailand stated that no one from Khao-I-Dang wanted to return.

A one-person repatriation

January 1988. Talks concerning return, including that of single individuals, had reached an impasse. It was clear I would have to travel to Khao-I-Dang to identify candidates. To prepare for the trip, I called on the Phnom Penh office of a French agency which I knew well, Handicap International (OHI), which specialized in artificial limb fitting and war-victim rehabilitation. I asked them to contact their Khao-I-Dang office, and ask whether any of their patients had ever talked about coming back home. The response was positive, and by the time I travelled to Thailand and reached Khao-I-Dang, one person who wanted to return had been

---

11 I am indebted to Mr. Patrick van de Welde for his comments on UNBRO'.

12 For an account of this camp's establishment, see Barber 2015.

found. Speaking in French, OHI Khao-I-Dang introduced me to her, calling her 'Madame' Seng Long. From then on that is how I addressed her.

Originally from a small village in Kompong Cham Province, Madame Seng Long had lost the use of both legs after hitting a landmine on her way to the border camps. Before going to Thailand, she had been suffering from a gynaecological problem which had not improved with local treatment, nor with that provided in Phnom Penh. Having heard that the refugee camps in Thailand offered good medical care, she decided to travel there. Although the journey could be dangerous, due to military activity and the presence of landmines, Madame Seng Long knew that health travel across the border was not uncommon, while black market smugglers moved constantly between the border and Phnom Penh. The prospect of being cured was stronger than her doubts, and, as thousands of people had done before, she headed for Khao-I-Dang.

Madame Seng Long left Kompong Cham with a woman from her village, a long-time friend. Using various means of transport, the two women reached a location near the border where they were joined by a group of three men and their wives. The group set off together, determined to cover the last part of their journey on foot. But disaster overtook them as they moved across a rice field. Seng Long activetd a landmine whose impact hit her from the back, damaging her spine and paralyzing her from the waist down. Inexplicably, none of the others were hurt. While two of the women did what they could to stop Seng Long's bleeding, the others looked for help in a nearby village. Once in Khao-I-Dang, Seng Long gradually recovered. Armed with patience and willpower, and sustained by Handicap International's physiotherapy and encouragement, she eventually was able to walk, albeit with some difficulty, with orthopaedic appliances on both legs and two walking sticks.

I met Madame Seng Long when she had spent just under three years in the camp. Although her legs remained weak, and she often made use of a wheelchair which OHI had assembled for her, she had recovered psychologically and was strong enough physically to think of going back home. Her husband, her children and her life in Kompong Cham were waiting. She was ready to face them in her new condition, for there had been many letters between them, and the family knew what to expect.

One issue, however, which was crucial for her acceptance by Phnom Penh, had still to be settled – her politics. That was soon resolved. She clearly had had no contact with the resistance during her difficult recovery. As for her life in Kampong Cham, the more I delved into it, and into her reasons for coming to Thailand, the more politically inoffensive she appeared. I could see nothing to which Phnom Penh could object. One thing was clear, she had not fled the PRK from a distaste of the regime. She had left to seek treatment, and had planned to return home immediately after her intended cure. Her long stay in Khao-I-Dang was not something she had wished for, only her damaged legs had forced her to stay.

* * * * * * * *

February 1988. Back in Phnom Penh, I approached Mr. Uch convinced that he would have to agree: a person with a disability returning in a wheelchair was not a security threat. Also, I thought, Mr. Uch would not be blind to the prestige that the PRK would gain by approving the return of a humanitarian case. I was right. Despite some initial reticence, and a long discussion, he gave the green light. The political gains attached to the return had outweighed the risks. Incredibly, however, I learned that some officials in the Ministry of Foreign Affairs, and the Ministry of the Interior acting behind it, were still unconvinced, as was consistent with the government's inflexible policy of repatriation blockage. This, I hoped, would continue to be waived after Madame Seng Long came back, even if in 1984, one of my UNHCR predecessors in Phnom Penh had been disappointed to find that his one returnee (the first ever official individual returnee to Kampuchea), rather than being followed by others, turned out to be first and the last.[13] For the time being, I could only be sure that Madame Seng Long would be coming back.

While still in the camp, I had worried about Mr. Uch's possible refusal, but I never imagined that difficulties would come from the United Nations in New York. Madame Seng Long was almost ready for her return, when UNHCR Bangkok transmitted the UN's message: neither the Bangkok nor the Phnom Penh UNHCR offices could be publicly associated with the return. UNHCR was a UN agency. Any public participation of a UNHCR official in the return of a refugee to the Popular Republic of Kampuchea from Thailand, could be interpreted as *de facto* recognition of the PRK, a granting of international approval to an illegitimate political entity. If the return were to be publicly backed by UNHCR, there could be strong reactions – from the Khmer anti-PRK Coalition operating in Thailand under Prince Sihanouk, and from the main Western powers and China. Only with the establishment of an internationally recognized government in Phnom Penh, and the setting up of an internationally valid Repatriation Framework, could UNHCR be officially involved in returns.

The practical consequence of the message was that I did not accompany Madame Seng Long on any part of her journey back. I flew back to Kampuchea on my own and Madame Seng Long travelled later, accompanied by two Phnom Penh-based NGO staff who were returning from their break in Thailand, and whose involvement could not be seen as political. Isabelle and Claire worked with Handicap International and the French NGO, Enfants du Cambodge. When the three women arrived at Phnom Penh's Pochentong airport, I stood waiting with Monsieur Puy from the

---

13 See Wetterwald 2014:49 concerning the authorities' blockage of individual repatriation cases after the return of the elderly Mme. Suon Morn.

Seng Long, her family and the Kampuchean Red Cross upon her arrival in Phnom Penh.

Kampuchean Red Cross, Madame Seng Long's husband, her children and a few relatives. The plane touched down and came to a stop. The door opened, and I saw Madame Seng Long holding on to Isabelle and to Claire. We all watched in silence during her long descent from the plane, holding onto the railing. Isabelle, descending backwards, watched her every step, while Claire held her by the elbows from the back. She managed the last step into the tarmac and was helped into a wheelchair. In this her new condition, she was about to meet her family, her husband and children. Although her letters had explained what had happened, we all dreaded this first meeting. The initial moments were not easy, but once everyone had regained their composure, a group photograph captured the smiles that a family reunion called for.

Two weeks later, I joined the Kampuchean Red Cross to call on Madame Seng Long at her village. Isabelle from Handicap International came also. She needed to check that all parts of her home were easily accessible, and we all wanted to make sure that she counted with the authorities' support. Mr. Uch had been suspicious of the motivations of returnees. I, in turn, remained cautious of the authorities' approach.

We crossed the river by ferry, and as soon as we drove into Kompong Cham territory, we knew that security was a serious business. We got out of our vehicle just outside town, and met the local Red Cross delegation. They were waiting by the side of the road. Having greeted us, they pointed to a military escort whose seven members would be with us throughout the visit, armed at all times. The unexpected arrangements showed special concern for our security in an area which had faced some Khmer Rouge activism.

We wanted to look at the economic conditions to which Seng Long was returning. Walking briefly in Kompong Cham town, with the unavoidable seven-man escort at our heels, we could see that the townsfolk were just making ends meet, against the rundown buildings of the formerly prosperous town. For the time being, Isabelle and I agreed that Seng Long would be better off in the village, where the land, however poor, would provide. The following day, however, I was not so sure. The scenes I saw from our vehicle were not promising. Driving slowly in the heat, across the exhausted landscape of the dry season (it was March), we looked in the distance at the crumbling earthen dikes. They zigzagged in all directions before us, keeping the water-starved fields separate, the earth lying like sawdust abandoned by termites. As we drove along, the villages stood close to the road, each of them reachable by way of a small bridge that arched over the empty course of a waterless canal. By the wretched-looking shacks and under the colourless sky, the cows showed their bones and reached for the few visible tufts of grass. The emaciated sugar palm trees stood close by. Faced by such desolation, I wondered how our one returnee would be able to cope. But Isabelle was more clear-minded: Madame Seng Long was not alone, and her family and the villagers would know what to do. She would be provided for. Her family would make sure of that.

When we finally reached the village, Madame Seng Long was sitting in her wheelchair outside the family homestead, surrounded by relatives. Smiles were on everyone's faces. Isabelle went into the house to make sure that access was good, while I sat chatting with her, with the help of a Red Cross interpreter. Everything she said was positive, there was no criticism, no complaint, no mention of Khao-I-Dang. She said everything was fine.

Back in the village, Seng Long's family and neighbours, Kompong Cham.

19

THE IMPACT OF
LIBERALISING MEASURES

A Khmer woman prepares bundles of firewood for sale 1988.

My small office continued its routine work: regular monitoring visits to the displaced person projects, occasional meetings with Mr. Uch to discuss the possibility of more individual returns. But often, when faced with lack of progress on the return front, and looking back at our one and only achievement, Madame Seng Long's return, we could feel demoralized. Fortunately, some (marginally) positive developments concerning international efforts towards peace, provided an incentive to go on. Another boost came from the government's new liberalicing policies which, we hoped, would transform the environment into a substantially better place for the struggling local population, and for those in the Thai camps who would perhaps, eventually come back.

Opening up the economy (1988-1989)

I arrived in Kampuchea at a time when the PRK was fully engaged in a comprehensive liberalisation of its policies, a radical ideological shift and departure from communist orthodoxy, which a group of ambitious transformers had imposed, to ensure the regime's survival on the international scene. Among the innovative policies, priority was given to the economy. To improve performance in this field, rigid centralization and close control was replaced by a more open system which permitted economic initiatives by private citizens, promoted the creation of small-scale businesses, and encouraged all manner of commercial activity. The model probably followed the example of Vietnam, where liberal reforms had been introduced in early 1978, with encouraging results.[14] I saw evidence of the change in the most active market in town, the New Market, *Psah Thmay*. An endless variety of items were available there: food, soft drinks, beer, clothing, bicycles, motorcycles, tires, ventilators, all of which reached Phnom Penh from Thailand, despite daunting obstacles: uninterrupted fighting between government and resistance forces, and the widespread presence of landmines. As I could easily witness, the illicit trade was booming, and was taking place openly. Sitting one evening at a riverside restaurant, for instance, I saw black market merchandise being unloaded onto the embankment from a medium-sized boat, a few metres away from my table. Ironically, such activity was linked to the growth of the Khmer camps in Thailand, the bastion of anti-PRK forces. As the various coalition camps in Thailand had grown, and become semi-permanent settlements, so had smuggling into Kampuchea prospered within a stable system which benefitted military and civilian profiteers on both sides of the border. Years of war had generated the know-how to smuggle and sell goods everywhere inside Kampuchea, where goods travelled along routes where well-oiled payoffs made conditions safe for traders. In Phnom Penh, the goods were readily available in the markets or on the sidewalks, being offered in small quantities by persons of all ages.

Different generations sell cigarettes, Phnom Penh 1988.

14 The reforms were partly intended to make up for the financial losses which military responses to the Khmer Rouge along the Khmer-Vietnamese border had provoked. See Elizabeth Becker 1998: 436.

In the capital's relatively relaxed atmosphere, I could see trade picking up, bringing back to life some of the city's lost commercial dynamism, and pulling pedestrians, cyclos and bicycles onto streets where, up to very recently, only a very small number of official vehicles circulated. Low-level government employees or small businessmen sold goods to complement their limited earnings, while the poor found a way out in the food trade. They brought in their produce from the outskirts of town, where it was bought and sold at a profit. The people's inventiveness in making ends meet seemed to have no limits. A host of services were offered: fortune-telling and palm-reading by the women, quick-fix repair jobs or transport services by the men.

In town, some old family businesses were being revived: ice production and distribution, or the baking of bread which generated a chain of jobs for bakers, distributors and salesmen.

Not everyone benefitted from the new commercial freedom. I could see a lot of begging, practiced by war victims and other disabled persons, but also by children and many single women, some of them war widows. And outside the markets' many entrances, the cyclo-taxis stood idle, their large number and occasional fares only slightly diminishing persisting high levels of unemployment.

Cyclo drivers carry their clients' produce.

Bread being made and sold Phnom Penh, 1988.

Concessions to a princess – early signs of the PRK's monarchical revisionism (1988)

Changes in the economy were accompanied by a partial revival of Buddhist practice, and by a certain openness towards the monarchy, two processes which represented clear political gains for the PRK. As the example of neighbouring Thailand showed, reinvigorating Buddhism and the cult of kingship could serve as solid institutional props for the government[15], and a means of gaining international prestige.

Being aware that a more conciliatory image vis-à-vis the monarchy could yield important political advantages, the PRK softened its former absolute rejection of everything royal. Among the possible benefits, the PRK identified the opening of a line of communication with Prince Sihanouk. As recognized Father of the Khmer people, important player on the world stage, head of the anti-PRK Coalition, and a friend of China (the arch enemy of the Vietnam) the prince could help the PRK gain the international legitimacy

The persistent presence of the monarchy under the communist PRK: the Royal Palace Phnom Penh, 1989.

which the West and China denied it. A possible way of reaching him was through a PRK government official, who was also a member of the royal family. This was Prince Sihanouk's first cousin, Princess Lyda Sisowath[16].

---

15 The revitalization of Buddhism and the monarchy occurred in Thailand most significantly under the government of Marshall Sarit Thanarat (1957-1963) and later, in the period following the first ever and only effective experiment with democracy in the country (1973-1976).

16 Princess Neak Ang Mechas Sisowath Sovethong, 'Lyda' (1945-1994). Her father, Prince Sisowath and Sihanouk's mother (Princess Sisowath Kossomak) were full siblings. Prince Monipong had five wives and thirteen children; with his fourth wife Neak Moneang Son Sunneary, he fathered Lyda, the eldest of four full siblings, with one surviving sister at my time: Neak Ang Mechas Sisowath Pongneary, known as Lolotte.

I first saw Lyda in 1988 during a meeting of the Women's Association of Kampuchea, of which she was president. She held this humanitarian-political position in addition to her other roles: Deputy Secretary General of the National Front for the Salvation and Defence of Kampuchea, and Vice-President of the Kampuchea-Cuba Association. On that day, speaking in her high-pitched voice and slightly nervous manner, she pleaded persuasively for the hundreds of women who had lost their husbands in the country's succession of conflicts. The room was crowded with humanitarian agencies, many of which had been contributing financially to the Association's projects. During the break, I thanked Lyda for the invitation, and caught her interest by mentioning one UNHCR project which supported war widows by providing their communities with reliable sources of agricultural produce. Her response was immediate: she invited me to Takeo Province which she had represented in Parliament since 1981, eager to hear more about the project and about UNHCR's efforts to encourage repatriation from Thailand.

In Takeo, Lyda proved to be much more than a high-ranking official. She was three persons in one – a politician, a royal princess and, most interesting to my anthropologist self, an active spirit medium. I had studied spirit mediums in Northern Thailand as part of my postgraduate studies in the late 1970s, and Lyda's own practice in that field created an immediate understanding between us. She would later tell me the full story of her initiation as the spirit medium of her deceased royal ancestors. But just then, she chose to talk about her life under the Khmer Rouge, not however, without first commenting on the sinister background of our meeting place.

No location in the PRK was free from the spectre of the Khmer Rouge, and so it was with Takeo, the former Khmer Rouge Southwest zone. The area had been under the control of Ta Mok, leading Khmer Rouge military commander and prominent member of the leadership. Known as the 'Butcher', he was famous for the massacres that were perpetrated under his command before 1975 and, when Democratic Kampuchea came to power, for his role in directing murderous purges for the regime. Unlike other members of the DK leadership, he was never a victim of the purges, even when they became generalized practice. His position within

Ta Mok's former centre of operations, in the middle of a lake, Takeo.

Visit to Takeo. Back row: the Provincial Governor, Lyda and myself.

the leadership (at one point Commander of the Army) was solidly entrenched, as was his closeness to the supreme leader, Pol Pot. Once the PRK had taken over, he was arrested by Hun Sen's military in March 1999, and later charged with crimes against humanity. His trial, however, never took place, due to several postponements, ill health and eventual death in July 2006.[17] My encounter with Lyda and the Governor of Takeo, two representatives of the strongly anti-Khmer Rouge PRK, was taking place on the very spot where the residence and centre of operations of one of the most bloodthirsty Khmer Rouge commanders had once stood: an apparently unblemished and even idyllic small island, which was linked to the mainland by a narrow bridge.

Lyda turned to her own story. She had known the horrors of the Khmer Rouge period, but unlike many members of the royal family, she had survived. 'I was forcefully evacuated from Phnom Penh with my family. Having reached the border province of Battambang, I was separated from my husband and children, and never saw them again. My sister Lolotte and I resisted the hardship, but we had lost a lot of weight and were exhausted, the result of hard work in the rice fields, and little food. We were luckier than others, though. After a time of endurance, a sympathetic Khmer Rouge cadre took pity on us, got us out of our work brigade, and had us taken to a monastery close to the Thai border. We were never called

17 For further details, see Strangio 2014: 242.

back, and stayed in the monastery until the Vietnamese arrived. By that time, we were strong enough to make our way back to Phnom Penh.'

Lyda and Lolotte lived there in anonymity, but their neighbours soon discovered their royal identities, and in time, the news reached the government. It is not clear how the authorities initially contacted Lyda, but she, rather than her sister, was approached for employment, perhaps because of her former work experience in a government dependency, a passport-issuing department under Lon Nol's US-backed, anti-communist government. I would have expected such a former work profile to have excluded Lyda from PRK employment, but the PRK's need for qualified personnel probably helped cancel out the unfortunate association, as had been the case with many other PRK recruits. In any case, her royal association could not but be decisive in her recruitment. She explained, however, that once she was in, she kept questioning her choice: 'After joining the communist PRK, I was tormented by doubts. Not that the PRK's communism bothered me. I just didn't like some of its actions, like the way it dealt with the outside world – the Soviets, for instance. Actually, one time I went to Moscow officially to participate in a women's conference. I came back disappointed by the Soviet's non-committal attitude to Kampuchea and, once back in Phnom Penh, by the government's hesitations about how to react. I was upset by its passivity. Feeling unhappy about that, and about many instances of inefficiency inside the bureaucracy, I decided to quit. But my resignation was not accepted, they wanted me to stay. I stopped going to work all the same, remaining at home for eight months, with the government paying my salary regardless. They kept contacting me, asking me to return to work. But I really did not want to go back, especially since I kept receiving messages from the royal family in exile, who urged me to pack my things and leave. It was all very difficult. I didn't know what to do, but in the end, after much wavering, I decided to stay.'

As Princess Neak Ang Mechas Sisowath Sovethong, and Prince Sihanouk's first cousin, Lyda was in a position to liaise with the prince, and by that token possibly influence the stormy relationship between the PRK and the Thai-based coalition of anti-PRK forces. On the Phnom Penh side, she was connected with government officials of the highest order, among them her immediate superior, the Minister of the Interior, Chea Sim, and the then Foreign Minister, and future absolute leader of Kampuchea, Hun Sen. As for Prince Sihanouk, she had kept in touch with him through the years, despite the political differences between them and her own commitment to the PRK. The letter she wrote to him on December 20, 1984,[18] frankly expresses her disagreement with some of the prince's political options, while showing a wish to remain close:

---

18 See Norodom Sihanouk 1986: 407 for the French original (translated into English by the author).

'Oh Monseigneur, why must you, my beloved cousin, whom I have worshipped more than anyone else in my heart, why must you become the leader of these blood-stained monsters (i.e the Khmer Rouge[19])? You are admired by the people who consider you as their father. Why do you now betray them in this way? My heart bleeds every time I hear that you are siding with them, they the murderers of your innocent people... Oh, Monseigneur, what makes you associate with these bloodthirsty people? Beware, Monseigneur. Once the lemon is pressed, it is thrown away. When you were in Beijing, Ieng Sary had already shown off (with these words): "We have worked a lot for Sihanouk. Now, it's his turn to serve us, he will be our buffalo and help us cross the river (...)." Monseigneur, forgive these words which are perhaps too straightforward, but that's the way I am. Respectfully, your cousin Lola or Lyda, whichever you prefer.'

When Lyda wrote the letter, two years had passed since Sihanouk had become the president of the Coalition Government of Democratic Kampuchea (CGDK) within which the Khmer Rouge, Lyda's 'blood-stained monsters', had gained a new lease on life, with international blessing. At that point, the PRK could hope that Lyda's family links would translate into concrete political advantage.

* * * * * * *

Lyda performs as a medium at home in Phnom Penh, 1989.

The Phnom Penh leadership made a point of recognizing her value, and in that vein, made a major ideological concession by allowing her to exercise her skills as the medium of her royal ancestors. Lyda had in fact been operating as a medium at home for some time, acquiring a reputation for curing a variety of ailments. The various aspects of her practice, including the medical, interested me, but I was

---

19 Author's note.

mostly intrigued by her political mediator role. Promoting peace and reconciliation was not an easy task, she said, and only with the support of her possessing spirits was she able to attempt it. It was they who encouraged her in that direction, and gave her strength, both when they possessed her, or when they just spoke to her. All of them were her own royal ancestors and on the whole, they treated her well. Among them, her absolute favourite was without doubt Prince Si Votha, her paternal great grand-uncle.[20]

Prince Si Votha was known in popular lore as a royal revolutionary who had fought against French colonial rule. But historians affirm that he was in fact a disgruntled royal younger brother, who had fought for the throne against the claims of his elder siblings. His grudge against the French was that they had backed his elder half-brother, King Norodom, as legitimate claimant to the throne. The historian Chandler has recorded the interesting occasion, in February 1877, when four columns of troops, including French, Cambodian and pro-French Vietnamese elements, came to the hills of Ba Phnom in pursuit of Si Votha. The rebellious prince had established himself with his followers in the area, and started recruiting an army. Chandler leaves us with the picturesque image of the defeated pretender escaping on an elephant with a following of only a few men, then surrendering without a shot, and finally being pardoned within the terms of a general amnesty by the lenient King Norodom.[21] Lyda understandably never mentioned that version of Si Votha's struggle. Instead, she chose to emphasize her great grand-uncle's more attractive image as royal fighter for justice, and his romantic aura as lone rebel, fighting valiantly against the French. She considered herself Si Votha's intellectual heir, the Red Princess who had opted to operate from Phnom Penh's international marginality out of nationalist conviction, very much as *he* had acted in his time, from the margins of the state. She was proud to be descended from a man who, she was convinced, had fought to free her country from French control, one of the first Indochinese patriots and radical nationalists.

---

20 Lyda's connection with Prince Si Votha, her possessing spirit and great grand-uncle. Si Votha was the youngest son of King Ang Douang (reigned 1840-1860), a kind of venerable Khmer founding father, famous for trying to stand his ground in defence of a more autonomous Cambodia despite the threat of foreign encroachment by Siam or Vietnam. Ang Douang's eldest son was Prince Norodom (reigned 1864-1904), Lyda's great grand-uncle. Ang Douang's second son was Prince Sisowath (reigned 1904-1927), Lyda's paternal great grandfather. Following King Sisowath's death, his line inherited the throne, in the person of Lyda's paternal grandfather, King Sisowath Monivong (reigned 1927-1941). At his death, his son, Crown Prince Sisowat Monireth (Lyda's father's elder brother) should have been king, but the French decided otherwise, and gave the throne to the Crown's Prince's sister's son: Prince Sihanouk, Lyda's first cousin. Since Sihanouk's mother Kossomak had married a Norodom, from that time the Norodom branch superseded that of the Sisowaths (Lyda's branch) as holders of the Cambodian throne.

21 Chandler 1996: 119-120.

Lyda's great grand-uncle King Norodom: his equestrian statue at the Royal Palace.

Lyda had not always been enthusiastic about becoming a medium: 'Mediums are common in Kampuchea, but I never expected to become one. For one, I have always detested traditional Cambodian music – that 'ting-a-ling-a-ling type of music' used to get on my nerves…. The whole thing was very difficult. The eight months I stayed away from my government job was a period of great stress. First, I was tormented by doubts about the government, and then there was the mediumship business. One day, when I was alone, resting in bed, ready to fall asleep, the spirit of King Norodom approached me.[22] He spoke to me with great conviction and authority. He said: "you have important political work to carry out. You have been chosen to work for the country's reconciliation because you are pure of heart. You will do this by becoming a spirit medium. Your possessing spirits will give you strength. Your main possessing spirit will be the god Indra, who demands that you give yourself totally to his service. You will have to venerate the god by dancing in the traditional Cambodian way."' Lyda resisted. She told herself she would never become a medium, unable as she was to commit herself exclusively to Indra because she was married. In any case she was ignorant of Indra's rituals. As for dancing, she was forty-two years old. How could she find the flexibility required to perform? To these objections, the spirit of King Norodom answered simply 'ca viendra tout seul' – 'the gift will come to you of its own will'.

Lyda held her medium sessions at home, but one day, in early 1989, she obtained the authorities' permission to perform in the palace grounds. The event was to take place in front of the Silver Pagoda, where the ashes of several monarchs were kept in their respective urns. The revered site, like the rest of the royal palace, had been

22 King Norodom was Lyda's great uncle, see note 15 above.

carefully maintained by the PRK according to their policy to preserve the country's cultural heritage, one among a number of features which set them apart from the Khmer Rouge. Lyda invited me to the extraordinary ceremony, with the condition that I bring along my video camera, and film the proceedings. Camera at the ready, I arrived at the Silver Pagoda in the early afternoon, and found her standing by the equestrian statue of her great grand-uncle and mentor, King Norodom I. She greeted me and continued to check on all the last-minute details. As she squatted, I zoomed in. She was looking closely at the dozens of small flower arrangements, and decorated banana leaf cones which had been arranged in rows, and placed over wide carpets. Lyda stood up. The camera followed her as she walked towards a tall *chedi*, next to which the members of her traditional orchestra were busy dressing. She and the camera caught the men putting on their ceremonial costumes, white formal jackets over wide, dark blue *sampot*s, the traditional trousers which leave the calves and the feet uncovered. The zoom lens isolated the musicians' faces, which remained taut while the men finished dressing, and then showed their respectful devotion. Some were survivors from the pre-Khmer Rouge days, and knew her from before. She was their long-lost princess who, transformed as a medium, was about to perform an ancient rite. They were proud to provide the best of traditional sounds for her, and when Lyda approached, they sank to the ground and raised their joined hands to greet her, while she lowered hers, palm against palm, in their direction.

The ceremony started after sunset. A reflector provided enough light for the camera to capture Lyda in respectful prostration, immobile, with joined hands high above the forehead. Beyond, in semi-darkness, a row of monks sat crossed legged, chanting. Several guests moved quickly past Lyda from the right, their bodies half bent, their heads lowered in sign of respect. And when the monks stopped their chanting, and we heard the traditional musicians starting to play, we all knew that Lyda was about to be possessed.

She bent forward slightly, raised her joined hands above her head again, and paused. Slowly, she rose to her feet. The possessing spirit, an authoritarian prince, then forced her bare feet to stamp hard on the ground, to the beat of the orchestra. All eyes were on her, until the princely spirit left Lyda, allowing other spirits to enter. As possession followed possession, the music and Lyda's dancing quickened, mirroring the mood of each of the spirits. As the last one left, I zoomed in again on Lyda, now un-possessed, and down on her knees. She made a last sign of gratitude with her raised hands, and thanked the spirits.

Lyda trusted that news about the ritual would reach Prince Sihanouk, soften his attitude towards Phnom Penh, and perhaps make him more amenable to meeting the PRK. She knew of the prince's closeness to the supernatural, his use of omens, and his respect for mediums and astrologers. That facet of the prince was in fact

Lyda's ceremony took place by the Silver Pagoda, Royal Palace Phnom Penh.

well known, and serious foreign writers on Cambodia have confirmed it. For instance, Milton Osborne[23] mentions Prince Sihanouk's strong devotion to the spirit of Princess Nucheat Khatr Vorpheak, his royal ancestor, whose body was said to have been recovered in the late 19th century in extraordinary circumstances, when she was extracted from the stomach of a crocodile… Sihanouk was devoted to the spirit of that princess; he approached it occasionally as his advisor, even consulting it on matters of foreign policy through a medium. Osborne further mentions the prince's reliance on the advice of soothsayers concerning his own safety when moving from one residence to another. He notes Sihanouk's devotion to the remains of his beloved daughter Kanthi Bopha, deceased in 1952 at the age of four from leukaemia, and his practice of placing the urn containing the child's ashes by his bedside, as a means of protection during his sleep.[24]

Prince Sihanouk *was* sensitive to the supernatural and could therefore sympathise with Lyda's activities as a medium, but it was not clear whether news about the Silver Pagoda event ever exerted any influence on his attitudes to the PRK. In any case, Lyda's success in obtaining permission to perform a royal rite inside the royal palace was, in itself, a major achievement. She had managed to extract from the PRK leadership a strong signal of openness to the country's monarchical past

---

23 Milton Osborne 1979: 46.

24 When the Khmer Rouge had held Prince Sihanouk hostage at the palace, and he noted the disappearance of the revered urn containing Kantha Bopha's ashes, the KR, probably aware of the supernatural value which he attached to the ashes, assured him that the urn had been stolen during the Lon Nol days, blaming their enemies and former persecutors for the disappearance (Norodom Sihanouk 1986: 132). Although the KR had shown little respect for the symbols of royalty, they probably saw political advantage in distancing themselves from the urn's disappearance, at a time when they were about to use the prince as a source of international legitimation, with China's full support. At that late stage, the KR may have been advised by their Chinese mentors to respect the symbols of royalty in Phnom Penh for reasons of political convenience, a line they had themselves followed concerning the sacred Potala in Llasa, capital of Tibet. This reminds us of the Pathet Lao's instrumental respect for the integrity of Luang Phrabang and the king before they took power in 1975.

and, by implication, a readiness to speak to the other side. For only that reason, I felt I could add the Silver Pagoda session to Lyda's other political achievements, including those performed as a member of the National Assembly, the Women's Association, the National Front for the Salvation and Defence of Kampuchea, and the Kampuchea-Cuba Association.

* * * * * * * * *

Beyond its political significance, Lyda's spirit mediumship had a significant impact on the revival of Khmer classical dancing. The PRK had previously proscribed all art forms associated with the royal past, and Lyda's performances as a medium, which comprised traditional dancing as a central feature, had helped weaken persisting political resistance to a refined art form which was closely linked to the court. The resuscitation of the Phnom Penh School of Dance in 1988 cannot be ascribed to Lyda, but she surely contributed to create the context in which the Royal Ballet's revival was possible. And once the revival was under way, she was a constant source of support, including by developing close cooperation with a French NGO specializing in oriental dance as a spectacle. Lyda's own dancing cannot be said to have provided a model for aspirants; she was characteristically frank on that count, and willingly referred to her late entry into mediumship and associated dancing, as an important limitation to her art. But even her limitations were the basis for a further encouragement to the Royal Ballet. Being candid about her need for professional advice to make her performances meet minimal standards, she recruited as her dancing advisor and support one former member of the original ballet instructing team. Devoted to ballet and to Lyda's mediumship, the elderly expert became Lyda's permanent instructor, constantly attentive to ways of improving Lyda's movements and postures. She also assisted her before each performance, helping her in the complicated make-up process, and getting into

The rebirth of the traditional School of Dance Phnom Penh, 1988.

her very elaborate costumes. Lyda benefitted enormously from the old veteran's support, while her patronage to a recognized expert of the ballet at its peak was another signal that the art had to be revived.

The reinvigoration of classical dancing in Phnom Penh took place at the same time as it was being similarly revised in Thailand's Khmer refugee camps, also with inputs from members of the former Royal Ballet. It was clear even then, when repatriation still stood in the distance, that dance and music could eventually help understanding between the two sides. As a leading member of the Women's Association of Kampuchea, and reviver of a form of spirit possession of which classical Khmer music was an integral part, Lyda helped develop the institutional framework which, once peace was restored, would bring together the best exponents of Khmer traditional dancing, one important aspect of reconciliation.

* * * * * *

It is not clear that the government officials who approved the Silver Pagoda evening of royal ritual, including Ministers Chea Sim and Hun Sen, felt genuine empathy for Lyda's spiritual practices. Consulting mediums was common in town and in the villages, and those who gave their authorization were probably familiar with the practice since childhood, although they were not necessarily adepts. In any case, they were surely aware of the devotion which spirit mediums generally enjoyed, and of the political credit which the government could gain by being publicly associated with Lyda, both a spirit medium and a royal princess. They knew that respect for the monarchy, represented by the charismatic Sihanouk, and devotion to pre-revolutionary religious practices, including spirit-medium cults, were deeply embedded in popular consciousness.

Moving forward in time to the period that followed my departure, it is clear that Minister Hun Sen's personal sympathy for Lyda never wavered, giving her his full support until her death on October 9, 1994. According to Lyda's sister Lolotte, he often spoke about her in public, expressing his appreciation. When she became seriously ill, he offered her the government's financial support, grieved for her at her death and, together with other ministers, attended the royal cremation by which she was honoured at Oudong. The event was well suited to her station, for the old royal capital is studded with a number of royal funerary *chedi*, among them one that contains the remains of her paternal grandfather, King Sisowath Monivong, and those of her father, Prince Monipong. Thanks to her close royal connections and to her links with the PRK, Lyda continued to act until the end as a bridge between the two sides, including when the strong rivalry between the former enemies had been replaced in the 1990s, by a measure of coexistence.

In my time, in the 1980s, I knew Lyda for being outspoken, invariably frank in her opinions, and critical of the entire political spectrum; of Sihanouk (for his closeness to the Khmer Rouge) and of the PRK (for its inefficiencies). Given her independent-mindedness, and despite her links with the former PRK, I cannot help but wonder what she would have thought when, in the early 1990s, under a newly established royalist context, King Sihanouk, back in Phnom Penh, bestowed the title of *Samdech* ('Lord' or 'Prince') to several members of the former PRK leadership, among them the then second Prime Minister Hun Sen, President Heng Samrin, and the Minister of the Interior, Chea Sim. And after Sihanouk's new occupancy of the throne and eventual death, I cannot help but wonder how Lyda would have responded to the spectacle of the ancient Khmer royal house being reduced to being the legitimating instrument of a self-perpetrating, strongly authoritarian state.

The communists become Buddhists (1989)

The PRK leadership advanced its construction of a new image of itself by adopting a more open attitude towards the Buddhist Sangha. More than that, wishing to distance itself from the Khmer Rouge's almost total destruction of the monkhood, and from its own initial, closely controlled and distant revival of Buddhism, the leadership decided to show itself publicly as fully engaged with Buddhist practice. Taking observers by surprise, the highest levels of the PRK made a display of their devotion as practising Buddhists, occupying centre stage at a ceremony in which a set of historic Buddha relics were reinstalled in one of the city's most prestigious Buddhist landmarks.

Everything started at Wat Ounalom, the administrative centre of Khmer Buddhism, and residence of the country's leading monk. The famous relics had been placed there for safeguarding, following their removal from their original reliquary, perhaps during the Khmer Rouge period, or in the first years of the PRK. They were now to be taken back to their original emplacement at Seakmony *Chedi*, an emblematic Buddhist monument whose pale blue and cone-shaped outline had been for years one of Phnom Penh's distinctive landmarks.

Standing outside Wat Ounalom, I saw a group of officials, unexpectedly dressed in pre-communist formal white jackets, and the traditional *sampot*. They carried the relics with evident deference, with lowered heads, and placed them at the centre of a large float. Two elderly monks added other sacred objects, making the moving platform into the procession's centre. And when the procession got started, I spotted a second platform which showed a group of musicians playing traditional music in the lotus position. Next to them, a set of sacred manuscripts had been placed on an elevated stand. Throngs of people surrounded the floats, as close to them as they could without pushing.

Relics being moved from Wat Ounalom to Seakmony Chedi, 13 April 1989, Phnom Penh.

The procession's destination, Seakmony Chedi, rose high above the ground, its back towards the Phnom Penh railway station behind it, and facing east over a long esplanade that ran eastwards towards the river. It was a site of maximum visibility, a suitable location for a powerful symbol of religious resilience that had survived fourteen years of communist rule. The *chedi* had suffered years of abandonment, but now stood some thirty metres above the ground. It was ready for the event in its elevated position and pristine pale blue, with a temporary set of steps which led up to where the relics were to be placed. On the esplanade, a crowd of men and women squatted, holding their hands together in the direction of the *chedi*, in a sign of devotion. The monks were also there. Sitting cross-legged under a dais, they waited for the procession to reach its destination. Not far from them, a group of women put some order to the mountains of food which the laity had donated as

Above and right: Regained Buddhist devotion in communist PRK: devotees look towards the elevated *chedi* from the esplanade, against the background of the railway station.

Politburo member Say Pouthang (left) and Minister Hun Sen (centre) fill the monks' rice-bowls.

a form of merit-making. The offerings were as abundant as those that had been offered to the monkhood in pre-communist days.

I walked towards the *chedi*. As the procession approached, I caught sight of a wide red and gold parasol. A royal parasol? I wondered. The crowd prevented me from seeing who was walking under it, but when I came closer, I could barely take in what I saw. It was Foreign Minister Hun Sen carrying a silver offering bowl in Buddhist devotion, advancing slowly behind President Heng Samrin and the Minister of the Interior, Chea Sim. The former paragons of communist orthodoxy had gone Buddhist! They walked under the parasol right up to the *chedi*'s steep flight of steps, and following four monks, ascended to the top, and prostrated themselves before the shrine.

The PRK leadership and their wives later made a further public display of Buddhist sentiment, when they squatted respectfully to listen to the monk's chanting, and joined the devotees by filling the monks' rice bowls.

The elements of political opportunism and manipulation were evident, but the communist leaders' enactment of standard Buddhist practices were so convincing as to suggest previous Buddhist schooling, and perhaps even sincere engagement. For instance, Strangio[25] has noted that Minister Hun Sen was exposed to Buddhism from his early years, having been sent from his village to a monastery in Phnom

25 Strangio 2014.

Penh at thirteen years of age, when he paid for his upkeep by carrying food and running errands for the resident monks. That early learning surely helped him perform convincingly as a Buddhist in 1989, regardless of his inner convictions.

However that may be, this was one of the first significant public demonstrations of the government's new approach to religion, which favoured both the presence of high-ranking government officials in Buddhist ceremonies, and an intensified participation of monks at official gatherings. However, the innovation did not put an end to the party's control of religion. This was enforced by government officials who personally spelt out the rules, regulated Buddhist practice in each monastery, and reiterated the message that entering the monkhood was not to be encouraged among the young, for the war continued unabated, and young men had to be available for army service.

President Heng Samrin and Ministers Hun Sen and Chea Sim descend from Seakmony Chedi.

Below: The PRK leadership listen to the chanting of monks by Seakmony Chedi: President Heng Samrin, Politburo member Say Pouthang, Minister Hun Sen (squatting at the front), Minister of the Interior Chea Sim (standing). Ms. Bun Rany, Minister Hun Sen's wife (squats at the back, extreme left).

I asked myself why the PRK had decided to participate in the reinstallation of those particular relics, in that particular *chedi*. As Marston's work suggests[26], over the years, Seakmony *chedi* represented a key aspect of Phnom Penh's identity, being saturated by a multiplicity of political and religious associations, including those that link it with Prince Sihanouk. It was indeed he who ordered the *chedi*'s construction in 1957, to celebrate the creation of his own 'modern' Cambodia, established under his leadership to mark the country's independence from French control. The monument had been designed by a group of monks; its purpose, to exhibit a set of Buddha relics which Sri Lanka (the recognized centre of Buddhist excellence) had donated to Cambodia to commemorate the 2,500th anniversary of the Lord Buddha's Birth, Enlightenment and Nirvana (*Visakabochea* in Khmer[27]). To enhance the importance of the 2,500th commemoration, the Sri Lanka-based World Federation of Buddhists had redefined Visakabochea as an international festival, and in Cambodia, this was elevated from being a merely local event (carried out only in certain monasteries and at court) to a religious celebration of national significance. As this happened, the relics and their *chedi* became national referents and sources of national identity, comparable in that role to other nationally significant sacred objects of the Buddhist world, such as Sri Lanka's Buddha Tooth Relic, inside its shrine at Kandy, the Emerald Buddha in Bangkok, or the precious Phra' Bang in the royal capital of Laos.

In their search for a new image of themselves, what better example than the 1957 conspicuous display of religious conviction could the PRK leaders wish to follow? We know that the PRK was perennially in the shadow of Sihanouk, based on the prince's continued role in international negotiations concerning the country's future, and on his key influence on the PRK's own political survival. The PRK, therefore, had everything to gain from following the example of a man who was nationally and internationally recognized as the Cambodian people's 'Father', and whose indestructible international authority since the 1950s rested partly on his continual activation of the monarchical and Buddhist traditions. The consolidation of Sihanouk's power by the memorable collective performance of 1957 provided the PRK with a recipe for the strengthening of their own case.

We can speculate that some of the older members of the PRK may have witnessed the 1957 events. They were the right age. President Heng Samrin was born in 1934, Minister of the Interior Chea Sim in 1932, and Veteran Politburo member Say Phoutang in 1920. Others like Hun Sen, who was born in 1952,

---

26 See Marston in Alcedo, Ness and Maier (ed) 2016.
27 Held annually at full moon of the 6th lunar month, between April and May.

would at least have heard of the festivities' grandiose scale, and known that the *chedi* had become a major national shrine and centre of all Visakabochea celebrations, not only under Sihanouk, but later, under the Lon Nol regime, right up to the Khmer Rouge takeover. The PRK knew that the monument was deeply embedded in popular consciousness, and that a ceremony centred on it could effectively serve the double purpose of transforming its own image, and consolidating its power. However, the 1957 events were not something the PRK could have replicated. Imitation would have been ideologically problematic (the original celebrations had been too deeply permeated with royal ritual), some of its aspects were impossible to reproduce (the king and queen had participated throughout) and the expenses of the original had been prohibitive[28]. Something more modest was required, which nevertheless could yield results similar to those which Sihanouk had achieved. In the end, the PRK opted for a simpler reinstallation of the same set of Buddha relics, in the very *chedi* which Sihanouk had inaugurated in 1957.

Negative aspects of liberalisation, the trend towards greed and inequality

The impact of the PRK's liberalicing trend on the economy was raising standards in town, but it was doing that selectively. While it left the poorest groups largely untouched, to families with some material resources and personal determination, were able at least reach the point where they could make ends meet. The new measures also gave rise to isolated, but highly visible pockets of wealth, which showed in a number of renovated colonial villas pointing to the emergence of a new class of rich Phnom Penh buyers, to the birth of real estate speculation, and to the creation of small islands of privileged living for the city's political elite. The liberalicing policies were as much indicative of the leadership's self-serving tendencies, as they were a sign of its concern for general standards of wellbeing.

The trend started when private money entered the country, and was fueled by a handful of visionaries who sensed that the Peace Process was moving forward, and foresaw that the eventual international recognition of Kampuchea would be accompanied by an influx of UN agencies and NGOs who would pay very high rents. Whether reached by way of business acumen or political flair, the gamble to invest in the emerging real estate market in Phnom Penh flourished. The first signs of the trend were accompanied by the promise of financial advantage for potential

---

28 As Marston notes, the lavish preparations included temporary structures crowned by immense awnings to seat 10,000 guests; pavilions to house visitors from all provinces; the ordainment into the monkhood of 2,500 men from the civil service, the armed forces and the laity; spectacular fireworks showing the image of the Buddha; acting out by the Royal Ballet of scenes from the life of the Buddha; the liberation of prisoners; travel arrangements to Sri Lanka for King Norodom Suramarit, Sihanouk's father, to receive the relics personally; provision of a fleet of planes to transport the relics to Cambodia.

Contrasting means of transport mark the birth of unequal Phnom Penh, 1988.

investors from outside the country. Many of them were oversees Cambodians who had thrown in their lot with the PRK, had gambled on the regime's stability, and were of the opinion that, despite the international political deadlock, the Phnom Penh government was there to stay. Also, business delegations from Thailand started travelling to Phnom Penh, following the Thai government's conciliatory policy towards its communist neighbours, which culminated in January 1989 with Thai Prime Minister Chatchai Choonhavan's pledge 'to transform the Indochinese battlefield into a market'.

The arrival of substantive investment was soon accompanied by the first signs of enrichment, the conspicuous display of wealth and a consequent, ever-growing level of visible inequality. There were flagrant although isolated instances of extravagance; for example, the insulting presence of luxury vehicles, such as a brand-new Mercedes Benz coupe which, I was astonished to see, had been parked by the morning market.

Such displays of wealth were particularly provoking in the context of enduring transport difficulties. Although the Khmer Rouge's almost total decimation of private means of transport was a thing of the past and, ten years later, motorbikes could be seen everywhere, carrying entire families, their goods and their animals, not everyone could afford a motorized two-wheeler. Now as in the past, therefore,

In the countryside, bicycles had been a key resource in the early post-Khmer Rouge period, but continued to be used, including to transport very heavy goods, 1988.

people in town and in the countryside had to rely on personal inventiveness. Bicycles were to carry piles of stuff, or to pull carts loaded with all manner of produce, while trucks transported fruit and vegetables, all stacked together with people who were forced by the low ceiling to double up. This was surely the context to drive around in a Mercedes.

People and merchandise are stacked together and transported in a truck.

Conspicuous markers of social differentiation such as luxury cars, however, had been known in the past. They had been a feature during Prince Sihanouk's royalist government in the 1960s, and under Lon Nol's republic in the early seventies. But in 1988, they pointed to a future of greed, materialism, corruption and displays of wealth among the elite which starting in the late 1980s, would be strengthened in the 1990s, and become the hallmark of Hun Sen's Cambodia after the year 2000. So much would be plainly evident on my return visit in 2016.[29]

Liberalisation and the repositioning of the political elite

It was not clear at the time what kind of debate had been unleashed within the government, by the process of liberalisation. I assumed that discussions had been highly animated and even confrontational, given the very significant consequences they entailed. Firstly, changes in the PRK's model of society, and a modification of former priorities of equality and social justice. Secondly, changes in the distribution of power among the highest levels of the political elite, and an alteration of criteria regulating access to posts within the government and the bureaucracy. Thirdly, possible negative reaction by citizens to the government's ideological *volte-face*. Fourthly, the unpredictable reactions to the country's transformation by the West and China, on the one hand, and by the Eastern bloc and Vietnam on the other.

It was only much later that the specialized literature clarified the issue[30], identified the protagonists and spelt out the impressive political and economic advantages they

29 See p.280-284 below.
30 See Strangio 2014: 21-41 for an exhaustive discussion.

accumulated.[31] The literature also showed that the liberalisation process did not entail, as could have been expected, a confrontation between a strong, intransigent, communist old guard and the modernizers. Vickery[32] indicates that long before the new measures started being implemented – only two years after the creation of the PRK – a large part of the Administration was in the hands of non-revolutionaries, survivors from the non-communist Sihanouk and Lon Nol periods. Also, within the national Assembly of 117 members, almost half had non-revolutionary backgrounds, and even in the cabinet where revolutionaries dominated, the ministers of Education, Health, Agriculture and Information had non-revolutionary backgrounds. Such personal histories did not entail lack of loyalty to the regime, but did permit an ideological laxity and casual approach to communist ideology, which eventually facilitated at least tacit acceptance, if not enthusiastic adoption of a new definition of priorities. I could not fail to remember that Princess Lyda, like many civil servants (including the President of the Red Cross, Madame Plech Pirun) had worked under the strongly anti-communist Lon Nol regime but had never seen her loyalty questioned, while her contribution to the PRK continued to be highly commended.

A curious hybrid was in the making. Against the background of the unresolved military and international conflict, the communist state was furthering an on-going process of change that included, a more open economy, respect for private property rights, the approval of a new foreign investment law[33], and as noted above, the revival of Buddhist practices and of aspects of its royal past. In April 1989, the logic of change even led to the abandonment of the country's communist identity, when the 'Popular Republic of Kampuchea' became 'the State of Cambodia', with a new flag, national anthem and coat of arms.

While it carried out its ideological, political and economic backtracking, the new Cambodia state allowed for increasingly accentuated nepotism, corruption and inefficiency in government circles, for continuing economic profiteering by the elite while the growing trend of socio-economic inequality remained unchecked. Also, being caught within the logic of its Vietnam-supported origins, the state continued, sometimes willingly, sometimes not, to submit to Vietnam's imposition of its military presence and to the meddling of its advisors at key levels of government. By so doing, it helped maintain one of the main impediments to an international resolution of the conflict. As we shall see below, only with the departure of Vietnam would real progress commence.

---

31 Prime Minister Hun Sen developed a formidable power base for himself in Kompong Cham, while his rival, Minister of the Interior Chea Sim did the same in Battambang. However, they each operated from different ideological standpoints: Chea Sim maintained unswerving adherence to the communist order while Hun Sen 'in the late 1980s had emerged as one of the PRK's most vocal advocates for economic liberalisation and was a driving force behind the constitutional reforms of 1989' (Strangio 2014: 47).

32 See Strangio 2014: 40.

33 See Vickery 1984: 242.

20

A DIFFICULT PEACE PROCESS
(October 1988-September 1989)

PRK/UNHCR High-level meeting

On October 21ˢᵗ, an urgent telegram from UNHCR Geneva asked me get in touch immediately by phone, immediately! Never more than then, was the lack of fit between the realities of Kampuchea, and outside expectations more apparent. As if the Geneva world of flawless communications could apply in Phnom Penh! The city had a total of two telephone lines which operated out of the Post Office, where they were used by all callers, the general public and *all* ministries. Making a call required hours in a queue which generally moved forward smoothly, without long pauses; but when one of the ministries required one of the lines, or both, then the queue had to stop. The interruption was not always brief, and at times, closing-time came before one's call could be placed. In that case, there was nothing to do but to come back the next morning, get back into the queue where one had left it, and wait once more. Eventually, one reached the booths, without however, being sure of getting through, since the line could be busy, or those being called could be absent.

On that day, however, telegram in hand, and hoping that written proof of my urgent need would make other callers give me precedence, I rushed to the Post Office. No luck. I had to stand in line for longer than ever: my place in the queue was kept for me from one day to another, for no less than seven days, seven days of mounting anxiety during which incoming wires insisted that I get on the phone. I was in the queue from Saturday October 22 to Friday October 28. When l finally got hold of the receiver, the confidential message was that Jean Pierre Hocke, the UNHCR High Commissioner Hocke, was to attend a meeting on repatriation. The venue was near Paris. The information had to be kept confidential. I was asked to attend. I was requested to head for France immediately. I did what I could, and made arrangements to leave on the next fortnightly flight out, hoping it would be on schedule. But it was not. As my luck would have it, the flight was cancelled. I was left with no alternative but to drive five hours along the pothole-filled road to Ho Ch Minh City, with an hour's wait at the Khmer-Vietnamese border. I finally reached Ho Chi Minh City in time to get on the Air France flight to Paris.

Once in Paris, I learnt by phone that the meeting was between the High Commissioner and Prime Minister Hun Sen. The event could not be made public for the time being, lest contact between the Head of a UN agency and the Prime

Minister be construed by the PRK's international opponents as a UN recognition of Kampuchea. Only after the fact could the meeting and its outcome be made public.

It was not unusual for a country representative such as myself to participate in a meeting between the country's authorities and UNHCR top management. In this case, there was an additional reason: the interagency competition that pitted UNHCR against the International Committee of the Red Cross (ICRC) for leadership concerning repatriation. UNHCR Geneva had learnt that the ICRC had instructed its Phnom Penh delegate to be present at its own separate meeting with the Prime Minister, at the same venue. UNHCR could not be seen to be less. To have me attend signaled to Prime Minister Hun Sen that UNHCR considered involvement with repatriation as much of a priority as the ICRC.

Neither UNHCR nor the ICRC appear to have got much out of the discussions. To UNHCR, the Prime Minister spelt out his reasons for stalling on repatriation in terms similar to those which Mr. Uch had used with me in Phnom Penh: 'repatriation equals destabilization', 'we cannot risk political sabotage'. The arguments were made in a tone which excluded compromise while, on his side, the High Commissioner could not deliver what the Prime Minister most wanted – recognition by the UN. Instead, he gave Hun Sen vague assurances of UNHCR's continual availability. I had expected some kind of breakthrough, at least concerning individual returns, but these were left to 'discussions in Phnom Penh on a case-by-case basis', while all UNHCR had transmitted was a serious intention of putting its know-how and resources at the service of repatriation 'when the time came'.

I returned to Kampuchea in mid-November. As I waited for the return of the PM's delegation from France, I shared my pessimism with a Geneva colleague in writing: 'The meeting was inconclusive, and I fear that the Ministry might harden its position. It is as if a year's patient perseverance has been thrown out of the window – months attending interminable meetings, trying to achieve some flexibility, and now this. I am waiting for the Prime Minister's delegation to return from France this coming week. I'll see then where we stand, but looking back at the months spent in Phnom Penh, I ask myself, have all these efforts really been for nothing?'

* * * * * * * * * * * *

It had been unrealistic to expect any real move on the repatriation front before any genuine political progress was made. But the meeting had put UNHCR in the Prime Minister's radar, and in the end, it had placed us as the top international repatriation player. Two months later, in January 1989, laborious negotiations led finally to the inclusion of Kampuchea in all international discussions for a political settlement, on a par with the other parties to the conflict. Phnom Penh then agreed to consider repatriation a necessary component of a comprehensive solution. The time was ripe for UNHCR to move, and so I approached the Ministry of Foreign Affairs, proposing an agreement which spelt out for the first time, officially and on paper, the practical arrangements for individual returns. As had occurred with UNHCR's statements at the high-level meeting in France, the document excluded all wording that could be interpreted as recognition by the UN. The text emphasized the purely technical nature of the proposed cooperation. It satisfied UNHCR by establishing it firmly as the lead agency for repatriation in Kampuchea, and contented the ministry by giving Kampuchea a kind of international respectability, while leaving concrete action regarding repatriation for the future.

The Agreement on Logistical aspects of Repatriation was signed by Vice Minister of Foreign Affairs, Long Visalo. My colleagues Marco Cabassi and Robyn Blake attended (at the back on the left), together with the ICRC and World Food Programme Representatives.

Returns are blocked, I focus on other issues

The agreement did not focus specifically on the immediate repatriation of single cases. But I had hoped that having signed the document and, given some improvement in international discussions on Kampuchea, permission for the return of individuals would be more easily granted. Not at all – approval continued to be postponed. I took stock of that, and with some frustration and a touch of anger, I decided to call less frequently on Mr. Uch, and spent more time overseeing

UNHCR's projects for internally displaced persons: commune-level schools, village-level dispensaries, tuberculosis prevention-centres, or prosthesis projects for landmine victims. These continued to make a difference, as did several weaving and tailoring production units, and the distribution of buffaloes to groups of women whose husbands had been injured by landmines or killed.

However, the projects' large number of locations, spread over a wide area made proper follow-up difficult for me to manage, even with the help of my assistant Robyn, most of whose time was taken up by administrative work. But as political circumstances changed, the authorities, who had for years refused to authorize the expansion of the UNHCR office, finally agreed to concede an entry visa for a third staff member. For the PRK, still caught in deep resentment against the West, China and the UN, this miniscule expansion seemed a major political concession. For us, it was a major gain. It meant more people to cover more ground, and the injection of new energy in the person of a new colleague, Marco Cabassi from Milan, accompanied by his wife Elizabetta. As the change coincided with the end of Robyn's two-year term, her replacement then joined the team: Marilyn Virrey, from the Philippines. Robyn's long stint in Phnom Penh had left her exhausted, the result of recurrent health problems, the limited satisfactions of her job, the frustrations of social life in confined Phnom Penh, and the deficient hygiene of the Monorom Hotel. Robyn had held the fort together with my predecessor Jean Claude, when for months and despite all their efforts, only few things had moved. The strain of long periods of dissatisfaction had taken its toll.

Revitalised by Marco who concentrated on the projects, and by Marilyn who dealt with the office, the team functioned with improved good spirits, and-as our capacity for work grew, we added more displaced-person projects to our visiting and monitoring agenda, including those in security-sensitive areas. As always, previous

The authorities finally allow the expansion of our office. With Marco Cabassi (left) and Marilyn Virrey (right) we were now three.

Typical project follow-up outing: UNHCR, the Red Cross and a military escort. Mr. Net Tun from the Red Cross, and Marco Cabassi from UNHCR stand on the far left.

official clearance from a complicated bureaucracy was required, but I noticed that in the slightly improving political climate, and with Marilyn's convincing Philippines-style networking, authorizations for project visits were more rapidly approved, or at least, less frequently postponed or cancelled. As Marco took over the follow-up of our out-of-town initiatives, I joined less often, but in all cases, as had happened since my arrival, each outing counted with the obligatory presence of an armed escort and the Kampuchean Red Cross.

The authorities were careful to authorize visits to areas they considered safe, far from heavy military concentrations and serious fighting. It was widely known that PRK forces and their Vietnamese allies operated along the distant Khmer-Thai border, along the 'bamboo wall', which had been built to prevent the various anti-PRK contingents from gaining territory eastwards, in the direction of Phnom Penh. As for us, circulating in the new, more sensitive areas which we were allowed to visit, the frontline was still very far, a long way west. Coming across military personnel there was a very rare occurence. Usually they were Kampuchean, although we did come across the odd Vietnamese brigade, deployed near our projects to help clear the fields of landmines, or repair the roads. In Phnom Penh, I had never seen even the shadow of one Vietnamese soldier, and only rarely a Kampuchean.

The Vietnamese soldiers we met were invariably friendly, and hardly fitted the descriptions of a formidable force that was holding back the peace. From our rare encounters, it was not clear how these inoffensive-looking road-repairmen could be part of a major invading military force. I personally had little direct evidence of

Vietnamese brigades repairing the roads near our projects.

their presence in the countryside, and despite the international news that reached me, I had remained skeptical of a really massive Vietnamese military presence. But when, following Hanoi's announcement of the troops' withdrawal, I saw the scale of preparations for the farewell ceremonies and after that followed the departing Vietnamese contingents, I had to accept the evidence of a massive deployment.

The Vietnamese troop withdrawal (September 1989)

In July 1986, the USSR had pressured Hanoi to reduce its military presence in the PRK. This was a major development, coming from Vietnam's longtime benefactor, and full supporter of Vietnam's presence in Kampuchea, but had little effect. However, the USSR renewed its pressure when its internal political and economic conditions deteriorated, and its foreign policy changed. From being combative vis-à-vis China (the leading force of the anti-PRK camp), its policy sought to normalize relations with its rival, and cease onerous commitments abroad, including in Vietnam. But since the USSR and Hanoi remained committed to the PRK's survival, and to a hoped-for international confirmation of its legitimacy, the withdrawal kept being postponed, Vietnam's troops remaining in place as a negotiating tool.

One thorny issue was indeed the PRK's legitimacy. The Phnom Penh authorities, in place since 1979, considered themselves the rightful representatives of the Khmer people, a claim strongly denied by the various China-supported, anti-PRK factions that operated on Thai territory – Prince Sihanouk's Coalition of Royalists, Republicans and the Khmer Rouge. These groups, many of them militarized, squabbled endlessly among themselves as they vied for dominance. But all shared the conviction that the PRK, a mere Vietnamese puppet, could not be a party to the Peace Process. The irreconcilable views held by the two camps were an intrinsic part of a polarized reality in which the Coalition and the PRK confronted each other militarily along the Thai-Kampuchean border, and were at each other's throats in a bitter and never-ending propaganda war.

The related issues of the PRK's status and its survival had been squarely faced when, on 4 December 1987, Prince Sihanouk met the then Foreign Minister of Kampuchea, Hun Sen at Fère-en-Tardenois (France). The unpredictable prince surprised everyone when he subscribed to a communiqué which stated that a political solution for Cambodia should include the Phnom Penh authorities. This accorded the PRK the status of legitimate interlocutor to the anti-PRK Coalition. As could be expected, China opposed the move, and Sihanouk backtracked. But the prince's readiness to meet Hun Sen, and issue a conciliatory joint statement, was a landmark. It ensured that all parties gradually accepted the idea, that once the Vietnamese troops had withdrawn, Phnom Penh would be included in all international discussions. This made sense, since Phnom Penh had been in control of the territory for the best part of ten years. Eventually, the PRK's full participation was ensured, notably in the so-called 'JIMs' – the Jakarta Informal Meetings (December 1987 to July 1988) – which brought together the PRK and the coalition factions for the first ever joint discussions on a Peace Settlement.

Such developments brought in high expectations of progress, which grew even more when Thailand, up to then unequivocally hostile to Phnom Penh, voiced its intention to replace political confrontation vis-à-vis communist Indochina with commercial links. But even more momentous was Hanoi's announcement in January, that its troops would be withdrawn from Kampuchea in September.

* * * * * * * * * * * * *

The September troop withdrawal was big news in Kampuchea and was widely publicized by Phnom Penh's propaganda machinery. A proliferation of panels and posters kept repeating the message that all Kampucheans should be eternally grateful to Vietnam for its help over ten long years of unflinching solidarity and generosity.

Propaganda panel proclaiming friendship between Kampuchea and Vietnam.

Vietnamese soldiers on
the way to their ships,
Kompong Som.

Messages of Kampuchean gratitude were transmitted in a succession of ceremonies which a profusion of national flags, military uniforms, and fervent speeches merged emotion with official formality. In the streets of Phnom Penh and in Kompong Som, the country's foremost port, busloads of departing soldiers responded to the cheering crowds. They smiled enthusiastically, and waved small Khmer and Vietnamese flags from their trucks.

In Phnom Penh, the main farewell ceremony was celebrated at Chaktomuk Theatre. President Heng Samrin and several ministers presided, flanked by the departing Vietnamese High Command. They sat with their backs turned to a large panel which summarized the objective of the event in Vietnamese and Khmer script: 'Medal presentation ceremony for the units of the Voluntary Vietnamese Forces who have successfully concluded their International Proletarian Mission in Kampuchea, and are going home'.

QUYET THANG! Victory! A triumphalist conclusion to ten years of fighting.

Vietnamese soldiers receive a 'krama' while their officers are given a painting of Angkor Wat, the symbol of Khmer greatness.

The triumphant message of a victorious military force departing after a good job done was repeated at all stages of the celebrations. Everywhere, a generous display of propaganda posters confirmed the fact that the 'heroic Vietnamese military had concluded its fraternal duty to sustain Kampuchea in its glorious road to victory'.

The festive atmosphere and the messages of success did not reflect the grim realities which the Vietnamese army had faced. The estimated death toll was 23,000, the equivalent of just under half the US army casualties during the Vietnam War (50,000 wounded and 10,000 missing).[34] Despite their laundered uniforms and smiling faces, the exhausted men were being withdrawn after years of pressure from a collapsing Soviet Union which could no longer provide them with financial support. Long gone were the days in the mid-1970s, when Vietnam had been able to respond to Khmer Rouge military provocations along the Vietnam-Kampuchean border, later sending 100,000 men thundering into Kampuchea to eradicate the Khmer Rouge, and give the newly created PRK full military support. Significantly, Vietnam showed the importance it attached to Phnom Penh by entrusting full supervisory powers to a prominent member of the political leadership, Le Duc Tho, founder of the Indochinese Communist Party, anti-colonialist revolutionary, and standing member of the Indochinese Communist Party. Le Duc Tho was known internationally for the role he played in 1973, during the negotiations that led to the Paris Peace Accords on Vietnam. His international prestige was at its highest following the signature of the Accords, when he was nominated but refused the Nobel Prize for Peace, a distinction he gained alongside his American counterpart, Henry Kissinger. Le Duc Tho was Chief Advisor in Kampuchea in the critical period when the PRK was being established.

---

34 Strangio 2014: 40.

Vietnamese forces
board their ship as
they leave Kampuchea,
Kompong Som.

Local and international political factors explained Vietnam's invasion of Kampuchea, its prolonged stay in the country and the eventual withdrawal of its troops. But there was one factor which kept being mentioned by the international media, diplomats and some PRK functionaries: Khmer recruits to the army had needed additional training before they could be trusted to fight against the anti-PRK Coalition without Vietnamese backing. This was evidently an additional reason for the Vietnamese military to have overstayed, over and above Hanoi's political calculations. Also, it gave credence to the claim, made by PRK critics, that the brunt of the fighting against the border-based anti-PRK Coalition had been carried out by Vietnamese soldiers. If that was the case, the numerous signs of appreciation which the PRK displayed in September 1989 were well founded.

Khmer-Vietnamese interaction after the troop withdrawal

Did the authorities' public pronouncements of thankfulness to Vietnam reflect what most people felt? If there was some warmth towards the departing men, I suspect that it was accompanied by a certain restraint. For there was (and still is) in Kampuchea, a deeply rooted anti-Vietnamese animosity, and this was bound to have inhibited strong expressions of appreciation. But beyond that, the pros and cons of Vietnam's presence vied against each other in people's minds, and resulted in a strongly ambiguous collective response.

On the one hand, there was no unanimous sigh of relief when Vietnam's troops boarded their ships at Kompong Som. Many Kampucheans knew that Vietnam had helped keep the country safe, and was leaving it weakened. And as the spectre of the Khmer Rouge lingered on in people's minds, the fear circulated that without Vietnam's protective shield, and with the country's military capacity much diminished, the Khmer Rouge might return.

On the other hand, certain aspects of Vietnam's presence were frankly criticized. For instance, officials I knew well, shared in private a strongly felt resentment against the many Vietnamese advisors in the Phnom Penh ministries, their invasive style, superior manner and controlling methods. Also, they deplored the allegedly large number of Vietnamese newcomers who, they said, were being encouraged by Hanoi to cross over to Kampuchea and settle. The newcomers, they said, seemed to meet few obstacles on their way in, and were known to make regular use of the bus service that linked Ho Chi Minh City to Phnom Penh.

That specific complaint seems to have been shared by ordinary people, and I heard of episodes of aggression against newly arrived Vietnamese who were accused by locals of threatening their means of livelihood. As far as I could see, tensions arose mostly between the Khmer and newcomers, while relations with long-established Vietnamese families were reportedly stable, both ethnic groups coexisting peacefully, perhaps even being pushed into solidarity by the new settlers.

Regular Phnom Penh-Ho Chi Minh City bus line.

The state faced a difficult dilemma. It had to respond to the complaints of its Khmer nationals, and avoid unnecessary friction with the nationals of its recognized Vietnamese mentor. To the extent that it was lenient with the settlers, the Cambodian state was acting differently from past Phnom Penh governments, who had been wont, almost by tradition, to face a given crisis by targeting the Vietnamese as the origin of all evils, transforming them into legitimate objects of public odium. Various governments had resorted to this tactic: Sihanouk's post-colonial monarchy, Marshal Lon Nol's anti-communist republic and Pol Pot's Democratic Kampuchea. At times, political manipulation had resulted in episodes of such violence, that large numbers of Vietnamese civilians had perished. Among the victimized Vietnamese subgroups, fishermen had often been targeted. Being more than the Khmer, fishermen at heart, the Vietnamese had opted and continued to opt to live in their boats, where their visibility made them vulnerable to accusations of attempted fish-trade monopoly by local or national power-holders in need of a scapegoat.

That did not happen under the PRK, and relationships between the Khmer and well-established fishermen, and other groups whose subsistence also centred around the provision of food, seemed to be reasonably smooth. The same could be said for the sizeable number of Vietnamese petty traders who could be seen mingling and competing freely with the Khmer in Phnom Penh.

At a higher economic level, restaurant owners of both groups operated in a spirit of mutual respect, while Vietnamese restaurants often maximized their

Kampucheans and Vietnamese wearing a cone-shaped hat on the river with a line of low-lying Vietnamese fishing boats in the background.

acceptability by catering to Khmer as well as Vietnamese clients. Next to the Central Market, for instance, a small Vietnamese 'Café-Restaurant' announced in both Khmer and Vietnamese script, a wide variety of high-quality Vietnamese *nem* and *chaiyo* (spring rolls), beer, cream-covered cakes and sweet tea. The café was run with remarkable efficiency by the Vietnamese owners. Their daughters acted as waitresses and were always impeccably turned out, in Vietnamese dress. Loud

Vietnamese and Khmer mingle as vendors and clients in Phnom Penh, 1988.

discotheque music completed the scene, while the harmony between the Khmer and the Vietnamese was confirmed by two posters, one showing the Vietnamese imperial palace at Hue, the other featuring classical Khmer dancers.

The Khmer and Vietnamese interacted smoothly at many levels. As for the state, its indebtedness to Vietnam required a policy which sustained smooth inter-ethnic relationships as a priority, regardless of negative stereotypes, and the occasional explosion of anti-Vietnamese sentiment. The state needed to strike the right note in a difficult inter-ethnic balancing act.

21
PEACE IN SIGHT

Mass repatriation: a key aspect of the Peace Plan

The Peace Process gained momentum when Australia's Foreign Minister, Gareth Evans launched an appeal for the creation of a Transitory Government – the Interim Administration for Cambodia – under UN supervision. The proposal required my full attention, for it included the repatriation of the 370,000 camp-based Khmers in Thailand who, it was specified, would be entrusted to UNHCR in the coordinating role. Apart from that, the ambitious proposal aimed at transforming Kampuchea into a viable democratic state, by means of a massive military/civilian UN operation which would conclude with internationally supervised, countrywide elections. The plan included the demobilisation of all fighting forces (abandonment of weapons, concentration of the demobilised in designated locations, provision of job-related training courses), and entrusted the maintenance of peace to an international civilian police force, acting alongside multinational military contingents.

Response to the clauses that concerned repatriation was generally positive: Sihanouk's coalition, the PRK and the Vietnamese authorities all agreed in principle to the returns, although, as expected, there was still in Phnom Penh a group of opponents who continued to fear that counter-revolutionaries could infiltrate returnee groups. As for the document as a whole, the Phnom Penh authorities and the people of Phnom Penh generally gave their assent. But there was one important concern: Sihanouk's Coalition had included the Khmer Rouge among its negotiators, and it was feared that the group would use its position to strengthen its influence, and perhaps even return to power. The fear that the group would undermine the process was amply confirmed years later by the various disruptions which the group attempted, including during the UN-organized elections in May 1993. Given the enthusiasm which the elections had generated, the political cost of disrupting them had been expected to dissuade the Khmer Rouge from intervening. But intimidation took place all the same, when threats against voters on election day were combined with sporadic shooting. After the elections, Khmer Rouge attempts to undermine the process persisted, remaining a factor until as late as 1998. The fears that Phnom Penh expressed in my time were fully justified.

Pioneering repatriation preparations and security risks

The mass return was not expected immediately. It in fact took place between 1993 and 1994. But once the Phnom Penh leadership had accepted the concept, it asked that preparatory work begin immediately. In a reversal of government policy which had systematically limited our work, my three-person team – Marco, Marilyn and I – was asked to get started. At the working level, however, old attitudes died hard, and the familiar top-down, suspicious-of-the-UN approach, continued to appear. All the same and at our insistence, we were granted authorization to visit regions beyond our UNHCR project areas. For each visit, we fought to get the required permits. These were approved each time, but always in the spirit of a special concession.

Up to then, our repatriation work had been limited to single persons returning to one location, such as Madame Seng Long. We now had to sketch out a plan for thousands of families who would be settling all over the country. My team of three was clearly too small to deliver, and I asked for a reinforcement of six from the Kampuchean Red Cross. Thus equiped, we agreed on our main objective, to determine the reception capacity of different locations. We had no difficulty in determining the available supply of health and schooling facilities. But when it came to the complex issue of land, I decided to recruit Francois Grunewald, an agricultural expert with years of work in the country. He assessed the land's productive potential and legal status, and showed that a relative abundance of productive land was available.

But he also pointed to a major obstacle: the widespread presence of landmines. We knew what that meant – more war victims. The problem was particularly acute in the western region, close to the Thai-Kampuchean border, where much military confrontation had taken place. The area was adjacent to the returnees' main point of entry into the country, where a large proportion of returnee families was expected to settle. We thought hard about safer alternative entry points and roads, but concluded that all possible avenues of access required extensive landmine clearing, a massive deployment of technicians, and an extended timeframe which would inevitably delay the return, perhaps considerably. The same applied to the rice fields, which none of the warring factions had spared as ideal sites for explosive ordinance.

We concentrated our surveying efforts in Battambang and Pursat, the country's westernmost provinces, along the Thai-Kampuchean border. Until then, security risks had excluded all visits by foreign civilians. Our trip was therefore an absolute first for foreign humanitarian workers like ourselves. As for travel arrangements, our long-standing cooperation-cum-competition with the International Red Cross led us to organize a joint mission. ICRC and UNHCR flags, tied to our vehicles, and our logos and those of the Kampuchean Red Cross, provided a symbolic humanitarian shield which, we hoped, would make us safe. But the authorities would have us take no risks,

UNHCR, ICRC and KRC vehicles and military escort in the first ever humanitarian mission to Battambang.

and made available a truckful of armed soldiers for our protection. This was accepted by all, albeit with reluctance by the ICRC, whose principled commitment to neutrality among all warring parties, tended to outweigh concern for their own security.

With escort and all, we headed west through areas which were still under Khmer Rouge control. The drivers' and our own nervousness increased when potholes and cracks on the road made us slow down, for we knew that speedy driving could minimize risk. The threat seemed real enough, for we represented the Peace Process which the Khmer Rouge opposed. However, concern with security did not prevent us from looking closely at our surroundings. As we moved on the unpaved road, leaving clouds of dust behind us, we caught sight of a richer Kampuchea than we had ever seen, the red earth and solid wooden houses reflecting an unexpected prosperity. This increased as we approached Battambang, the country's second largest city. Once there, we could see nothing that would signal the damage of war. Contrary to expectations, we faced a neat outlay of wide, tree-lined streets, and fine villas. Not only had we driven unscathed through potentially dangerous territory, we had reached a centre of former prosperity which stood solid and complete, a long cry from the war-scarred reality of our imaginings. Our fears had been baseless, we had reached Battambang town.

A brief meeting at the Governor's Office on the logistics of repatriation was followed by a visit to the returnees' expected point of entry, fifty kilometres away, at the border town of Sisophon. Across the Thai-Kampuchean border, Sisophon faced the Thai town of Aranyaprathet, for years the centre of border relief operations for the displaced Khmer, including those living in Khao-I-Dang camp, where I had found Madame Seng Long. Sisophon was the main gateway into the country, and for that reason, a place to visit. But even more atrocious road conditions, and uncertainty about the presence of landmines, made a visit premature. The governor's technicians, however, helped fill in the missing elements in a key chapter of our developing Repatriation Plan.

The peace process and the humanitarian agencies

Political progress internationally and the prospect of peace and returns had a strong, impact on all humanitarian agencies in Phnom Penh. It gave UNHCR a primacy in repatriation matters, gave other UN agencies and the International Red Cross a prospect of permanence and even expansion, and rewarded the Phnom Penh-based NGOs for their tenacious support of a previously marginalized Kampuchea. I noticed that irreversible political progress had given rise to a new feeling of solidarity among all agencies, even mellowing past polarization between those who strongly supported the PRK, and those that did not. In this new hopeful Phnom Penh, all differences seemed to have been put to rest.

As for the Thailand-based agencies, they were confronted with a different kind of issue: the possibility that mass repatriation could cost them their jobs. They therefore started to consider following the returnees to Kampuchea, and working for them there. However, this required some adjustment to their political perceptions of the PRK. When I had visited Khao-I-Dang in early 1988 in search of a repatriation candidate, the staff's opinions vis-à-vis Phnom Penh had varied from indifference, to reluctant understanding, to frank hostility. The more intransigent had even accused all Phnom Penh-based humanitarian workers of encouraging the survival of the 'illegal Phnom Penh government'. Critics did distinguish between Phnom Penh NGOs and UNHCR as a UN agency, but politically, my small Phnom Penh-based team was placed by the most critical in the same bag. For this minority, we were traitors, working with the enemy. These opinions, I knew, resulted from prolonged exposure to a political reality our critics could not control: years of Chinese and Western support to the unsteady Coalition of Royal/Republican/Khmer Rouge political and military forces; prolonged UN recognition of the coalition; systematic channeling of most of the aid for Cambodia to the border camps; the constant battering of propaganda.

With news that the Peace Process was progressing, such political perceptions started to crumble. And as political flexibility spread in the camps, humanitarian workers sought more information about Kampuchea, and began to consider coordinating with Kampuchea-based NGOs until, eventually, a group of border NGO representatives travelled to Phnom Penh, a welcome first step towards cross-border cooperation.

Within this trend, discussion seminars were organized in Bangkok to bring together opinions and expertise from both sides. I also participated, contributing my team's recent findings in a surprisingly cooperative context where Phnom Penh-based agencies were being sought for the information which only they could provide. The border agencies needed the data to prepare camp populations for the return, and those who planned to follow their beneficiaries into Cambodia needed the information to prepare for possible future jobs. The days when they could focus single mindedly on assisting and protecting the camp population were numbered.

The agencies' visits to Phnom Penh and those of an ever-growing number of humanitarian, diplomatic and commercial delegations diminished our isolation. But our initial positive reaction gradually changed into forced abnegation – the country was being subjected to an invasion of forces which we could not control. Never was this sense stronger than when a UN mission reached Phnom Penh. Seventeen UN technical experts reached Pochentong airport with a typically UN ambitious time-table in which the conditions for the return were to be evaluated in a few days.

When the mission left, it was clear that plans were being made for the expansion of the UNHCR Office in Phnom Penh, from my three-person outpost, created to secure UNHCR's foothold in anticipation of a future prominent role, to a major office that would manage hundreds of staff, and coordinate all activities connected with mass repatriation. The expectation that UNHCR Phnom Penh would be growing dramatically was already on the table in early 1989. And in 1990, the time to actually expand had come, as it was now certain that UNHCR would be at the helm of one of the largest repatriation movements ever, within the framework of a massive UN Peace-Keeping Operation. Within UNHCR, the stiff competition for posts with much higher gradations in the hierarchy than those to which I could aspire, was one signal that my time in Phnom Penh had come to an end.

Departure

As I prepared to leave, all Phnom Penh old-timers in the UN and NGOs met with an unexpected novelty: the authorities now allowed us to live outside the hotel ghettoes, and rent separate accommodation. Marilyn, still in charge of administration in our office, left her one-room existence at the Monorom Hotel, and rented part of a house that belonged to the editor of a local newspaper. Marco and Elizabetta chose to stay in their bungalow at the Samaki. I decided to wait in mine, while new premises for our office were being refurbished, in a spacious former private clinic. When this was ready, the era of UNHCR's narrow working conditions in our two Monorom Hotel rooms had come to an end. The clinic was larger than UNHCR's working arrangements then required and had sufficient space to provide me with a new home. I therefore left my Samaki bungalow in early 1990, a move which not only confirmed my imminent departure, but marked the end of an era in which recent UNHCR Heads of Mission had lived in the forced but comfortable Samaki confinement.

Working and living in the former clinic gave me a welcome sense of being my own master, out of the foreigners' ghetto. It also allowed me to rediscover the value of privacy which had largely been absent from my former living arrangements. Once the new place's gate was shut, I was in my own space, away from the close proximity of bungalows inhabited by other agencies. Work wise, the available space gave our activities a new dimension, away from the cramped, insalubrious conditions of the two-room office at the Monorom. The size of the building reflected UNHCR's changing status, as did its large, well-tended front garden, which separated the building from the enclosing walls and the street. It was part of a new UNHCR chapter to which I did not belong.

I had left the Samaki, but I still organized my farewell party there, by the swimming pool, in a space which was part of a reality that was about to vanish, but where all guests would feel at home. My office still consisted of only three people, Marco, Marilyn and me, but still, I was the Head of a UN agency, and this required a level of formality which was expected by the attending guests, government and embassy officials, and the humanitarians NGOs, the UN agencies and the ICRC. As tends to happen at a time of departure, the food, the drink and the official speeches created a feeling of togetherness. Among those present, there had been casual acquaintances, competitors and even rivals, but also many allies and friends. Each one of them stood separate, with their own individual expertise and political choices, but they also were part of a group of old-timers, who had shared a fleeting but significant moment in history that was now giving way to a more durable, more stable reality.

My time of confinement and uninterrupted subjection to political control was coming to an end, while I watched the government's policies opening up day by day. And yet, the country's international isolation remained. Flights out of Phnom Penh to Bangkok were as infrequent as ever, and continued to follow the round-about route via Vietnam. As had often been the case in my three years in Phnom Penh, the flight I chose for my departure was cancelled. But I was firm, the time had come to let go, and so I made arrangements to be driven to Ho Chi Minh City where I would be boarding the flight to Bangkok. I packed my trunks on the new office's wide terrace and, with the help of Sam, the office driver, loaded them on the back of a truck. Sam had been the first Khmer to welcome me upon arrival at Pochentong airport three years before, had spied on the office and reported on my movements, but had now become a close collaborator, almost a friend. Driving out to Vietnam with him on 28 August turned out to be the best way to leave. In three years, I had grown fond of the country and the people, and moving gradually out of Phnom Penh and Kampuchea, while looking at the fields from the truck's front seat, helped soften the blow. The potholes this time went unnoticed, as the stark scenery of under-populated Kampuchea absorbed me. On the other side of the border, the full impact of the Vietnamese crowds confirmed that I had really left.

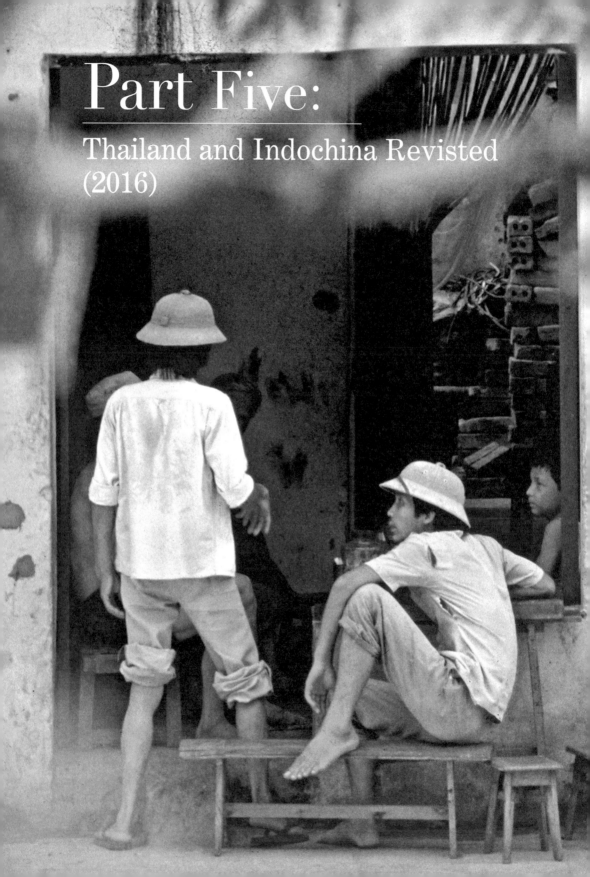

Part Five:

Thailand and Indochina Revisted (2016)

22

THAILAND
Economic continuity and
Monarchical-Buddhist stability

Twenty-six years after I left Phnom Penh and Southeast Asia, I boarded the American Airlines/South Korea flight to Bangkok at Mexico City's Benito Juarez airport. High-rise buildings and infernal traffic similar to those I had just left behind awaited me in the Thai capital. I had first seen it in 1972, and since then, the sprawling city had continued to evolve steadily in the same direction, according to the logic of unequal development: first-world urban growth in the capital and larger towns, third-world progress elsewhere.

I skipped Bangkok and headed immediately for the North, my stamping ground during my PhD research days, in the late 1970s. Chiang Mai was as I expected, bigger, noisier and with more traffic than I could remember. But I was shocked when I left town and headed on public transport to my old village, Ban Panya Chomphu. The village, where I had lived and worked on my thesis for the best part of two years, was no longer self-contained and rural. It had become a Chiang Mai suburb, its sturdy houses speaking of middle-class prosperity. The small wooden house on stilts where I had lived had gone, as had the grounds of which it was a part – the Health Station, the lotus-flower pond, the grass and the trees. All that had vanished, bulldozed over and replaced by cement and the Saraphi Bowon Hospital.

I found my former landlady living nearby, enjoying a comfortable retirement in a largish house with a wide porch and terrace, shaded by a thicket of *lamyai* trees – the picture of middle-class suburban comfort. Like the village, she had been transformed. From being a provincial government midwife, born and bred in Thailand's Northeast,

My house and the grounds of the local Health Station in 1987 (right) bulldozed over and replaced by the Saraphi Bowon Hospital in 2016 (left).

Opposite page: A Hanoi tea-shop in 1985, inviting but out of bounds for Westerners, a far cry from the easy access of today in Vietnam and elsewhere in Indochina.

The image of the Buddha is everywhere in Thailand an unquestioned object of devotion. The Buddhist Sangha and the monarchy otherwise continue to function as the Thai state's pillars of stability. (Photo taken at Doi Suthep, Chiang Mai)

she had become in speech, in dress, and in the house she occupied, a well-to-do retired professional, according to the channels of upward mobility in an area where the economy had not ceased to expand since my time.

The transformation of Ban Phaya Chompu illustrated the positive side of development, but I could not forget that chronic poverty continued to plague other areas, including my landlady's birthplace, the Northeast. Nor could I fail to remember the country's other less positive continuities, including in the political sphere. With the exception of the period between 1973 and 1976, a new version of authoritarian government, military or civilian, had reappeared over the years, presenting itself invariably in the trappings of democracy.

In addition, the Buddhist Sangha and the monarchy continued to be objects of strong devotion throughout the country. They also operated as highly effective state instruments of legitimacy and social control, which were reinforced by laws which condemned any behavior indicating disrespect to the monarch. Following the death of King Bumiphol on 13 October 2016, strict *lese majeste* laws started being applied in exacerbated form under his son, King Vachiralongkorn, fueling previously unimaginable scenes of political mobilization, which sought to reform the heretofore untouchable institution. The unprecedented protests, however, were put down by strong measures of state repression, leaving the throne solidly in place, although its prestige had been seriously dented internationally, and within a small minority inside Thailand.

In the wider regional context, we shall see that the questioning of this pillar of Thai stability took place at a time when a similar, recently reestablished Buddhist-monarchical edifice enjoyed full unquestioned solidity in former communist Kampuchea, now transformed into the Buddhist Kingdom of Cambodia. Similarly in communist Laos, Buddhist-monarchic ideas and practices had been selectively revived, albeit in limited form. The various ideologically dissimilar states had found a common political boon in the same ancient, persistently revered Buddhist/monarchical traditions and practices. And even Vietnam had sometimes resorted to royal/religious figures of the past within its own distinct religious tradition.

23

VIETNAM
Economic liberalisation and Communist orthodoxy

Crowded Quan Su Pagoda, Tet 2016.

Hanoi: 1985 and 2016 compared

The transformation of my village in Thailand surprised me, but that was nothing compared to the disorientation I felt when I reached Vietnam. I had first known the country in 1985 when, having left my first UNHCR post in Argentina, I had settled in its Hanoi office as Deputy Representative. Functioning in a peculiar isolated mode which the then strict authorities had imposed, the office coordinated, from its Hanoi confinement, the delivery of assistance to camp-based Kampuchean refugees in South Vietnam, and oversaw, through its Ho Chi Minh City-based 'Working Group', the historical Orderly Departure Programme. This allowed Vietnamese citizens to leave the country safely, rather than join the ranks of thousands of Boat People who were escaping the austerities of the then hardline communist state.

I had not been back for thirty-two years, and this time around, I was able to be fully part of its reality without a single barrier to stop me. Unlike 1985, I could move freely, walk and drink coffee wherever I wanted, enter any restaurant and order a meal, do anything that came to mind, without a nagging feeling that I was breaking a rule, or was being watched by the security services. After all these years, the strict confinement in which I had lived came forcefully to mind, heightening the sense of unrestricted movement which this new Hanoi was giving me. I had to take into account that I was no longer a UN official; I was just a tourist. But if my condition had changed, Hanoi had been completely transformed. Instead of the severity I remembered, austere and inward-looking, there was everywhere an almost palpable lightheartedness.

I had timed my visit to coincide with Tet – Vietnamese New Year. Hanoi was at its most festive and welcoming, as if all doors everywhere had been thrown wide open; even those of Trung Tuu, the enclosed compound where I used to live. I found it still facing the same small lake; the sign at the entrance, next to the gate, still read 'Diplomatic Compound', and the logos of several NGOs showed that westerners continued to be housed there. However, the guards in the large guardroom at the gate were unexpectedly relaxed, and let me in without asking questions. Of course, their casual approach was partly due to Tet (they were celebrating with food and drink), but there was more than that. The old single-minded concern with strict control and imposition of rules was gone. The presence of the state, though still palpable, had mellowed.

The same was also true at one of my former favourite spots, the Quan Su Pagoda, the Temple of the Ambassadors. Full access was given to a crowd that filled it to the hilt; inside, all temple buildings and altars were impeccably kept, and the intensity of feeling was everywhere. The diverse outfits of the visitors had replaced the drabness of the past, reflecting a new and freely displayed prosperity. No longer a gathering place for elderly women, there were people of all ages, young women and men.

I had entered the same pagoda during the Tet celebrations of 1985. What a contrast! The visit then had been an exceptional incursion into Vietnamese life, accompanied by a sense of intrusion into a reality that was normally out of bounds. Most visitors had been modest, elderly women. But I had been startled by the unusual sight of beggars at the entrance, and inside, by the unexpected presence of what were clearly members of the old bourgeois class, men as well as women. As if reviving their former identities for only that day, the men had worn a suit and a tie, the women an *ao zai* – the traditional tunic, which at a time of strictly observed dress codes (black pantaloons for the women), I had never seen in public. Tet had allowed on that day a

Devotees of all ages, women and men, flooded Quan Su Pagoda at Tet in 2016.

glimpse of what remained of the old social order. By contrast, 2016 showed the smart attire of the new Vietnam, a crowd of men and women who dressed as they pleased.

The rare sight of an *ao-zai* during Tet 1985, Quan Su Pagoda.

After a few days, I started seeing Hanoi as never before, as an integrated whole. In 1985, the city had appeared before me in the shape of an unassembled puzzle, whose separate pieces seemed to stand separately, with no relation to one another. Also, the city had seemed unreachable, living as I did, in the confinement of my foreigners' ghetto. Guarded and well-fenced Trung Tuu had effectively kept me and all other foreign officials, in a state of isolation. Whenever the official car drove me into town, all I could grasp was a fleeting passing image of one or other of its pieces. From the moving confinement of the official car, the Vietnamese crowd could only be sighted at a distance. I used to peer from behind the car windows, seizing snippets of reality on the way to the office, as we drove through, or around, the anonymous mass of bicycles. All I got from that and other drives, was a collection of blurred glimpses, caught in a hurry; and in the evening, I was back into the bounded reality at Trung Tuu.

In time, however, the authorities allowed me to use a motorbike, and then, I could drive among the bicycles and see who was in front of me, or beside me. I could go to a park and stop for a walk, or visit a market, or visit Hoan Kiem Lake gardens, where friendly teadrinkers, seated at low tables on tiny stools, would invite me to join them. There was real contact there. Well, to a certain extent. The customers, who were as interested to chat as I was, would lower their heads, and ask in a whisper where I came from. My few Vietnamese phrases were enough to reply, until, inevitably, a policeman would ask me to leave. Such contacts were never enough, but they were well worth the trouble. In time, I became bolder, and discovered places where I could stay longer without being asked to move on.

Such was the stuff of my old Hanoi, constructed out of small excursions and fleeting contacts, its separate pieces all the more precious for being so difficult to reach. In contrast, my 2016 revisit was made up of entirely free movements which allowed me to pull my collection of images into a new, nicely integrated whole.

Hanoi's composite identity

One evening, the heart of town at Hoan Kiem Lake was ablaze with lights. Strings of coloured bulbs spanned the road that encircled the lake; flowers were everywhere.

Affixed to the front of a tall building, a fatherly Ho Chi Minh holds a child and looks down benevolently on Trang Tien luxury mall.

An endless line of brand-new cars and four-by-fours paraded slowly, driving towards the farther side of the lake, near the Trang Tien Plaza, a first-world mall which offered a display of luxury shops, and international fashion brands. I reached it on foot. Across the street from the mall's entrance, I saw the unexpected: from the height of a brightly-lit panel, Ho Chi Minh, the highest symbol of the revolution, was looking sympathetically at the consumers' paradise, while embracing a child.

Down the road, reminders of the country's colonial past stretched before me, all of them flood lit. French-named establishments, destined for the rich and up-market tourism, such as the Café Lautrec, fitted in well with the architectural testimonies of French Vietnam – the Opera House of 1901, and the famous Hotel Metropole, in my time the very dilapidated Thong Nhat and home to a number of UNHCR pioneers who had lived there long before my time. The Metropole was now transformed into a symbol of colonial splendour. Inside, to add a historical touch to the air of nostalgia, the hotel walls displayed carefully framed black-and-white photographs. One showed the decisive Battle of Dien Bien, Vietnam's victory over French colonial forces, from an unexpected angle, with the wife of the defeated French Military Commander, General Christian de la Croix de Castries, holding on anxiously to a telephone just after the battle, listening hard to the latest news. Of course, celebrating Vietnam's historic victory did not exclude feeling sympathy for the French Commander's wife. But I missed a sign specifying that Dien Bien Phu was the culmination of Vietnam and Ho Chi Minh's thirty years' struggle for independence.

French colonial nostalgia: polished old-time sedans parked by the Hotel Metropole Hanoi.

The Presidential Palace, formerly the residence of the French Governor General of Indochina (completed in 1906).

As to the hotel itself, its magnificent presence showed Vietnam's capacity to put an end to French colonialism without eliminating everything French, its willingness to restore the buildings of the past to their original state. Apart from the Metropole and the Opera house, many other examples of colonial Hanoi had been maintained: the famous mix of Vietnamese and French architecture in the former Louis Finot Museum (the Vietnam History Museum since 1958), the boulevards lined with French villas, the Ministry of Foreign Affairs and the former residence of the French Governor General.

At Tran Tieng Plaza and other similar luxury malls, the communist state was accommodating pragmatically to a globalized world where the priority is to sell. But it was also enjoying the fruits of that other, older flexibility, which the Vietnamese have exercised from time immemorial when absorbing elements from the outside and making them theirs.[1]

Franco-Vietnamese syncretism. Inaugurated in 1932 by the École Française d'Extrême Orient, the building houses the Vietnam History Museum.

---

1 See Mus P: 1972.

Ho Chi Minh and the party's extraordinary achievement, after long years of anti-colonial struggle, was an independent Vietnam. It was also the preservation of a city which had denied nothing of its past, neither the beauty of colonial architecture, nor the testimonies of its darkest moments. Displayed in a number of well-kept museums, were the carcasses of B.52 American warplanes, photographic evidence of the Americans' bombing of Hanoi in December 1942, and at the Hoa Lo Colonial Prison, evidence of the torture perpetrated by the colonial regime on its opponents.

An aspect of French colonialism: militants accused of poisoning the French garrison on 27 June 1908 Hoa Lo Prison.

A taste of inequality: palatial villas for the very rich

When I visited Hanoi's surrounding areas, I recognised nothing. All I could see was a network of highways with buildings of ever-increasing height,

The anti-US struggle: Hanoi Central Post-Office destroyed by American B.52 war planes, 21 December 1972.

and other malls. But least expected of all, was a succession of villas, one bigger than the next, which spoke of new levels of inequality that in 1985 would have been beyond one's wildest imaginings. The most spectacular examples of personal wealth

Thanh Thang Palace on the Hanoi-Hoa Luu highway road, Ninh Binh Province 2016.

were to be seen on the Hanoi-Hoa Luu road; ostentatious affairs, some of them extraordinary palaces, which dwarfed the surrounding low-roofed housing, typical of Vietnamese urban and rural living. Among these, Thanh Thang Palace stood out for its scale and unprecedented opulence.

Some other examples of entrepreneurial success.

The palace, with two identical baroque buildings, stood by the side of the road, named after the owner's sons. Do Van Tien was the name of the fifty-two-year-old architect and cement tycoon who had them built. That was in 2016, but as I write these lines in 2022, the Google site shows that the two structures have been dwarfed by a third, more massive dome-covered palace, reminiscent of a Roman basilica. A friend in Hanoi tells me that the new building houses a three hundred-seat cinema with a gold-plated ceiling, while Google places the total cost of the site at between 300 and 400 billion Vietnamese Dong.[2] Thanh Thang Palace is unique in its excess and extravagance, but I saw many other lavish examples of entrepreneurial success on that, and other roads.

The ostentatious buildings could be seen from afar, some on the edge of the highway, which in the height of incongruity, also displayed symbols of the Communist Party. Placed at regular intervals, dozens of red flags and posters bearing the hammer and sickle, announced the Party's impending Twelfth Conference. They were everywhere, interspersed with the image of Ho Chi Minh, this time in the role of supreme symbol of communist authority, rather than as benevolent overseer of the liberalized economy, as I had seen by the Trang Tien Plaza.

Hanoi contradictions: Communist Party flags and propaganda posters stood on either side of a main avenue into the city, contrasting with the occasional luxury car.

2 https//www.oddiycentral.com/architecture/Vietnamese business

Alongside the rapid car traffic, were more rudimentary means of transport.

Apart from the highways, the same Communist Party placards could be seen off the side roads, protecting that other Vietnam, the country of rice fields and simple folk, who could be seen pushing or riding their own very different means of transport.

Such images of extreme social inequality, endorsed by a now flexible Communist Party, should not have surprised me. The transition from policies that fought for equality and modest standards of living, to ones which favoured prosperity with inequality, had already been initiated in the mid-1990s. One writer put it clearly at the time: 'Official egalitarianism, in so far as it existed, has been abandoned'[3]. But what I had seen in Hanoi in 1985, pre-dated those policy changes by ten years. The dramatic contrast between then, and what I was looking at in 2016, provoked a strong reaction, especially when endorsed by the ubiquitous figure of Ho Chi Minh. To see the evidence of change is different from reading about it at a distance.

Ho Chi Minh: legitimator of the state's contradictions

In 1985, Ho Chi Minh was Vietnam's undisputed symbol and reference point. In 2016, his image had been given new uses, stretched to justify the strong contradictions that the economy's liberalization had brought in its wake. His figure was everywhere, exerting unquestioned authority, and giving a stamp of approval to all aspects of Vietnamese economic and political life. His image varied to fit different legitimating needs: in the high-tech environment of luxury malls, he was Uncle Ho, portrayed in softly-penciled sketches, the benevolent elder who protects

---

3   Bereford and Mc Farlane 1995 58 (quoted in Jerdal and Rigg 1999:45) in Evans (ed) 1999: 35-60.

the nation as his own child; in Communist Party venues, he was the revolutionary who appeared against the strident red and hard contours of propaganda posters; and in the former Ho Chi Minh City, Saigon, he was the authoritative statesman, sculptured in bronze, who embraced all contradictions of first-world neo-liberal excess.

For many decades, various aspects of his life and character had been used to consolidate his reputation in Vietnam and outside. In a process of careful editing, certain episodes of his life were deleted (the purges of Trotskyites and 'bourgeois' nationalists, widespread repression during the 1955-56 agricultural reforms[4]), while others were emphasised. For instance, his almost priest-like austerity, his scholarship in classical Chinese, his literary merits as poet and essayist, his linguistic competence (French, English, Russian, Cantonese and Mandarin), his internationalism, his direct knowledge of the politically significant states of his time. But beyond such attributes, his appeal ultimately rested on his undisputed leadership at the front of two historic processes of national resistance: his country's fight for independence from French colonial rule, and its unswerving opposition to the presence of the US, during the Second Indochina War. Ho Chi Minh's preponderant image as the unbending leader who led his people to victory against all odds, is consistent with the meaning of the name 'Ho Chi Minh', 'He Who Enlightens'.

In 2016, I could see that his qualities continued to be disseminated through a network of museums, among them his former, carefully maintained home in Hanoi: a minimal wooden structure on stilts, built at the back of the Presidential Palace (the former French Governor General's residence) which, the official narrative tells us, he only entered to exercise the functions of the Presidency (1945-1969) 'while maintaining his simple life-style in his modest house'.

Ho Chi Minh's house on stilts, now a museum, in the grounds of the Presidential Palace.

---

4 See Lacouture 2020.

Ho Chi Minh's mausoleum
Ba Dinh Square Hanoi.

I also revisited another persisting pillar of Ho Chi Minh's reputation, his massive mausoleum. Carefully maintained, and the object of a well-choreographed military ritual, it stands at the very heart of the republic, at Hanoi's Ba Dinh Square, where Ho Chi Minh announced the creation of the Democratic Republic of Vietnam on September 2, 1945. There was a time, including in the 1980s, when the site had an appeal to followers of a Mao-like, Lenin-like or Tito-like personality cult. From that point of view, it is significant that the mausoleum was inaugurated in 1975, the year when North and South Vietnam were united, and American forces were expelled. However, in the transformed climate of 2016, I suspected that Ho Chi Minh might have less appeal for the ordinary Vietnamese person, as the unapproachable Great Leader in a massive, grey building than in other more accessible venues.

In 1985, I had identified one such venue in a small temple on a side street of central Hanoi. Inside, I came across the unexpected sight of a small altar, complete with candles and incense sticks, dedicated to Ho Chi Minh. The mausoleum's inaccessible icon of the revolution, had become the object of an informal, more intimate and familiar devotion. This was clearly in the tradition of the cult that families dedicate to their revered ancestors. The national hero had been incorporated into the tradition, thus benefitting from its domestic intimacy. By 2016, the appeal of such a personal approach had gained ground; I saw several other such altars in the temples of smaller communities, outside Hanoi.

* * * * * * * * * * * *

Hanoi 1985. An image of Ho Chi Minh, the symbol of secular revolution, is placed at the centre of a small altar.

A strong religious imprint permeates Vietnamese culture. It can exert its influence even on the most consciously secular aspects of political life, as when the politically-based, secular reverence for a recognised national hero, such as Ho Chi Minh, is enhanced by being transposed onto a religious plane, where it becomes a feature of a specific cult.

There are also ways in which well-established cults, centred on nationally relevant figures of the remote past, can encourage reverential attitudes towards noteworthy individuals of the present, or of the recent past, without incorporating them into their respective pantheons.

Such cults are part of a vibrant Vietnamese nationalistic tradition in which patriotism and national pride, coexist with religious sentiment. They centre on kings and military commanders of the remote past, who are remembered for their historically recorded deeds in defence of the country's integrity, these being mainly acts of heroic resistance against Chinese incursions. The tradition is kept alive in a multiplicity of magnificently endowed shrines, which are carefully maintained, and assiduously frequented, and encourage attitudes of intense, cult-like devotion.

The relatively recent exploits carried out by Ho Chi Minh, fall naturally into the mould of such cults. Although these have not, like the ancestor cults, incorporated his image, they have certainly strengthened his appeal by patriotic association. Admittedly, the heroes in the cults are known to have fought primarily against China, while Ho Chi Minh's struggle was against French colonialism and American imperialism. But all were equally engaged in the defence of Vietnam. They are all, to that extent, essential pillars of the country's identity. Moreover, there is no contradiction in claiming that the image of a communist revolutionary can be strengthened by a tradition that hallows royal or feudal military figures. The tradition does not glorify the systems of which the heroes were a part, it focuses on the national relevance of the heroes' courage and military skill, on their ability to preserve the integrity of Vietnam.

Hanoi and its surrounding areas boast many such shrines. In 2016, they continued to remind the visitor of Vietnam's succession of unyielding national defenders, and of its firm stand against outside aggression. Outside Hanoi, for instance, the ancient village of Duong Lam preserves the memory of two important kings, Phung Hung and Ngo Quyen, both of whom rebuffed China's assaults, the latter by famously placing stakes with iron points in the estuary of the Bach Dang river, where the Chinese were enticed to battle at high tide, but whose ships remained impaled by the stakes and immobilized, when the water receded.[5]

* * * * * * * * * * * *

The glorification of heroic exponents of the past, despite their monarchical and feudal backgrounds, have operated elsewhere in communist Indochina.

---

5   King Phung Hung defeated the Chinese in 784, while King Ngo Quyen repelled them in 938.

King Fangum, a royal figure of the 14th century and founder of the Lao Nation, is a revered national symbol and source of national identity in the communist Lao Popular Republic. And in communist Kampuchea, both the Khmer Rouge, and the Vietnamese-sustained PRK glorified the achievements of ancient Angkor to enhance the prestige of their respective regimes. So much for the *remote* past.

As for the use of royal figures of the *recent* past, as recognised national reference points and sources of national identity, communist Kampuchea (the PRK in particular) never ceased to sustain the cult-like devotion that surrounded a royal prince, king and politician, Sihanouk. The cult continues in the present Kingdom of Cambodia, although in modified form, since the coronation of King Sihamoni, Sihanouk's son. By contrast, Laos and Vietnam have avoided the co-option of recent royals. Laos excluded the possibility when it abolished the monarchy, a process which the monarch and his immediate family did not survive. And in communist Vietnam, no value has been attached to any member of the imperial family that preceded the establishment of Ho Chi Minh's Democratic Republic in 1945. Although, the republic did temporarily incorporate the recently demoted emperor Bao Dai as Advisor, that cooperation was short-lived, and was never revived, following Bao Dai's joining the French, and partaking in their defeat at Dien Bien Phu. Present-day Vietnam can both unequivocally condemn or ignore Bao Dai, and even the relatively recent Nguyen dynasty to which he belonged (only established in 1802), but extol the virtues of General Quan Cong and other such historical/mythical paragons of ancient patriotic fervour, despite being strong exponents of feudal states.

In a further twist to the accommodating meanders of ideology, however, the Vietnamese communist state has not hesitated to maintain selected sites associated with the Nguyen dynasty in the interest of tourism, including the former Imperial

The heroes of the remote historical past share Ho Chi Minh's firm stand in defence of the Nation. The oldest shrine dedicated to one such hero (General Quan Cong) is the Tran Quoc ('Defence of the Kingdom') Pagoda'. First built in 545 on the banks of the Red River, it now stands by the West Lake in Hanoi.

Palace at Hue. For similar commercial reasons, Laos has revived selected aspects of its prerevolutionary Buddhist-monarchic tradition, while Cambodia has done the same with Angkor Wat. But unlike Vietnam, the latter two states have found in that tradition, a source of national pride and identity.

Excluded from the pantheon of national heroes: Emperor Bao Dai and Empress Nam Phuong (Photo courtesy of Mr. Chinh).

* * * * * * * * * * * *

In 2016, the broad range of issues which Ho Chi Minh's image had been used to legitimate, by far surpassed anything I could remember from 1985. Most noticeable was the juxtaposition of this iconic revolutionary leader, with massive commercial malls, palatial villas and luxurious facilities for a booming tourist trade, all of which stood amid highly visible evidence of sharp economic and social differences. I found a final visual expression of Vietnam's contradictions, when I stopped briefly in Saigon on my way out of Vietnam. Dominating the city centre's wide esplanade, the bronze statue of a saluting Ho Chi Minh turned his back on the magnificently restored symbol of French colonialism, the former Hotel de Ville, now seat of the People's Council, while his statesmanlike gesture embraced the glass-plated skyline of the new Vietnam.

Ho Chi Minh stands between the colonial past and the neoliberal future, Saigon 2016.

24

CAMBODIA
Economic Liberalism and One-Man Rule
under Chinese Protection

Improved standards of living but marked inequality

In 2016, a full quarter of a century after my departure, the former dereliction of Cambodia's capital had vanished. Alongside the upgraded boulevards, reconstructed colonial villas, impeccable monasteries and carefully spruced-up Royal Palace, an air of wealthy self-sufficiency permeated the dynamic skyline of its new high-tech buildings, massive five-star hotels, luxury car dealers and huge casino, which attracted gamblers from all over Southeast Asia.

Phnom Penh's selective metamorphosis was as puzzling in 2016, as my exploration of the war-scarred capital had been in 1987. Rather than a few renovated buildings standing in the midst of dereliction, I now saw extensive new areas destined for the rich, although poverty was far from having been stamped out. Following its modest beginnings in 1989, real estate speculation had evidently boomed, most expensively at the 'Diamond', the new self-consciously elitist development where, alongside shopping malls and entertainment halls, three or four-floor villas were offered behind the walls of guarded, fortresslike residential compounds. By the entrance of the 'Elysee', perhaps the most exclusive among them, a large panel showed French-style buildings, an image by which promoters invited potential buyers, encouraging them to identify with stereotypes of European sophistication and high living. Thinking of my own country, Mexico, and of similarly developed Thailand, I knew that this type of urban development was commonplace in the globalized world, but it was nothing short of miraculous when set against my memories of wartime Phnom Penh.

Entering the 'New Diamond' complex.

A villa inside a residential compound.

The massive Sokha Hotel soars at the confluence of the Tonle Sap and Mekong rivers.

The many hotels that marked the city's landscape had been built to respond to the needs of the booming tourist trade. While sites such as Angkor Wat attracted the largest numbers (crowds of tourists now dominated the landscape of the ancient ruins), Phnom Penh catered for a wealthier, if smaller group of demanding Southeast Asians, in addition to Chinese officials, businessmen and politicians. As already noted, China's economic ventures and unconditional political support, accorded without demands for human rights, or the rule of law, were a major element in Cambodia's economic performance.

I missed the town's former placid rhythm and silence, which the infernal confusion and noise of motorbikes and cars had swallowed up. Despite a sweltering 40 degrees, I was able to reason that hundreds of motorbikes circulating in compact proximity, transporting piles of articles, or unexpected numbers of passengers (many without a helmet) were surely a sign of a new prosperity. Still, I could not help but notice the hierarchy of wealth which showed in the occasional air-conditioned four-by-four, which glided along half a metre above the tarmac, dwarfing the motorbikes. A glimpse of inequality showed in the traffic, but also, more clearly, in the neglected sidestreets. Walking down one of them, I saw piles of uncollected rubbish by the rundown buildings, while groups of people, probably unemployed, stood chatting and smoking in mid-morning, having taken over the street and the sidewalks. Further along, by the entrance of the well-restored terracotta Museum of Archaeology, two children and their young mother in shabby clothes, lay half asleep on a mat, probably tired of begging.

And yet, despite the differences and the contrasts, Phnom Penh as a whole had been pulled out of the depths of hopelessness which, with few exceptions, had been general when I first reached town in 1988. There was now enough of an economic breathing space among a sufficient number of families to give the town a new sense of lightness. I sensed that one evening when, in advance of King Sihamoni's

The floodlit image of King Sihamoni.

birthday on May 13, a public celebration was organized along the riverfront, close to the Palace. Throngs of young couples sat on the promenade benches, and looked across the river to the brightly lit 'Diamond', and the Sokha Hotel. Further down, beyond a row of cyclos, vendors offered sweets or multi-coloured balloons for the children. The scene was eons away from my Phnom Penh, taking place as it was by the king's illuminated image – a figure who had not existed under the communist PRK. Prince Sihamoni, the son of the charismatic Sihanouk had been crowned in November 2004, thereby sustaining the country's identity as a functioning monarchy. And although he was known to reign in the shadow of the ever-more powerful Prime Minister, Hun Sen, I could sense just then, his unquestioned appeal. His brightly lit presence was reassuring.

I sat on one of the benches facing the river, and reflected on the changes which the Cambodian state had undergone. In 1988, I had seen the PRK leadership, including PM Hun Sen, legitimizing the use of Buddhist and royal symbols for the first time. In 2016, I was witnessing the successful culmination of that strategy in what was now royal Cambodia: the king, and the entire royal-Buddhist apparatus were now, by all accounts, at the disposal of the leadership and the prime minister, to enhance the government's prestige, reassure the people, and reconcile it with the new leadership's implacable exercise of power.

The origins of Phnom Penh's development for the rich

The new high-tech Phnom Penh of 2016, and that of the 1980s, belonged to two separate worlds, but I could see how they were linked. The towering glass-plated buildings, upmarket malls and living areas for the rich were the culmination of a process which had been born before my eyes in the late 1980s. At the time, the use of property as a means of enrichment was an offshoot of the communist regime's recently launched liberalizing trend, an expression of its new proclivity to accumulate wealth, of an emerging ethos among its ranks of materialism and greed. There were many factors behind the trend, but one came to mind via my former incarnation as a UN official: the unintended, but perverse consequences of the massive United Nations operation, put into place in 1991 to implement the Paris Peace Agreement for Cambodia.

Such long-lasting influence should not come as a surprise. Already in the late 1980s, the more experienced pioneers in real estate investment had sensed that the Peace Process, which was already on the horizon, would require a massive UN presence and an abundance of funds, which would spill over into the economy, and the real estate sector. They had correctly anticipated that the operation would bring in an unprecedented number of staff, all of whom would have to be housed. Indeed, in 1993, the United Nations Transitional Authority for Cambodia (UNTAC) counted 15,000 soldiers, nearly 3,000 civilian police, 1,300 civilian support staff and 600 UN volunteers, totalling an estimated 20,000 people; numerous NGOs further inflated that number. This was a boon for those who had space to rent out: rental costs rocketed to several thousand US dollars a month for the best accommodation, astronomical amounts if compared to the average income.[6]

UNTAC's economic impact was, of course, an unintended consequence of its intervention, and occurred independently of the pursuit of its objectives (the cessation of hostilities, the establishment of a new, viable Cambodia with functional democratic institutions, a fair electoral system, an independent Judiciary). Also unintended but perhaps more pernicious, was UNTAC's impact on the country's moral fiber, among its leadership particularly. As with other peacekeeping operations, UNTAC's unprecedented levels of investment, display of international wealth (2.8 billion US dollars) and massive deployment of personnel, created inflated expectations about the future among those who had some money, and wanted more. And for those in positions of power, the political elite and its dependents, international funding also created tempting opportunities for enrichment, rather than obligations to follow international standards of governance and administrative practice. It gave rise to a taste for easy material advancement, and generated visible examples of newly acquired wealth, which did not pass unobserved, but continued, despite UN complaints. It did not help, of course, that the UN operation itself featured some instances of corruption, particularly among some of its military contingents.

In this context, a deep groove of chronic unaccountability was created, which became deeper in time. When, in the decade following the year 2000, Cambodia's economy underwent remarkable expansion (almost ten percent between 2001 and 2006[7]) and international aid flowed freely, the demands of western donors for compliance with best practices and respect for human rights fell on deaf ears. But aid continued to flow regardless, as if donors had decided that the Phnom Penh government should not be antagonized but maintained. For despite its shortcomings, the regime was perceived as a guarantor of political continuity. Notwithstanding

---

6 Riddle 2000: 63.

7 See C.Hughes and Kheang Un in Hughes and Kheang Un 2011: 10-12.

the visible social inequalities, violations of human rights and disregard for the rules of good governance, the donors' choice was to sustain the regime; too many international funds had already been invested in Cambodia, and no one wanted to upset the balance. Efforts that favoured international standards were otherwise undermined by China's readiness to provide economic aid without preconditions, a strategy of penetration that was being practiced in Cambodia but also in Laos.

On the lookout for my personal Phnom Penh

Sitting pillion on the back of a motorbike taxi, I started to look for what remained of the past. My driver Sinat and I had been on the go since early morning, but baffled by so many transformations, I kept giving him wrong directions. Nothing seemed recognisable, until I finally entered familiar territory as we drove past the morning market. In the eighties, the area had been filled with extraordinary, decaying, architectural treasures. One was the collapsing carcass of the Grand Hotel, an Art Nouveau beauty which, following years of abandonment, had been taken over by the urban poor. With a little effort, Sinat and I found what remained of it, standing half-hidden behind a makeshift wooden fence, ready for demolition.

As we drove on, there was a second flash of recognition, when I caught sight of something out of the corner of my eye, and I asked Sinat to stop in front of a renovated town house. At the top of the façade, the central balcony was framed on either side by the outline in stucco of a snake, ready to enter a vase. My zoom lens showed the shapes clearly. They were the very same snakes and vases I had

A house survives in a brand-new version of itself.

1988.   2016.

The former Samaki Hotel,
now Raffles Le Royal 2016.

photographed in the past, but instead of brown, they were now gleaming white, and attached to a brand-new yellow housefront. Incredibly, they had survived.

Encouraged by this finding, we drove towards the French colonial Post Office. Like the town house, it stood under a coat of fresh paint but otherwise kept the memory of the endless hours of queueing which I had been forced to endure before making a phonecall through one of its two telephone lines – the only two functioning in town. Sinat now drove towards my main objective for that morning: the Samaki Hotel. In my time a well-guarded ghetto for Westerners, I had lived there in one of its bungalows for the best part of two years. As Sinat's motorbike rolled into the drive, I was faced with a newly renovated, five-star hotel, which in the restored Kingdom of Cambodia was now called "Le Royal".

In this new version of itself, it looked strangely domesticated, less aloof and impressive than the weatherworn building I remembered. Inside, the former bare interiors had also been altered to fit five-star hotel standards. I was confronted with a profusion of antique furniture, carpets, vases and mirrors which made the building look smaller, comfortable but stifling if compared to its former spacious austerity. I looked on, past a smart European couple, and headed for the gardens at the back. Stepping outside, everything I knew had gone. My former swimming pool, deficient in maintenance but a welcome spot for my daily swim, had now been replaced by two very large pools, both of them glowing an unnatural turquoise blue.

My bungalow at the Samaki in 1987.

In 2016, the bungalows had been obliterated
by the hotel's new wing and swimming pool.

Two or three five-star looking clients lounged by the water on their *chaises longues*. I walked towards the compound's western wall, where my bungalow used to stand, next to many others. None had survived. I stood there in a daze, facing the white columned entrance to the hotel's new wing.

On the trail of Buddhist Phnom Penh

I asked Sinat to take me to Seakmony Chedi, a landmark monument whose re-inauguration in 1989, was one of the PRK's leadership's first public displays of Buddhist devotion, a key aspect of Kampuchea's then nascent revisionism.[8] Sinat parked the motorbike in front of the old railway station, where I had last seen the *chedi*, but all that was visible was a dilapidated fence surrounding what looked like an unused plot of land. I crossed over, pushed open a rusty door, and entered. The abandoned garden was overgrown with bushes, and had a small shrine at the centre – nothing like the one I had in mind. Rather than towering over the surrounding area, the shrine stood level with the road, dwarfed by the glass-plated highrise buildings behind it. It was coloured gold, not blue, and was crowned by a smallish Buddha image in a glass-protected lantern.

I thought that the original monument must have been dismantled, but careful examination of my photographs after the visit, showed that the tops of both the 1989 and 2016 *chedis* were the same. The original blue *chedi* had not been demolished at all, but had been reduced in size. Its former base, which had raised it high above the ground in my time, had been taken away, making its upper part stand directly on the ground.

This change tells us much about the political use of Buddhist monuments in Cambodia, before and after I left in 1990. I have already described one such

The blue elevated *chedi* in 1989 (left) and the gold *chedi* I found close to the ground in 2016 (right) were the same.

8   See Part Four p.236-241.

historically significant political use, the reinstallation of relics in Seakmony Chedi in 1989. Another similar instance occurred after my departure from Phnom Penh when, following the UNTAC-organized elections of 1992, the Kingdom of Cambodia was reestablished, in a process that culminated in Prince Sihanouk's coronation in September 1993. The momentous series of events were accompanied by the revival of certain Buddhist practices and by the downgrading of a number of Buddhist sites, among them Seakmony Chedi. As for the sacred relics the *chedi* contained, it was decided that they should be placed in a new structure, better suited to the dignity of the newly relaunched royal and Buddhist Cambodia.[9] In this process, the old structure was not to be dismantled, but would be given a more modest use. Seakmony Chedi's long-lasting symbolic primacy under Sihanouk (1957-1970), Lon Nol's US-sustained Republic (1972-1975) and the communist PRK (after 1989) was thus effectively obliterated.

It is not clear how the momentous decision was actually reached. Probably, a variety of experts, members of the Sangha, soothsayers, astrologers or spirit mediums were consulted, while Sihanouk, in his new investiture as king of Cambodia, gave the final stamp of approval. Among the likely advisors, the anthropologist John Marston has pointed to Sihanouk's first cousin and spirit medium, Princess Lyda Sisowath, the very same Lyda whose various activities I have described in Part Four. As a royal medium, and Prince Sihanouk's first cousin, Lyda had attempted to act in my time as a bridge between the PRK and the prince, a function I know she continued to exercise when he returned to Phnom Penh, first as prince, then as king. By that time, Lyda's persistent efforts to communicate with Sihanouk seem to have been recognised, as is attested by a 1993 proclamation which raised her and her sister to royal rank[10]. Given Lyda's and her sister's newfound closeness to Sihanouk, it is not surprising that Lyda was involved in the process that led to the *chedi*'s demotion. Among the many opinions which would have been brought to bear, the weight of Lyda's well-respected opinion could well have helped tilt the balance in favour of a new reliquary. In any case, Lyda's involvement shows her continued relevance in the recently re-established kingdom, a well-deserved recognition, I feel, for her persistent efforts over the years, to promote national reconciliation and peace.

The identification of a suitable location for the new reliquary was an arduous process which lasted several years, and cost millions (US\$ 4 581 966).[11] In the end,

---

9 See Marston: 2013 for a detailed discussion of the issue.

10 Marston 2016 Note 5.

11 See Marston 2013 for a detailed description of the process. For instance, he shows that Wat Phnom, the mythical originating hill of Phnom Penh was initially selected for the erection of a new more appropriate monument, with construction progressing for over two years, but finally abandoned due to the terrain's unsuitability.

Symbol for the new post-communist Cambodia: the monumental new *chedi* which Prince Sihanouk inaugurated at Oudong in December 2002 (photos by courtesy of J. Marston).

the chosen location for its construction was Oudong, the former royal capital, a site of historical and mythical associations, famous for a concentration of *vats* and royal funerary monuments. The foundation stone was placed in August 1996, but the monument was only inaugurated on 19 December 2002, in a ceremony that was attended by hundreds of thousands of devotees who travelled from all corners of the country. The figure of one million participants was even mentioned, a number commensurate with the national importance which Sihanouk desired for this grandest of symbols for the royal, internationally validated, post-communist Cambodia.

The continued political use of religion

The tumultuous history of Kampuchea shows the repeated instrumental use of Buddhist and royal symbols, and the symbols' extraordinary resilience, despite having been the object of systematic desecration in the past, as under the Khmer Rouge. As for 'my' Seakmony Chedi, a photograph taken in April 2021 shows the monument still standing in its former location opposite the railway station. No longer hidden behind a fence, it is entirely visible, and I am told that it is now a minor centre of devotion. In the evolving landscape of Phnom Penh, it has stood its ground, not as the single most important religious complex in the country, but as one Buddhist site, which together with Phnom Penh's numerous Buddhist landmarks, attests to the continued vigour of Buddhism.

To that vigour should be added its persistent political relevance, specifically its use by political figures as a source of prestige and legitimation. Concerning the new Oudong structure of 2002, Marston notes that donors associated with its construction included Hun Sen's Cambodian People's Party, and Hun Sen himself.[12] And at a much later date, in 2013, when the PM's political power had reached its peak, his display of Buddhist devotion continued. Strangio mentions his regular visits for counsel and solace at Vat Champuskaek[13], a lavishly endowed monastery which developed into a major centre of meditation practice and Buddhist devotion, thanks to the generous donations of the regime's most loyal and wealthy supporters.

In 2016, Sinat and I approached Vat Champuskaek by the front gate. The path leading to it was bordered by a succession of stone carvings,

The Seakmony Chedi in 2021 against Phnom Penh's most recent skyline.

gods on one side, and demons on the other, in clear imitation of the stone figures which flank the access roads to the Gate of Victory at Angkor Thom.[14] 'Why not?' I thought. Associating a brand-new Buddhist foundation with the symbol of Khmer political power, and undisputed pinnacle of Cambodian architecture, was an effective status-enhancing measure, and a persuasive way of legitimating the prolonged exercise of political power.

Status enhancement by imitation of the past: Angkor Thom's Gate of Victory (left) is reproduced at Wat Champuskaek (right).

---

12 See Marston, in Whalen-Bridge and Kitiarsa (ed) 2013.

13 Strangio 2014: 203.

14 The Gate of Victory, which leads to Angkor Thom (12th century) is preceded by two rows of beings on either side of the road. The demons and gods illustrate a famous legend: they pull at the ropelike body of the *naga* in order to churn the Sea of Milk and extract from it the elixir of eternal life, *amrita*.

Fully consistent with the political significance of the *vat*, a small but highly visible office of the Cambodian People's Party (CPP) faced the monastery, across the road from its main gate. The party is heir to the communist Kampuchean People's Revolutionary Party (KPRP), whose name was changed to CPP in 1991, another move by the country's leadership to sever all links with its communist past, and consolidate its new identity as the non-communist State of Cambodia. In addition to the army, and the variety of government-dependent economic operators, the CPP functions as a countrywide instrument which consolidates Prime Minister Hun Sen's regime.

Inside Vat Champuskaek, the massive, recently built monastic compound comprises a garden of lush vegetation, where many temples compete with each other in size, in the wealth of their gold-leaf decorations, and in the social importance of their patrons and donors. These are in all likelihood members of the political, military or business elite who, like the prime minister, seem to believe that material proof of their Buddhist devotion fully legitimates their accumulation of wealth, and political prominence. A long row of meditation cubicles is in line with the patrons' intention of making Vat Champuskaek into a centre of religious excellence, which will positively reflect on each of them.

Inside the monastery, the various temples compete in magnificence, while meditation cubicles speak of the donors' religious devotion 2016.

Twenty-six years after I left Kampuchea, the political benefits of a Buddhist revival had been fully exploited, in a process that was continuing. But perhaps not all was political manipulation: the mix of political convenience and religious interest could be genuine. I thought also of the attraction of the esoteric dimensions of Buddhism. Rituals that generate extraordinary powers, both aggressive and defensive, strongly appeal to holders of power who need protection from the very dangers which the pursuit of power generates. At a time when a growing fear of assassination plagued the topmost members of the leadership, religion and its esoteric aspects could serve as a powerful source of protection against real or imagined enemies. It is perhaps not by chance that the Prime Minister's public Buddhist devotion developed as the number of his personal bodyguards grew, becoming a veritable 'personal army of more than 1,000 men backed by tanks, armoured personnel carriers and helicopters'.[15] The army, the police and other units are clearly the regime's main sustaining force, but Buddhism as practiced in selected monasteries has continued to function as an inexhaustible source of political strength.

The Red Cross past and present – the ubiquitous presence of the Prime Minister

I was disappointed that old friends and colleagues could not be found. With one exception, however: thanks to Sinat's perseverance, we located the former President of the Kampuchean Red Cross, Madame Plech Pirun at home, close to the Faculty of Medecine.

Madame Plech Pirun with King Sihamoni (courtesy of the late Madame Plech Pirun).

We rang the doorbell, and a housemaid showed us to her bedroom, on the first floor. Now well over ninety, and moving with difficulty, she offered us a cool drink, talked about her health, and pointing to a set of framed photographs on a side table, reminisced about the past. Spanning many decades, the pictures showed her at centre stage in a succession of Cambodias: saluting Prince Sihanouk in the 1960s, standing by Prince Ranariddh in the 1990s, and more recently, being greeted by Prince Sihanouk's son, King Sihamoni.

As Madame Plech Pirun showed me her photographs, remembered common acquaintances (many of them deceased) and commented sympathetically about the present regime, she demonstrated the meandering line that linked her days in Kampuchea to the Cambodia of today. This, she, of course, considered better than the Khmer Rouge days, and an improvement on the Vietnamese-sponsored PRK, while omitting to mention the continuity between the PRK and the present, ensured by the person of the perennial Hun Sen. I did catch sight on a side table, however, of a recent picture that placed Madame Plech Pirun squarely in Hun Sen's

---

15 Strangio 2014: 73.

world. It showed her next to the prime minister's wife, Ms. Bun Rany, the new President of the Red Cross who, like her husband, ensured the political continuity between the 1980s and 2016. By assuming the institution's presidency, Ms. Bun Rany had consolidated the charity's subordination to government, and made it into yet another instrument of her husband's ever more absolute political dominance.

* * * * * * * * * * * *

The Red Cross had become a new bastion of power, as the outward appearance of its new headquarters showed. Sinat drove me there, on the other side of town. Compared to the old Red Cross building where I had attended many meetings, this one was unexpectedly grand. It stood pompously in the guise of a ministry, at the end of a drive, carefully fenced in, and guarded at the gate. The guard, visibly unimpressed by the sight of a foreigner arriving on the back of a motorcycle without any official business, would not let me in. However, with Sinat's help, I was able to convince him to contact the administration inside, and give the names of former contacts, one of whom, Madame Plech Pirun had told me, collected his and her pension every month. I had known this person well in the old days, as a regular participant in joint UNHCR/KRC initiatives. The guard called three officials in succession on his cell phone, and gave the names, but none were recognized, not even that of the former Red Cross President, Madame Plech Pirun. I insisted. To no avail. No one was willing to see me. I was far from the casual Red Cross of the 1980s and its informal surroundings. This new incarnation struck me as having become barricaded, more like a ministry, such as the Ministry of the Interior which embodied the defensive state, aloof, inaccessible and unresponsive. The new Red Cross stood before me as an apt symbol of the real, closed Cambodia, where the overbearing state, economically prosperous and politically authoritarian, jealously guarded its power behind closed doors.

A one-man authoritarian state and a malleable king

Authoritarian government is nothing new in Cambodia. Since the late 1960s, the country has harboured a succession of heavy-handed regimes, some more mellow than others, but all of them cast in the authoritarian mold. Some have featured democratic elements, as with Prince Sihanouk's paternalistic and intransigent variety of the monarchy, or with Lon Nol's US-sustained anti-communist republic. Ohters have been closed authoritarian systems, such as the Vietnamese-backed PRK and, before that, in a class of its own, the genocidal Khmer Rouge regime. And today, a strong, domineering state persists in Cambodia's lastest mutation. In the guise of a newly revived Buddhist monarchy which boasts a liberal economy, it masquerades as a democracy under the intractable authority of a one-man leadership, who in fact rules in the spirit of the now defunct PRK's one-party system.

As my 2016 revisit concluded, I could sense the powerlessness with which ordinary Cambodians experienced a state which focused on the interests of the small elite groups who controlled or sustained it. Besides the 'open' Cambodia of the tourist brochures, which welcomed anyone who wanted to enter, or could pay for the luxuries it offered, this was the Cambodia where the opposition was persecuted, where opposition leaders were threatened with incarceration or forced into exile, an opposition immobilized by the police and the armed forces, who could not question the power to which the country was subjected. This was the new Kingdom of Cambodia, Hun Sen's Cambodia that had replaced Kampuchea, economically improved, and politically authoritarian, dismissive of the opposition, oblivious of human rights, and legitimated by the indispensable dyad, Buddhist Sangha, and the monarchy, the nation's two pillars of stability. From the angle of the government's international acceptability, Hun Sen had achieved the perfect solution. He had kept the reins of power, and held the ideal legitimating instrument: Sihanouk, first as Prince and, after 1993, as king. Then, after Sihanouk's abdication in October 2004, and death in 2012, Hun Sen's position improved even more. He no longer had the indomitable Sihanouk to deal with, but instead Sihanouk's son, the infinitely more malleable Prince Sihamoni, who provided unconditional legitimation while he, Hun Sen, was fully in control. The prime minister made use of the Buddhist-monarchic apparatus at will, the economy prospered, the opposition had been virtually eliminated.

What I saw in 2016 was what remained of the democratic system which the UNTAC mission had introduced in 1993, but which had gradually been eroded, leaving only vestiges of the original. Since then, the decline of democracy had continued. Described in the specialized literature[16] , the process of deterioration culminated in 2017, in a series of blows that transformed Cambodia's *partial* democracy (which allowed for limited democratic competition) into a *closed* *system* that lacked all basic democratic features such as an independent media, a functioning multi-party system, a vigorous opposition, a fair and transparent electoral system, an independent judiciary and legislature. The political legacy of the historical UN mission had been effectively obliterated after twenty-four years, a period which coincided almost exactly with my absence from Cambodia.

---

16 Loughlin and Noren-Nilsson 2021: 226 240.

25

LAOS
Survival Amid Encroaching Economic Giants

Luang Phrabang: tourist destination under persistent state scrutiny

The change that confronted me in Laos seemed less abrupt than in Cambodia. In Vientiane, high-rise banks and investment houses *did* soar above a few restored boulevards and parks, much of this, courtesy of China. But the capital retained its dusty provincial appearance and lazy rhythm, its characteristic semi-rural quality, and although some traffic filled the streets, this was a far cry from the infernal concentration of vehicles in the much more populated cities of Phnom Penh and Hanoi.[17]

I saw a similarly gentle transformation in Luang Phrabang. My former two-floor teak house still stood where I had left it, on the side of the Phou Si. It had become a guest house, and the few alterations it had undergone mirrored what had happened in town: slight adjustments here and there, to meet the needs of the tourist trade. The city had responded well to an endless line of visitors. It had made good use of its buildings, adapted them when needed, but had not defaced them. The happy blend of French and Lao buildings was still there, the former Royal Palace was in good shape and now housed a museum, the many *vat* were well kept, and boutique hotels, cafes, restaurants and souvenir shops filled the townhouses, whose structures, mercifully, remained untouched. The deforming impact of architectural modernization had been avoided, thanks partly to the town's status as a UNESCO World Heritage site.

The former hospital, now a luxury hotel.

An upmarket guest house.

---

17 Vientiane, 2015 : 620 000; Phnom Penh, 2020: 1 573 544; Hanoi, 2015: 3 657 210.

The main street: tourist shops within the town's untouched housing structure.

The available facilities, ranging from luxury hotels to guest houses for backpackers, could respond to all levels of demand. Some establishments were owned by recently returned, formerly well-to-do families, many of whose members had been refugees. They were back, and were now tolerated and even welcomed by the regime, provided they had sufficient resources. Among them, I found a former student and general's daughter heading an antique shop. I heard of an investor who had refurbished the former colonial-style hospital to top-notch conditions; his fabric designs, known internationally, were available for very steep fees in the hotel shop. Such businesses could belong to Laotians, but many were in foreign hands – Chinese, Japanese or French, this raising the question of how much of the profits ended up abroad. On the other hand, these nationalities added to the town's atmosphere, in particular the French, who gave a certain corner of town a special touch, a more casual version of the atmosphere of colonial nostalgia which I had seen in certain areas of Saigon and Hanoi. All seemed to be going well for the buildings and the people who were linked to the tourist boom.

A vintage 1953 Citroen, parked as decoration in front of a French-owned restaurant.

By walking off the main road, along the side streets, I found another Luang Phrabang, different from its glossy, tourist-brochure façade. In my two old neighbourhoods, I looked for houses where friends had lived, but found that they were long gone, having settled abroad by

Flashback to 1972: the son of my neighbour (first from left front row) and leader of the band, an essential component of my neighbourhood at vat Sen Luang Phrabang.

way of Thailand and the refugee camps. As had occurred in Phnom Penh, it was easier to find buildings than people, but I did find some. A plump woman in her late fifties attending clients in a small shop turned out to be a former student. And, as I stopped in front of my former first house of 1972, the ground floor of a colonial building at Vat Sen, I found my former neighbour in the person of a very elderly woman who stared at me from her front door. Now haggard and grey-haired, but formerly striking in her good looks, she was the widow of a handsome government cadre, who used to drive off on his motorbike early in the morning and wave, precisely as was also about to leave for work. I remembered her small son, the head of a band of brats, who filled our small side lane with constant movement and turbulence.

Luang Phrabang tourism and the state

I was amazed at the town's extraordinary touristic development. For a start, it was truly remarkable that private investors willing to set up the required accommodation infrastructure, had been identified and brought in. But more impressive, once the touristic project was launched, was the consensus reached among those involved, to preserve the town's single most valuable asset: its buildings and their unique location, between two rivers. In addition, the decision was eventually taken, surprising in a communist context, to carry out a revival of particularly magnetic Buddhist and royal ceremonies from the town's prerevolutionary past. This notable development appears to have followed from a tough debate between two opposed camps, conservative ideologues versus progressive tourism-backers. Determined to succeed, the progressives opted for a tactic of flexibility, and agreed to the edited revival of certain festivities, included those carried out for the Lao New Year. These festivities had been discontinued after the Pathet Lao's takeover in 1975[18], but had been resuscitated in the early nineties, and thence performed each year in modified form in the wake of Luang Phrabang's commercial/touristic awakening. The process of repackaging rescued certain Buddhist and royal ideas and practices, and eliminated others, thus allowing the authorities to claim to be true to their communist tenets, and pose as the defenders of the country's cultural heritage.

---

18 See Trankell 1993: 192 in Evans (ed.) 1999: 191-213.

I wondered what the last Pi Mai festivities had looked like. The description I was given recalled the celebrations I had seen in the 1970s, though they lacked what I regarded as their essential components. In their original version, the succession of rituals had ensured the renewal of the kingdom and its placement in the cosmos, within the context of the Lao people's foundation myths (see Part One). The new version lacked the essential historical and mythical aspects, and progressed, of course, without the main activator of Laos' cosmological system – the king. Pi Mai was being performed as a carnival, nothing more, as just one more aspect of the new commercialized Luang Phrabang, now no longer the proud capital of Laos' most

Statue of King Sisavang Vong in the grounds of the former palace, now a museum.

ancient traditions, but a showpiece for consumption, part of a place of hotels for all budgets, souvenir shops and tourists.

I witnessed one instance of the partial, and distorted revival of the past, when I visited the former Royal Palace, turned museum. Standing with a group of tourists, in the former palace grounds, next to the massive bronze statue of King Sisavang Vong, I heard the guide stating that this sovereign (reigned 1946-1959) had been the last to reign.

King Sisavang Vathana, who reigned when I lived in Luang Phrabang, was not mentioned, nor was it noted that he had assumed the monarch's responsibilities upon the death of his father, King Sisavang Vong, mistakenly referred to by the guide as Laos' last sovereign. The guide's explanation was that Sisavang Vathana had never been crowned, and could not therefore be described as a former king. But it was not mentioned that once Sisavang Vathana had assumed his responsibilities as sovereign, he purposely postponed the coronation, wishing that its celebration coincide with the end of the war.

A false version of history was being used to hide actual events, and relegate the royal dynasty to a fossilized past, which left the secular communist present uncontaminated. In actual fact, King Sisavang Vathana's demise took place in stages, beginning in 1975 with his forced abdication and nomination as 'Special Advisor' (which he refused) and ending in 1977, when he was confined to a so-called 'reeducation Camp' of Houapanh Province, in the distant Northeast. Living in isolation there, he, Queen Khamphoui and Crown Prince Vong Savang are known to have met their deaths, although the exact date and circumstances of what may amount to regicide have not been clarified, the issue being systematically avoided by the regime, in a tactic where unwieldy aspects of the past were cancelled.

* * * * * * * * * * * *

The edited version of the New Year celebrations, the invention that King Sisavang Vong was the last king of Laos, and the obliteration of King Sisavang Vathana's reign provided foreign and local tourists with edited fragments of the past. These reflected well on the present by way of their aesthetic and enjoyment value, while the regime's Marxist-Leninist convictions, and the society's actual dynamics, remained unseen by passing tourists. Visitors were encouraged to enjoy

Performance of the *Ramayana* at the Palace Museum Theatre, 2016.

a visit to the former Royal Palace and the monasteries, a performance of classical Lao ballet or a *baci*, as part of a well-organised schedule available at a price.

Also, according to a popular fad, young couples were encouraged to pose for pre-wedding photographs against the background of carefully restored traditional buildings in costumes which imitated the fashions of the past. Elsewhere, I saw similar encouragements of a selectively-based nostalgia, in Cambodia, by the Victory Gate at Angkor Thom, or at Hanoi's Temple of Literature. By encouraging young couples to pose for photographs in traditional dress, the authorities presented

<table>
<tr><td>Luang Phrabang</td><td>Angkor Vat</td><td>Hanoi</td></tr>
</table>

Neo traditional styles of dress in Laos, Cambodia and Vietnam 2016.

a superficial ideological flexibility that paid lip-service to the vanity of the young, but left the axioms of their respective regimes untouched.

My reflections above show that initially I was seriously put off by Luang Phrabang's new tourist-oriented reality. I was looking at it from the perspective of the 1970s, when the former royal capital had been the proud repository, and annual activator of Laos' most ancient traditions. Today, however, I admit that for all its trivializing and distortions, tourism saved Luang Phrabang from abandonment and relentless decay. It was the only form of development for a town whose only substantial resource was its cultural patrimony. At the national level, moreover, Luang Phrabang's fight for a demonstrably successful tourist industry, and its success in fostering a certain ideological flexibility locally, probably had a mellowing influence on communist orthodoxy elsewhere in the country. In any case, the central government could not but recognize that its ideological concessions had paid off. Enveloped in the aura of a UNESCO World-Heritage site, and international tourist destination, Luang Phrabang had become an economically profitable venture. It was also a source of national prestige which helped promote the authorities' new image of the country – an economically liberal and internationally-oriented Laos.

Viengsay and the northeast: pillars of orthodoxy to counter ideological revisionism

While Luang Phrabang's tourism could seem counter-revolutionary to the more orthodox, or even a threat to fundamental values, the regime used a number of ideological props to offset criticism and put concerns of political laxity to rest. These props included an unlimited number of statues and photographs of recognized revolutionary leaders; recurring patriotic celebrations to bolster the memory of the revolutionary past (including the five-yearly Lao People's Revolutionary Party's Congresses); a network of museums, which promoted the image of Laos as a revolutionary, forward-looking, secular country; and last but not least, a number of historic sites, the most influential of which stood in the heartland of the Pathet Lao, the northeastern provinces of Houaphan and Xieng Khouang.

At the height of the conflict in the 1970s, the area had been totally out of bounds for a foreigner like myself, who lived in the royal capital. But in February 2016, it was possible to travel there by land. I therefore headed straight to Viengsay town, the sanctuary of the revolution and former bastion of Pathet Lao power. Heavy with the mythical connotations of prolonged revolutionary resistance, the small town confronted me with the craggy outline of its eerie rock formations, and the solid cliff-like mass of limestone, which hid the maze of caves where the PL's headquarters had operated during the long years of relentless US bombing.

The well-hidden former Pathet Lao Headquarters: caves in the limestone mountains of Viengsay.

2016: Monument dedicated to Laos' victory over the US, Viengsay Town.

Perhaps most memorable and chilling was the sight of the bomb craters, all of them marked by signposts recording the date of the blast. A picture of systematic destruction was completed in the museums of the area, in Viengsay and in the provincial museums of Houaphan and Xieng Khouang. They showed the scale of past devastation, and the persistence of unexploded ordnance (rockets, bombs, artillery shells and mortars) with their unending heavy toll of incapacitating injuries and death. Such incontestable evidence explained the presence in Viengsay of a monument which, dedicated to Laos' victory over the US, commemorated the victims and denounced the perpetrators of the carnage. I photographed it from all angles.

My visit to Viengsay refreshed my memory of Pathet Lao history. Among other aspects, it reminded me of the PL's geographical, ideological and military closeness to Vietnam. In a building occupied by the provincial Memorial Sites Committee, a small exhibit of maps showed Houaphan Province jutting into Vietnamese territory, almost being surrounded by it. Outside the museums, in the streets, I could see the Vietnamese connection on display with almost palpable sympathy. I sensed it along the main avenue of Samneua town, where the red ground and yellow star of Vietnamese flags, alternated at regular intervals with posters announcing the 12th session of the Vietnamese Congress. These were the same flags and posters I had seen a few days before along a highway leading to Hanoi. Clearly, such reminders of Vietnam could not have been displayed in other parts of Laos, where the real or imagined presence of the Vietnamese after 1975 was deplored and at times even deeply resented[19]. But I was standing at the heart of Pathet Lao territory, the spot where the myth of the revolution and its principal Vietnamese ally had been constructed, and was being maintained.

The search for nationally relevant symbols

Xieng Khouang and Houaphan provinces, and Viengsay town made me understand, almost made me experience the extraordinary physical challenges which the Pathet Lao leadership had faced. It was the stuff out of which the myth of their struggle had been made, a revolution fought in terms of a David and Goliath confrontation with American power and American bombs.

Lao-Vietnamese Solidarity: Kaysone Phomvihane (Secretary General of the Lao People's Party) and President Ho Chi Minh in Hanoi,1962.

However, the various locations and museums failed to clarify the internal workings, and order of precedence within the LPDR leadership. At the provincial Memorial Sites Committee in Viengsay, a set of ageing photographs of the leadership, displayed in a row of identical pinewood frames, had a flattening, equalising effect. Emphasis on the fraternal links among them, imposed an artificial stamp of uniformity on the group, although an isolated photograph on a different wall, gave a certain prominence to Kaysone Phomvihane, Secretary General of the Party (1955 to 1992) sitting with Ho Chi Minh.

The visibility of Kaysone's image, compared to that of other leaders, reflected the time, after the PL's 1975 victory, when he emerged from the shadows of secrecy as the movement's strongman. In the photograph, however, I wondered why he was shown in the status-enhancing presence of Ho Chi Minh. Did he need the prop of the charismatic Vietnamese leader to reinforce his image? I knew that efforts had been made to build Kaysone as a national figure and political reference point, including by means of the nationwide distribution of his statues or busts. But he seems never to have become the object of a vigorous national cult, never a unanimously popular, uncontested symbol of the revolution and model of

---

19 Before the revolution such resentment appeared sporadically. During the colonial period, for instance, Lao patriots occasionally complained of Vietnamese over representation inside the colonial bureaucracy. On the positive side, established Vietnamese communities have been and are an integral part of Laos' urban landscape, including in Vientiane and Pakse. In Luang Phrabang, the Vietnamese constituted a well-respected elite. Similar ambiguities concerning Vietnamese residents are also evident in Cambodia (see Part Four p. 255-257).

King Fangum's monument by the Mekong in Vientiane: a new royal national symbol for a communist state.

excellence for the new Popular Republic, never the Laotian equivalent of Vietnam's Ho Chi Minh, or Cambodia's Sihanouk. Was the reason his own apparent greyness and lack of charisma? Or were his strong links with Vietnam an issue? Had his being born Nguyen Cai Song, of a Vietnamese father and Lao mother, prevented him from playing a national symbolic role, his importance being limited to areas which were physically and sentimentally close to Vietnam? Certainly, I came across several of his photographs in shops and hotels in Vietnam-sympathetic Houaphan and Xieng Khouang. But even there, in at least one instance, he seemed to need the prop of an uncontested political or religious figures of authority, to assert his symbolic preeminence. For instance, in the hall of a guest house in Samneua town, an altarlike display of symbols of moral and revolutionary fervour showed Kaysone's photograph next to the Buddha, Ho Chi Minh, and King Fangum, a Lao monarch from the remote historical past.

I have noted above the reasons for Ho Chi Minh's appeal beyond the borders of Vietnam.[20] As for King Fangum, he was propelled onto the national stage as a brand-new Laotian nationwide symbol on 20 December 2002. On that day, the highest levels of the communist leadership inaugurated his statue in an unexpectedly elaborate ceremony. Described in picturesque detail by Grant Evans[21], the ceremony elevated Fangum, monarch and founder in the 14th century of a unified Lao Kingdom, to the stature of national hero and source of national identity. Against all expectations, the monarch-centred event was carried out with emphatically Buddhist and royal pomp. It took place in a highly visible site of central Vientiane, on the left bank of the Mekong, where it received the full attention of the media, both national and international.

---

20 See Part Part Five p. 275.
21 See Evans 2009: 31-33.

Why the move? Why the publicity? Why an act that seemed to contradict basic communist tenets? Perhaps, at the conclusion of ten years of economic liberalisation, the LPDR wanted to give a signal, beyond its borders, that its initial closedness and rigidity had been left behind, as was consistent with its international economic engagements, and its unbending resolve to be a regional power that counts. Perhaps the move reflected the regime's need to counter the country's persistent regional and ethnic fragmentation, and occasional internal political disaffection.

Whatever the reasons, the leadership felt the need to display a new all-embracing symbol of national identity in the person of a king of the past, more appealing than the living leaders of the present or immediate past. As noted, efforts had been made to make Kaysone into a symbolically relevant national figure. But despite his exercise of preeminent roles when alive (Secretary of the Party for 37 years, 1955 to 1991, and President of the LPDR, 1991 until his death in 1992), the LPDR leadership in 2002 came to consider, ten years after his death, that he still did not fully meet the requirements of a nationally and internationally appealing national symbol. In the absence of a leader who could embody the achievements of the Lao revolution, and symbolise the construction of a new Laos after 1975, the leadership turned to the 14th century and to a more distant, but historically confirmed beginning: the unification of the Lao people by the nation's unquestioned Founding Father, King Fangum. There were therefore good status-enhancing reasons why the intriguing display of photographs in the Samneua guest house, showed Kaysone accompanied by King Fangum, apart from the Buddha and Ho Chi Minh.

Compared with the selective revival of Luang Phrabang's monarchical-Buddhist tradition in the wake of the development of tourism, the unveiling of King Fangum's statue seemed, because of its wider, national significance, a more blatant contradiction of the LPDR's ideology. But faced with biting criticism, including by the international press, the Vientiane authorities insisted that the ceremony was a *single* initiative which provided a stable, unquestionable anchor for the country's

Altar-like display showing King Fangum and Ho Chi Minh (left), the Buddha and Kaysone (centre and top right).

national identity, and was entirely compatible with orthodoxy. Using an argument we have noted above for Vietnam, the Lao maintained that resorting to royal figures of the distant past did not imply validating the monarchical-feudal system. It merely affirmed the antiquity of the nation's origins, the value of its culture, the power of a hero-leader who had ensured by his valour and leadership qualities, the integrity of an antecessor state, and by implication, that of present-day Laos.

The state and individual rights

After several days in Luang Phrabang, my various wanderings and conversations led me to conclude that all was not well for the rights of individuals. One afternoon, I happened to walk past the office of a small NGO, and stopped for a chat. The friendly American manager was sitting outside, by the office front, and asked me in. She knew the town's dynamics well, and was keen to talk. People were making ends meet, and on the whole lived comfortably enough, although there was a growing rift between those inside the world of tourism, and the others. But whatever the levels of wealth, everyone was living in a politically ambiguous environment which was flexible in some respects, but was ultimately subject to the control of the omnipresent state. A pervasive system of reporting by neighbourhoods functioned smoothly, thanks to the coordinated efforts of local officials and their adepts. Their uninterrupted information-gathering and reporting affected foreign-staffed NGOs and locals alike, although recently returned members of the former commercial class or the nobility were more targeted than others, except when they were well-connected politically, or outstandingly rich.

My first real encounter with the system took place one morning, as I walked out of Vat Mai. Once on the sidewalk, I accidentally bumpedinto my former next-door neighbour. We both recognized each other and, as she looked at me, I heard her calling out 'Monsieur Irvine'! We sat on a bench on the main road, by the *vat*'s entrance, and started chatting, speaking loudly enough for anyone interested to hear (I was speaking in my rusty Lao). After a while, we noticed a man, middle-aged and thin, who stood leaning against the *vat*'s wall, almost behind us, listening. We continued for another while, but the man's presence had become obtrusive. With our chat unfinished, my friend rose from the bench, said goodbye, and was off. Was the man just a busybody listening in? Perhaps. But my neighbour had been sure he was fishing for information. She told me so when I visited her at home some days later.

Another instance was when I called on the mother of a former student. She was managing a guest house in her old family home, while her husband worked in Vientiane. In the 1970s, she, her husband and the children had reached France on their own steam from Thailand, avoiding the refugee camps. Talkative by nature, she told me the story of her and her husband's return a couple of years before, difficult because the children had stayed behind in France, with relatives. After a long chat about the past, and as I was about to leave, she asked me to come again. She would tell her husband about my visit on the phone; he was sure to remember me from the time I was a teacher. But my second visit was short lived. Speaking frankly, she said her husband feared that my visits could mean trouble. Ever since she returned, she said, she was being watched. It was better to make this visit short. Mere paranoia? I doubt it.

I had left Luang Phrabang just as the Pathet Lao was taking control, and had therefore never experienced this pernicious aspect of the new Lao state. I immediately recognized it as essentially similar to the systems of control which I had known in Phnom Penh and Hanoi. The one element which had provoked so many people to become refugees was still operative. But in contrast to the time when it was first established, when it cut into people's lives with the sharp edge of a new imposition, the well-rooted system had now become part of normal life, and was accepted by most, including those who were very young in 1975, or had been born at a later date. Those who looked at the practice critically, and could be oppressed by it, were older, or were people like my friends (and the American manager), whose personal histories made them politically suspect

I had seen another aspect of the regime. Alongside the relative ideological flexibility it had exhibited vis-à-vis Luang Phrabang tourism, or in the creation of ideologically eclectic national symbols, the regime relied on a pervasive and highly effective system of community spying and reporting that gave rise to mutual distrust and, among a mistrusted minority, to generalised fear. Added to this were other means with which the government maintained its hold on power, and perpetrated itself: the authority of the Party, an effective propaganda machinery, the armed forces and the police. A deficient system of Justice completed the picture, and pointed to a reality that left little scope for the expression of individual concerns, or the defence of individual rights.

Chinese/Thai-sustained economic development versus community rights

Sitting in a small noodle shop near Vat Noong, I overheard two middle-aged women chatting. They were talking about the Chinese who, they said, were everywhere, and kept expanding their presence through their small businesses and companies. The Chinese border was too close for comfort, and Luang Phrabang would eventually be swallowed up. The snippets of conversation pointed to an issue which press reports had highlighted – the political and economic encroachment of China as a result of LPDR's economic choices.

Since 2016 and well into 2022, the concern of these two women is still fully relevant: Chinese investments have continued to expand as part of a logic of economic expansion which started in the 1990s. During that decade, the LPDR's new economic liberalization policy led it to engage with a group of countries that operated inside the Great Mekong Sub Region (GMS), all of whose members were committed to the coordinated development of their economies. Common efforts focused on the Mekong, which either bordered or traversed their territories. As a partner of Cambodia, Myanmar, Thailand, Vietnam and the Chinese Yunnan, Laos hoped to play a pivotal role in the system, being the only GMS member who had common borders with all the others, and whose territory included one third of the Lower Mekong. As the decade advanced, Laos gained ground as an active regional contributor, in a process that culminated in 1997 in its joining ASEAN (the Association of Southeast Asian Nations), two years after Vietnam, its similarly liberalising communist mentor.

Within this new grouping, Laos increasingly connected with GMS members. But although it followed a policy of careful calibration of forces, the general question arose as early as the mid-1990s, – the GMS mechanism lead to balanced, sustainable development for itself and all partners, or result in an unequal system of dominance and subordination, orchestrated by the demographically, economically and politically more powerful members. A clear answer came for Laos in the area of hydropower and large-scale dam construction. Laos had welcomed China's inputs in the sector as an opportunity to develop its economy, but the scale of Chinese engagement in project funding and implementation, ended up placing Laos in a state of dependency through indebtedness.

After my visit in 2016, Laos' wager on hydropower continued, despite persisting asymmetrical conditions. In addition, there were signals that Laos was moving towards over-production in respect of demand in Thailand, who had become Laos' major buyer of electricity. Laos's ambitious dam construction continued regardless of the risk that over-production might not yield returns commensurate with investment. In addition, the initiatives started provoking negative responses from neighbouring countries, as complaints mounted that Laotian implementation was occurring without sufficient pre-implementation assessments of the ecological and environmental impacts. Vietnam and Cambodia complained, but Thailand was the most vocal critic, focusing on a particular project, the Sanakham dam, which threatened to affect the flow of the Mekong waters along the Thai-Lao border, causing flooding or droughts in Thai territory. In a process of mounting tension, which alarmed Thailand's water authorities and even reached the Thai Cabinet, the Thai authorities also made complaints against China, one of whose companies was implementing the project.[22]

The Sanakham dam controversy is only one example of a multiplicity of debates where hydropower ventures have been seen as the origin of serious, deleterious effects on the entire Mekong. Looking at the wider picture, beyond Laos' borders, the systematic self-centred exploitation of the Mekong by poorly evaluated dam projects could expose wide areas adjacent to the river to unprecedented seasonal flooding or droughts, undermine the agricultural potential of such areas and negatively affect the livelihood of as many as 60 million people. Regionally, the most serious accusations have been voiced against China, not only for its role as investor and implementor of dam construction in Laos and elsewhere in Indochina, but also for its self-interested use of Mekong waters inside China, including Yunnan, with multiple ecological and apparently irreversible consequences down river.

In this controversial context, Laos plays the part of both victim and perpetrator. Victim of its northern neighbour and perpetrator in its own territory where it has victimized several localities, including the one town which, more than others, has been a main protagonist in this book: Luang Phrabang. The town stands perplexed before the Lao state which, having favoured the former royal capital's affluence by lending support to its tourism-based development, now promotes economic policies which are threatening the very basis of the town's prosperity, and possibly even its physical integrity. The immediate cause of concern in Luang Phrabang is a dam which is ready for implementation, with Chinese involvement. To add to this dam-related difficulty, Luang Phrabang finds itself in an area of road and rail development that will serve to promote Lao-Chinese and Thai-Chinese commercial

Luang Phrabang; a threatened town.

---

22 For a detailed discussion of the issue, from which these remarks are drawn, see Strangio 2020.

links. The process could make the town into a transit hub for transportation and commercial travellers, and require the expansion of its available accommodation stock. In a worse-case scenario, construction could modify the town's urban profile, cause irreparable damage to it as a UNESCO-recognised World Cultural Heritage site, and seriously undermine the touristic primacy with which it contributes significantly to the national economy. A further concern is that Chinese-organised agro-industry in areas close to town, and its accompanying land expropriation (without sufficient compensation) could encourage temporary or even permanent population displacements into the town in search of alternative employment.

The implementation of economic policy generally and that of hydropower projects specifically, advance with little concern for the interests of communities, their ecological and economic needs and those of the individuals within them. The situation of those negatively affected remains without hope of correction, in a social context that lacks well-defined avenues of social protest, and features human rights violations on a regular basis. It is a telling indication of the current state of affairs, that Laotian ecological and environmental activists concerned with the LPDR's Mekong initiatives, have resorted to Thailand's water and energy authorities acting with the blessing of the Thai Cabinet to put a brake on their own government's policies. It is unclear whether Thailand's measures and complaints will manage to make the Lao authorities change direction.

Vietnam and Cambodia, the other two Mekong-centred players, could decide to pull their weight even more than they have, and exert enough pressure for Laos to at least factor in the consequences of Lao projects on their own environments. But China's determination to dominate, its immense economic influence on the region, and the Lao leadership's apparently unceasing appetite for Chinese credits, makes such a course of action increasingly unlikely. In this context, we can see the persistent relevance of a question which was asked in the 1990s, when Laos first launched its economic reforms: what levels of external dependency can the Lao authorities concede, without jeopardising the country's sovereignty, endangering its ecological heritage, and negatively affecting the well-being of its people? Furthermore, how far can they go, without putting relationships with its immediate neighbours at risk?

A Laotian achievement outside Laos

While the LPDR faces innumerable challenges inside its territory, I have learnt that many of the Lao families who settled in Argentina in the 1980s have finally come to terms with their environment. The group's initial difficulties are known to the reader from my descriptions in Part 3, but having been unable to revisit South America, as I have Southeast Asia, I had not been able to provide fresher news.

However, a recently discovered doctoral thesis allows me to offer the following update on the Lao refugee families sent to Argentina. The effects of time, relative economic success, and the pull exerted by a Spanish-speaking second and third generations, have enabled the families to fit in, while maintaining their customs, and developing a Laotian/Argentinian identity. Many within the depressed group which the reader left in 1984, have since undergone an extraordinary transformation. The extent to which this has happened is attested by a recent refugee initiative to build a Buddhist temple in Misiones, a northern province whose Laos-like red earth, easy-going inhabitants, blue skies and intense heat and humidity, has facilitated the creation of a small, Argentinian Laos. And to further consolidate their presence, and commemorate forty years of the group's arrival in Argentina, the community has flanked the temple with a massive Buddha statue, the result of seven years of collective efforts which, the Lao proudly declare in Spanish, is the largest Buddha in Latin America. At least for some families, fleeing their own country, facing uncertainty, living in refugee camp confinement, and being transplanted to an alien land, has ended up being a boon and a blessing. For them and for their Argentinian-born offspring, Laos remains a reference point and a source of identity. But this is a Laos of the past, which remains untouched by the realities of the communist republic.

After 40 years, the construction of a massive Buddha statue marks the Lao refugee's community's reconciliation with their Argentinian environment, while asserting its Laotian origin and cultural specificity. Initiated in 2012, the monument was inaugurated seven years later, the proud achievement of a group of refugees from the 1980s and their descendants. Posadas, Misiones Province, Argentina 2017 (photo by Marcela Landazabal).

EPILOGUE

With my departure from Southeast Asia in 1990, I closed the first chapter of my career with refugees, moving on from there to other posts in Latin America, the Balkans and Western Europe. In this book, I have focused on that earlier period, in a region that faced the communist takeover in Laos, Vietnam and Cambodia, and the flight of refugees into countries that included Thailand and Argentina. I have described the evolution of events in these two countries and Indochina, from the vantage point of stable and officially recognised volunteer and UN jobs, which allowed me to become part of the environment as an active protagonist, and observe developments from the inside.

As a voluntary teacher inside Luang Phrabang, I saw the extraordinary spectacle of the Laotian monarchy moving inexorably to its extinction. As a research student in Northern Thailand, I saw the Thai state's defensive anti-communism, a strong countrywide response to the three Indochinese revolutions, including in border-based refugee camps where many of my former Luang Phrabang students had fled. As a UNHCR official in Argentina, I saw the grim reality of exile, through the eyes of Laotian refugees struggling with a (to them) excessively alien South American environment. As UNHCR Head of Mission in Kampuchea, I lived the quandary of an international official who tried to further the rights of refugees against the wall of politicians' intransigence, and the unbending political priorities of their governments.

My return visit to Indochina in 2016 showed the dramatic changes of an area which had witnessed a refugee crisis of catastrophic proportions, and now appeared transformed, each of its three countries showing the impact of liberalised economies, against a background of relative political, albeit authoritarian, stability. In this new reality, the complex links between Monarchy, Revolution and Refugees (the title of this book), were clarified. The former Lao monarchy had been replaced by a communist system, which remained in place in softened form, having moved away from its initial hardline, refugee-producing variety, to a country-specific mix of constraints in some areas, and flexibility in others. Concerning its pre-revolutionary culture, communist Laos had resorted to carefully selected aspects of the Buddhist religion, and to elements of its monarchical past as a basis for national identity and legitimacy, and also, more practically, as a magnet for tourism. In Vietnam, the communist state had remained, like Laos, loyal to its ideological beginnings, in a similarly mellowed form. It operated under the primacy of Ho Chi Minh's new, flexible, multi-faceted image, which portrayed him in turn as an austere revolutionary, a benevolent uncle, or an understanding statesman, who calmly oversaw the extravagance of luxury malls, or the unexpected expressions of blatant social inequality, thus legitimating those aspects of the country's liberalised economy which seemed most at odds with communist tenets. The country's feudal past remained present in the form of shrines dedicated to royal or military figures of the distant past, all of them sources of identity and national pride. As for Cambodia, it had continued to develop the liberal economy which I had seen introduced by the revisionist communist PRK regime in the late 1980s. All aspects of the country's Buddhist and monarchical past had been revived, a sharp swing of the pendulum from the excesses of the Khmer Rouge revolution, and the initial rigidity of the Vietnam-backed PRK. But royal Cambodia had retained, more than its two Indochinese neighbours, the authoritarian legacy of the preceding communist regimes, even intensifying it within a political system which placed the reins of power in the hands of a single man. 2016 also saw me revisiting the Kingdom of Thailand, where political change had continued to occur alongside the stable continuities of unequal development, combining it with the enduring presence of the two age-old pillars of stability, Buddhism and the monarchy. I saw that both institutions were still the object of unquestioned and unanimous nation-wide allegiance. In 2021, however, the role of the monarch faced unprecedented demands for reform by a vocal minority in the streets of Bangkok.

* * * * * * * * * *

In 2016, a kind of political and economic equilibrium had been reached in Indochina, following the evolution of its three countries, and the application in each of them of liberalising policies, in the economic field particularly. Though these had permitted high levels of inequality and left them unchecked, the policies played a key role in the region's visible material transformation. They also gave rise to other concerns. Having joined regional mechanisms of economic cooperation, Laos, Cambodia and Vietnam achieved unquestionable levels of material progress. But the presence of China and Thailand inside those mechanisms turned out to be problematic. Although they represented a welcome source of capital for project development, they also brought risk of longterm economic dependence and indebtedness, for Laos and Cambodia particularly. Although the new mechanisms had been designed to ensure reciprocity and fair play among members, both Thailand and China were quick to place themselves in positions of relative advantage, with China acting with particular grit.

Initially, Laos showed, more than Cambodia, the will to retain some independence by maintaining strong links with Vietnam and other donors. But it increasingly ceded to China's pressures, to the point of placing its very sovereignty at risk. As for Cambodia, it acted through its powerful prime minister, who continued to bank unequivocally on China, having found in Beijing the necessary dose of backing without conditions, which his uninterrupted exercise of autocratic power required. For unlike the West, who expected improvements on the human rights front in exchange for aid, China delivered aid without asking questions, and used economic cooperation to establish a permanent foothold.

China had, in 2016, and continues to have to this day, good economic/ political reasons for its evident objective of regional domination, with its focus on Indochina, on Laos and Cambodia particularly. Among the factors explaining this emphasis, is its ancient rivalry with Vietnam, strengthened by the recollection of its historical resolve to limit Vietnamese power, and by the memory of its leadership role within the international political and military onslaught against Phnom Penh's Vietnamese-backed regime in the 1980s. By means of its very visible presence in Laos and Cambodia, China can continue to express its traditional diffidence towards Vietnam. In this context, Vietnam has shown, perhaps more than its neighbours, a capacity to develop its dynamic economy outside the sphere of Thai and Chinese dominance, with the balancing, very substantial in-puts of other donors such as Taiwan, South Korea and Japan.

* * * * * * * * * *

The implementation of macro-economic policies in Indochina, with or without Thai or Chinese participation, has often been carried out within each of its three countries at the expense of local priorities, with frequent violations of the property rights of communities and individuals. This has been amply reported by the independent media, NGOs and some of the specialized literature, criticism focusing on the absence of effective avenues of redress, and on the unmovable power of 'big men' inside local or national elites, who play the part of benevolent patrons, and from that position pressure individuals and communities to abandon their grievances, and submit to the personal interests of elite members.

It is not clear to what extent the states of Indochina differ in terms of power concentration at the top of local and national hierarchies. Cambodia, however, appears to be a good candidate for the first prize, as it completes decades under the authority of the same strong man. For decades, and since 2017 in particular, Prime Minister Hun Sen has continued to impose his will, eroding all semblance of democracy, suppressing the opposition, while making all efforts to strengthen his position, secure his legacy, and ensure the regime's permanence. One way of achieving this has been through a dynastic model by which his family, and selected members of the various elites at the centre and in the provinces, have become entrenched in their respective centres of political and economic power, and handed over their privileges to the younger generation. In Laos and Vietnam, the authoritarian tendencies inherent in a one-party system persist, but the power of the state weighs more lightly on the individual, being exerted at the highest level through a system of collective leadership which is subject to periodic renewal. Unlike Cambodia, power is not centred in an almighty individual who, like most long-standing autocrats, is increasingly concerned with personal security and the perpetration of power, this leading him to impose increasingly restrictive measures on a closely invigilated and controlled population.

However, the differences should not distract us from the fact that the three states of Indochina share a common record of individual rights violations and abuse of power. In such a context, exceptionally courageous individuals have been keen to speak out, despite the ubiquitous presence of the state, and the threat of punitive measures. They have stood up and held their ground, even at the cost of their own freedom, and even at the risk of their own lives. The same courageous opposition has shown itself beyond the borders of Indochina, by way of recent anti-government demonstrations; in Thailand against the monarchy, in Hong Kong against China and, most violently, in Myanmar against the generals. While such resistances each attest to the continual vigour of conscientious dissension, the question arises whether the outbreaks of criticism regionally might lead individual states to opt for compromise, rather than intransigence and repression.

Beyond Southeast Asia

As new developments have transformed Indochina, leaving behind the refugee concerns on which I have focused in this book, other refugee crises have developed elsewhere, following the familiar pattern of political upheaval, mass departure and eventual resolution in the long term. However, in the face of very high numbers of refugees globally, and an exponential intensification of migratory movements, an increasing number of states have opted for nationalist isolationism and narrow self-interest, justifying their restrictive refugee policies in terms of a self-definition we have encountered more than once in this book: they see themselves as vulnerable entities threatened by a destabilizing outside agent, the 'dangerous' refugee/migrant. In Western Europe and North America, countries who were formerly at the vanguard of humanitarian concern, have tended to follow the trend. Rather than developing patterns of response which could serve as valid models of state behaviour worldwide, they have adopted narrow, closed-door policies which are continually eroding an ever-shrinking dose of international humanitarian concern. As a consequence, we have seen asylum seekers who flee situations of real danger at the peril of their own lives, being relegated to a limbo where their very survival is at risk.

Such is the difficult context within which UNHCR, NGOs and international organizations continue to work for refugees. It is an environment where international humanitarian solidarity varies with the changing migration policies of each state, in which the willingness of states to host refugees is uncertain, and the readiness of donor countries to fund refugee programmes is unpredictable. In such conditions, it is never clear whether governments will cover minimal needs, and for how long. And sometimes, unexpectedly, in response to certain crises, financial and other kinds of support can exceed expectations. As they did in 1979 at the Donor Conference organized in Geneva for the Indochinese refugee crisis. Or as has happened recently for Ukraine, with extraordinary levels of aid being made available to meet the consequences of Russia's recent invasion: incalculable material damage inside Ukrainian territory, an as yet uncertain number of wounded and dead among Ukrainian civilians and the military, and a massive population displacement which by March 24, 2022 had surpassed the 10 million mark, of which an estimated 4 million had fled the country as refugees. Over and above these aspects, the probable geopolitical consequences of the Russian state's assault, go a long way to explain current high levels of interest. For the invasion has alerted key political and military players: NATO, the capitals of Western Europe, Washington and Beijing, alongside a multitude of humanitarian organizations, including UN agencies, the ICRC, the IOM and NGOs.

The crisis has further revealed another aspect of the problematic working environment in which refugee agencies operate: the changeability of states' refugee policies. The unprecedented amounts of financial and other assistance for Ukraine, have been channeled to refugee-receiving countries, among them Ukraine's immediate neighbours, who are bearing the brunt of the refugee outflow. Significantly, some of these countries have shown an unexpected willingness to revise their restrictive refugee policies to accommodate the needs of the fleeing Ukrainians, moving away from the strict, sealed-border measures which they have been applying to deal with non-European asylum seekers. These measures have included technologically reinforced impediments to access (a mix of walls, barbed wire, observation cameras and high security reception centres), which in some cases have been accompanied by systematic push-backs. It is not clear what long-term impact the Ukraine-related, ethnic-specific surge of unanimous support will have on the refugee policies of states in the European Union, including the more restrictive. Perhaps it will give humanitarian concern a new, long-lasting impetus, favour more open policies for asylum seekers of all regions, and help erode the tendency in some states to give absolute priority to security concerns at the expense of humanitarian solidarity.

In the context of the surge of goodwill for Ukraine, there is another aspect worth considering: the variability of donors' enthusiasm. Commitment to a given emergency can be short-lived, and resources reduced or redirected to a new, emerging focus of international attention. Past examples of donor fatigue are legion, and as the Ukrainian catastrophe unfolds, we are reminded of a new example: Afghanistan, whose recent UN-organized international donor conference has secured pledges which represent only half of the set target (US 4.4 billion), when the country is witnessing an unprecedented fall in food supply. As for Ukraine, the independent media's courageous reporting of the mounting horrors has served to dispel whatever lethargy could have met the consequences of the invasion. The country is sure to remain in the limelight for the foreseeable future, although continued high levels of support will depend on the length of the conflict, and the cost of reconstruction following the ongoing high levels of devastation.

* * * * * * * * * * *

To the extent that I have focused on refugees as a major theme, I have shown, for Indochina and Argentina, that the negative destabilizing capacities attributed by an accusing state to another (e.g. by Thailand to Vietnam), can be projected onto selected individuals, including refugees, who are presented as being the demonized country's infiltrated agents, and are therefore targeted by punitive measures of varying intensity. The mechanism finds wide application worldwide, and in stages of my career which have not been included in this book, it has turned out to be an almost standard feature of states' approach to the refugee issue, a central component of anti-refugee state ideology, whether in Central America, the Balkans (exacerbated by strong interethnic rivalry) and Europe, with its restrictive refugee policies and exclusion mechanisms.

These locations, as with those I have looked at in the book, further show that each accusing state completes its demonization of others with a self-definition which heightens, almost sacralizes its own role: the state is the nation's sole protector against the onslaught of extraordinarily aggressive, destabilizing forces which must be effectively neutralized or destroyed by whatever means, be they relatively benign or violent. Faced with allegedly formidable threats, there are no limits to the measures which states adopt, always, in their view, with full justification. The Thai state fully vindicated the measures it adopted in the 1970s against Indochinese communism, and its alleged infiltrated agents, including refugees. Following the

Pathet Lao takeover in 1975, the Lao state unflinchingly the disciplinary measures it imposed on alleged 'reactionary saboteurs', including infiltrated Lao refugees from the camps of 'capitalist' Thailand. In the 1980s, the communist Cambodian state strongly validated the policies it adopted against the anti-Phnom Penh Coalition, and its alleged agents, including returning refugees. Also in the 1980s, the more extreme members of the Argentinian dictatorship stood by their own severe approach to Lao refugees who, despite having fled communist Laos, were seen as potential sources of communist infection. And at another level of ideological distortion, in Russia, where objective reality has been turned on its head by the state, the Ukrainian victim has become the aggressor, and the Russian aggressor the victim. Dressed by the state's ideologues in the garb of victim, in that of morally authorized caretaker of Russia's national integrity and redresser of wrongs, the Russian state has invaded Ukraine with a sense of righteousness.

We have seen in the text that a newly constructed reality acquires additional credibility by being linked to a vision of the past that combines historical fact with a sentimental/patriotic nostalgia for a glorious history. The training courses of Thai village scouts described the Thai polity at the peak of its power and extension, as a point of reference for a Thailand of the present being endangered by the communist threat. Similarly, the Russian state describes itself as under attack from forces which continue to eat into the 'legitimate' geographical frontiers which bounded the country's past powerful polities, the USSR and tsarist Russia. And in similar ways to my examples of Thailand and Cambodia, where added legitimacy was provided by the Buddhist Sangha, so has the Orthodox Church been a source of state reinforcement in Russia.

The above aspects of ideological manipulation are parts of a state's closed definition of itself and of its alleged assailants. Together they conform a self-validating microcosm which is impervious to criticism, a solid ideological fortress which is maintained by a narrow circle of inflexible defenders – members of the highest circles of the civilian and military elites, and their ideologues. In addition, the microcosms serve to exonerate states from answering for actions which follow from their ideological positions. These actions, we have seen, range from exactions imposed on individuals, to social arrangements which can lead to widespread discontent and, in some cases, to refugee movements of different sizes. Such movements are never seen as responding legitimately to the imposition of refugee-producing policies and measures; they are regarded as proof of the inability of individuals to adapt to a new, allegedly improved political order. Refugees might reach hundreds of thousands, but their departure is explained away as a welcome salutary outflow which rids the state of potentially destabilizing elements. This is presently happening with the as-yet-unknown number of Russian citizens leaving Russia in protest for the invasion of Ukraine. It was the case with the hundreds of thousands of fleeing nationals from Laos, Vietnam and Cambodia, in the 1970s and 1980s. The stigma which departees carry as they leave, tends to stick. When the authorities of their country of origin remain in power overrtime, they can use the stigma to block repatriation, as I have amply documented for the return of a single person (Madame Seng Long) to Cambodia.

* * * * * * * * * *

The above specific examples of ideological manipulation, demonization of states and scapegoating of its alleged agents, including refugees, show the difficult context in which refugee work is carried out by the plethora of organizations which seek to respond to refugee needs, among them UNHCR. Following a twenty-seven-year career in the UN's refugee agency, I am convinced that an institution which navigates in such difficult waters, battles continually to ensure that its budgets are filled by unevenly forthcoming donors, and faces intractable dilemmas in a frequently hostile political environment, is an indispensable counter to the vagaries of human solidarity. I have described some of UNHCR's dilemmas and shortcomings, but this should not distract us from the value of the agency's commitment and globally recognized mandate to protect and attend the needs of persecuted groups or individuals who are forced by their states' excesses, and violations of their rights, to flee their own countries and seek protection elsewhere. It is clear that without the agency's efforts, and those of the refugee-focused agencies it coordinates, thousands of refugees would find it difficult, if not impossible, to reach their safe, if temporary and often imperfect destinations. As for me, UNHCR has offered an extraordinary variety of learning experiences. It has allowed me to apply my skills in a succession of collective efforts of which this book has provided a few examples, all of them derived from an earlier, decisive exposure to Southeast Asia and to political upheaval, radical change and exile in Laos.

Sunset on the Mekong
Luang Phrabang 2016.

BIBLIOGRAPHY

Anderson, B. 1977, 'Withdrawal Symptoms: Social and Cultural Aspects of the October 6 Coup', in *Bulletin of Concerned Asian Scholars*, July-Sept: 13-30

Barber, M. 2015, *Blinded by Humanity: Inside the UN's Humanitarian Operations*, London: IB Taurus

Becker, E. 1998, *When the War was Over: Cambodia and the Khmer Rouge Revolution*, New York: Public Affairs.

Bizot, F. 2000, *Le Portail*, France: Editions de la Table Ronde.

Bowie, K. 1997, *Rituals of National Loyalty*, Colombia University Press

Chalo Utakhapat 1976, *Yaa Somun Phrai kap Rook nai Prathet Roon lae Vithi Chai Bambat Raksaa*, Bangkok: Phrae Phitaya International.

Chandler, D 1996, 'Royally Sponsored human sacrifices in Nineteenth Century Cambodia: the Cult of Nak ta Me Sa (Mahisasuramardini) at Ba Phnom' in Chandler *Facing the Cambodian Past*: Chiang Mai, Silkworm Books

Davis, R. 1974, 'Muang Metaphysics – a Study in Northern Thai Myth and Ritual' Thesis submitted to the Faculty of Arts, University of Sydney, for the degree of Doctor of Philosophy.

Evans, Grant 1999, *Laos - Culture and Society*, Chiang Mai: Silkworm Books.

Evans, Grant 2009, *The last Century of Lao Royalty*, Chiang Mai: Silworm Books.

Finot, L. 195? 'Origines legendaires' in *France Asie Revue Mensuelle de Culture et de Synthese*, Tome XII: 1047-1049

Gunn, Geoffrey 1982, 'Theravadins and Commissars: the State and national Identity in Laos', in Stuart-Fox,

Contemporary Laos', 1982: 76-100 University of Queensland Press.

Hearne, R.M. 1974, *Thai Government Programs in Refugee Relocation and Resettlement in Northern Thailand*, Auburn New York: Thailand books

Hughes, C. and Un, K. 2011, *Cambodia's Economic Transformation*, Copenhagen: NIAS (Nordic Institute of Asian Studies) press

Irvine, W. 1982, 'The Thai-Yuan "Madman" and the Modernising, Developing Thai Nation as Bounded Entities under Threat: a Study in the Replication of a Single Image'. Unpublished PhD thesis , School of Oriental and African Studies, University of London.

Jerndal, R and Rigg, J 1999, 'From Buffer State to Crossroad State' in Evans G. (ed) *Laos, Culture and Society'* 1999: 35-60

Keyes, C. 1971, 'Buddhism and National Integration in Thailand' in *Journal of Asian Studies*, 30: 551-567.

Lacouture, Jean, Biography of Ho Chi Minh www.britannica.com

Landazabal-Mora, M 2019, 'Lo que resiste entre el exilio. Una genealogia de la diaspora laosiana en Guyana francesa y Argentina'. Unpublished doctoral thesis Universidad Nacional Autonoma de Mexico (UNAM)

Landazabal-Mora, M. 2021, 'La historia (des)bordada: imagenes de los refugiados Laosianos en America Latina' in *Nomadas* no. 54 (Enero-junio 2021) Universidad Central de Colombia

Lemoine and Mougne 1983 'Why has death stalked the refugees', in *National History*, Vol 92 n. 11: 6-19 Nov 1983

Loughlin, N. and Noren-Nilsson, A. 2021, 'Introduction to Special Issue: the Cambodian People's Party's Turn to hegemonic Authoritarianism: Strategies and Envisaged Futures' in *Contemporary Southeast Asia* Vol. 43/2 (August 2021).

Marston, J.A. 2013, 'Post Pol Pot Cambodia and the Building of a New Stupa' in Whalen-Bridge, J and Pattana Kitiarsa (ed) *Buddhism, Modernity and the State in Asia*: *Forms of Engagement* 95-113 New York: Palgrave Macmillan,

Marston J.A. 2016, 'Relics from Sri Lanka and the post-independence Buddha-Jayanti Celebrations in Cambodia' in Alcedo, P; Ness, S; Maier,MJ (ed) *Religious Festivals in Contemporary SouthEast Asia 2016: 71-93* Manila: Ateneo de Manila University Press

Mc Coy, A. 1972, *The Politics of Heroin in Southeast Asia*, Singapore: Harper & Row Publishers.

Muecke, M. 1980, 'The village Scouts of Thailand', in *Asian Review*, April 1980, Vol. XX – 4

Mus, P. et McAlister, J. 1972, *Les Vietnamiens et leur revolution*, Paris: Editions du Seuil

Mysliwiec, E. 1988, *Punishing the Poor: the International Isolation of Kampuchea*, Oxford: Oxfam Publication.

Norodom Sihanouk 1986, *Prisonnier des Khmers Rouges*, Hachette.

Osborne, M 1984, *Before Kampuchea. Preludes to Tragedy*, Sydney: George Allen and Unwin Australia Pty Ltd

Perez Gay, J. 2004, *El Principe y sus guerrilleros, la Destruccion de Camboya*, Mexico: Ediciones Cal y Arena.

Randi, J and Rigg, J 1999 'From Buffer State to Cross-road State' in Evans, G (ed) *Laos, Culture and Society*' 1999: 34-60

Somboon Suksamran 1977, *Political Buddhism in South East Asia. The role of the Sangha in the Modernisation of Thailand*, London: C Henst and Co

Somsak Ponkeo, 'A new national symbol is born in Vientiane'' *Vientiane Times* December 24-26, 2002 in Evans *'The Last Century of Lao Royalty'* 2009: 31

Strangio, S. 2014, *Hun Sen's Cambodia*, New Haven and London : Yale University Press

Strangio, S. 2020 'Thai official warns Laos on Power Purchases from Controversial Dam' in *The Diplomat*, November 27, 2020

Strangio, S. 2021 'Not Sufficient. Thailand rejects Report on the Lao Hydropower Dam' in *The Diplomat*, January 26, 2021

Stuart-Fox, M. 1982, *Contemporary Laos*, University of Queensland Press.

Stuart-Fox, M. 1986, *Laos: Politics, Economics and Society*, London: Francis Pinter Publishers.

Trankell, Ing-Britt 1999, 'Royal Relics: Ritual and Social Memory in Louang Phrabang' in Evans, G (ed) *'Laos – Culture and Society'* 1999: 191-213

Vickery, M. 1984, *Cambodia 1975-1982*, Sydney and London: George Allen and Unwin.

Vickery, M 1986, *Kampuchea – Politics, Economics and Society*, Sydney and London: George Allen and Unwin.

Wekkin, G. 1982, 'The Rewards of Revolution: Pathet Lao Policy towards the Hill Tribes since 1975', in Stuart-Fox *Contemporary Laos',* 1982: 181-198. University of Queensland Press

Wetterwald, JN. 2014, *D'exils, d'espoirs et d'aventures Un Suisse a la rencontre des réfugiés*, La Chaux-de-Fonds Suisse Editions du Belvedere

Winichakul, Thongchai 2020, *Moments of Silence. The Unforgetting of the October 6, 1976 Massacre in Bangkok*, University of Hawai Press.

ABBREVIATIONS

CGDK (The Coalition Government of Democratic Kampuchea) was set
up in July 1982 to bring together the strongly anti-communist KPNLF
(Khmer People's National Liberation Front) created in 1979 under former
Prime Minister Son Sann; the monarchical and politically conciliatory
FUNCINPEC (Front Uni National pour un Cambodge Indépendant, Neutre,
Pacifique et Coopératif) created in 1981 by Sihanouk; the Khmer Rouge,
renamed PDK (Party of Democratic Kampuchea) as part of an effort to
whiten their internationally damaged image. CPP: Cambodian People's Party

CNRP: Cambodian National Rescue Party

DRV: Democratic Republic of Vietnam

ICRC: International Committee of the Red Cross

IOM: International Organisation for Migration

KRC: Kampuchean Red Cross

LPDR: Lao Popular Democratic Republic

LPLA: Lao People's Liberation Army

NLHS: Neo Lao Hak Sat (Lao Patriotic Front)

PL: Pathet Lao

PRK: Popular Republic of Kampuchea

RLA: Royal Lao Army

RLG: Royal Lao Government

UNHCR: Office of the United Nations High Commissioner for Refugees

UNICEF: United Nations Children's Fund

WFP: World Food Programme

ACKNOWLEDGMENTS

All those relatives, friends, acquaintances and colleagues whose presence has left their mark on the experiences I have described. Among them I wish to mention:

In the early 1970s in Laos: my students at the Lycée in **Luang Phrabang,** and the Lao people who helped me enter and understand their culture.

In the late 1970s in Northern Thailand: the people of **Ban Phaya Chomphu,** for their unconditional hospitality; the health professionals in the hospitals and the villages in and near **Chiang Mai** who shared their knowledge and personal experiences in support of my doctoral studies; my assistant Suvet, companion of arms during my PhD field-work.

In the mid-1980s in Argentina: the team of social workers attached to UNHCR Buenos Aires and all UNHCR colleagues and friends, with special mention of Belela Herrera, Carmen Cattaneo, Maria Mercedes Pinto, and Roberto Rodriguez.

In the late 1980s in Cambodia: in the government, Princess Lyda Sisowath; in UNHCR, colleagues Robyn Blake, Marco Cabassi and Marilyn Virrey; in the Kampuchean Red Cross, Madame Plech Pirun, Dr Mi Samedi, Monsieur Net Tun, Monsieur Khek Poui; in the ICRC Violene Dogny and Peter Lutolf.

* * * * * * * * * * * *

During the writing of this book, I have received many suggestions, useful comments and encouragement. I wish to thank all those who have dedicated time and given their full attention to the text, among them, the following persons:

First and foremost, the sorely missed **Dr. Andrew Turton,** my PhD thesis supervisor at the School of Oriental and African Studies in the late 1970s, and strong sustainer of my work through the years.

In Bangkok: Raymond Hall. With his year-long attachment to Laos and UNHCR-based expertise on refugee issues, Ray has been an important source of encouragement since the first stages of the writing. And his specialised knowledge of Pakse during his VSO days in the 1970s have helped sharpen my understanding of that area, so different from my own in the North. **Patrick van de Welde.** As a former UNBRO official, Patrick's information on the functioning of the camps for Cambodians in Thailand has been invaluable, serving as an important corrective to more politically-biased descriptions'.

In Corke: the writer **Alannah Hopkin**, for her invaluable suggestions on style.

In Cuernavaca, Mexico: photographer **Alfredo Tooru Ebisawa,** who helped clean, digitalise and restore my slides with infinite patience; **Peter Falck,** distant family connection and meticulous commentator.

In Dallas and Mexico City: my sisters **Veronica** and **Jean** for their patient and always enthusiastic reading of the various drafts.

In Geneva: UNHCR colleagues **Marilyn Virrey and Anne Davies,** old time colleagues in Hanoi.

In London: **Martin Barber**. With his in-depth knowledge of Laos and extensive experience of refugee work in UNHCR and elsewhere, Martin has provided me with important insights, based on his very meticulous reading of the text. **Tiao Khamtoune**, former Luang Phrabang teacher-trainee in the 1970s, has been an unconditional source of precious information, always ready to help'.

In Mexico City: **John Marston**, Professor-Investigator at the Colegio de Mexico.

In Philadelphia: fellow social anthropologist **Professor Marjorie Muecke**, who shared many moments of field-work in the Chiang Mai area in the 1980s and has patiently read through the text, including the first indigestible first drafts. Marjorie has kindly shared some of her photographs for inclusion in the book.

In Rome: **Pietro Andruccioli**, patient reader and steadfast source of encouragement.

* * * * * * * * * * * *

Over the years, the following institutions and colleagues within them have shared successes and failures, friendships and rivalries, good and bad times, all of which are part of a common past that remains in my memory: Voluntary Service Overseas (**VSO**), International Voluntary Service (**IVS**), the School of Oriental and African Studies (**SOAS**), and for 27 years, the Office of the United Nations High Commission for Refugees (**UNHCR**).

INDEX